FLY PATTERNS FOR THE RIVERS & LAKES OF WALES

Dymuniadau gorau

Roe Morgan

First Impression—November 1984

© Moc Morgan

British Library Cataloguing in Publication Data

Morgan, Moc
    Fly patterns for the rivers and lakes of Wales.
    1. Fly tying
    I. Title
    688 7'912 SH451

ISBN 0 86383 135 4

Printed in Wales
at the Gomer Press, Llandysul, Dyfed

Acknowledgements

The Author and the publishers would like to thank the following people whose expertise and generosity have helped to make this book a reality.

For fly patterns: Tony Bevan, Llanilar; Ken Bowring, Cardiff; Emrys Evans, Blaenau Ffestiniog; Major T. Ernest Hughes, Llandeilo; Dewi Edwards, Liverpool; Roy Jones, Blaenau Ffestiniog; Dr Graeme Harris, Brecon; W. J. Williams, Llanffestiniog; Emyr Lewis, Llanbrynmair; Norman Closs Parry, Treffynnon; Leslie Peters, Brecon; Tomos Jones, Tregaron; Dave Cole, Tredegar; Hywel Evans, Llanfarian; Father Gargan, County Mayo; Mike Howells, Llanidloes; Dilwyn Richards, Llandeilo; Taff Price, Surrey; Illtyd Griffiths, Capel Bangor; Winston Oliver, Llanegwad; Jean Williams, Usk; Gwilym Hughes, Wrexham; Eirwyn Roberts, Dolwyddelan; John Braithwaite, Bristol; Steve Pope, Bristol; Arthur Owen, Ganllwyd; General Sir Thomas Pearson, Hoar Withy; Harry Lewis, Glyn-neath.

For Illustrations and Photography: Valerie Ganz, Llandeilo; Ryan Peregrine, Llandeilo; Elgan Davies, Aberystwyth; Nicholas Thirkell, London; Ian Rolls, Carmarthen; The Wildlife Department of Dyfed College of Art, Carmarthen; Victor Gollancz Ltd. and the executors of the estate of the late C. F. Tunnicliffe for some of the text illustrations which appear in *Portrait of a Country Artist* by Ian Niall; the estate of the late Negley Farson for permission to use the wood-engraving by Charles Tunnicliffe from his masterly, *A Book of Fishing*; and Col. G. H. F. Chaldecott, Nantgaredig for illustrative material and very special thanks to the sage and generous Ieuan Jones, Llanwrda, for permission to use engravings and illustrations from his magnificent private collection.

Fly-tying: Mike Green, Corwen, the most gifted of fly-tyers, for expertly tying some of the 'old masters'!

Production: The staff of the Gomer Press for their patience and expertise and to Nellie Jones of Pontrhydfendigaid for so ably typing the manuscript.

Finally, to Lynn Hughes of Llandeilo for his Foreword and his editing of this book with firmness and sensitivity and any success accruing to the publication must and is willingly shared with him.

Moc Morgan

Foreword

The origins and background of fly-fishing in Wales

Fly-dressing, that rare combination of intensely practical and instinctive artistry, has a thoroughly absorbing historical development in Wales. It is a genuine—surviving and thriving—vernacular folk art-form which, on examination, reveals local techniques and customs that draw from a general fund of knowledge and, at the same time, contributes back innovations, based on experience, that add scientific and imaginative dimensions.

The Coch-a-bon-ddu and its many variants are known and used by trout fly fishermen throughout the world—from Canada and the USA, to Kenya and New Zealand. It has its origin in the Drop Fly described by George Scotcher for use on the Usk over a hundred and fifty years ago and, by the way its name is torturously mis-spelled, it is clear that many attribute its nativity either to Scotland or Ireland. Lures now commonly in use in reservoir and lake fishing were, in many instances, pioneered by enterprising Welshmen in an attempt to outwit that wily and still abundant fish, the sewin. Descendants of those pioneers, the present generation of Welsh anglers have not, in return, been slow to adapt the weird and wonderful artefacts of the stillwater fly-box to the purpose of night fishing for sewin.

This book itself is approached in something similar to this pioneering spirit—for, not since George Scotcher's delightful classic, *The Fly Fisher's Legacy*, published in Chepstow around 1820, has there been what he himself would have called a 'Fisherman's Grand Desideratum, or long wished-for Instructions' on flies and fly-dressings as put to use and practised in Wales.

It should, in this connection, be noted that the section on trout-fly tyings in George Agar Hansard's later *Trout and Salmon Fishing in Wales*, (London 1834), is a word-for-word plagiarism of Scotcher's book and is itself the studiously pilfered piece of patchwork that Scotcher warns his readers against in a declamatory prefatory note headed: 'Caution!'

It is to be hoped that no such warnings are required here, but there is a long-overdue need to fill the gap, to break the silence of a hundred and fifty-odd years after Scotcher's seminal work, with a statement—which has no pretensions of being definitive but is a modest summary of the state of the art at the present time—on the basis of information available.

Fishermen, as a species, are famous for their ability to colour the truth: and often the tendency is—the better the man the better the lie! Some successful anglers are very secretive about their 'killing' patterns—keeping the fly they are catching with, covered—while talking to a fellow fisher on the bank. These traits have not made research particularly easy, but they have been the exceptions, and anglers all over Wales and elsewhere have helped in forthcoming and generous ways to make this book a reality.

But, whatever boastful claims may have been made for certain patterns, where the originals themselves exist, they speak for themselves. The work of Pryce Tannatt, Dai Lewis, Rev Powell and many others is available for us to see and the practical worth of their ingenuity is demonstrable. Study of these men's individual contributions, each with their local characteristics, discovers for us aspects of angling custom that are of fascinating interest to angler and naturalist alike. They provide valuable data towards the continuing discussion on the practice of angling in Wales.

In former times, as indeed today, fish and fishing have occupied a special place in the economy of Wales and in the imagination of the Welsh people. When man first settled in Britain some twenty thousand years ago it is in the west and south of Wales that he left earliest evidence of himself, his habitation and way of life. From the artefacts that he fashioned from stone and bone there can be little doubt that the migratory fish which filled the rivers—and the native fish that otherwise occupied the rivers and lakes—provided a seasonal harvest and permanent food source. They were a persuasive factor in determining the positioning and growth of settlements. Shakespeare's Fluellen, in *Henry V*, makes the point when he says that there is a river at Macedon and the river Wye at Monmouth 'and there are salmons in both'.

Shakespeare, well-versed in natural history, must have known that the first reference to salmon angling was by the Roman poet Martial, who flourished after 43AD: and that Aelian in his *Natural History* c.200AD says 'I have heard of a Macedonian way of catching fish, and it is this: between Beroea and Thesalonica runs a river called the Astraeus, and in it there are fish with speckled skins. These fish feed on a fly peculiar to the country which hovers on the river. When a fish observes a fly on the surface it swims quietly up and gulps the fly down'.

The metal-crafting people who began to settle in Britain as many years before Christ as we now live after His birth left coracles, pronged spears and barbed hooks enough in their burial mounds to convince us that they were not only fishermen but had expectation of some fishing heaven which lingers in the race memory of all true fishers! As to what baited these hooks—if anything at all—we cannot tell, nor can we determine precisely when feathers and fur first adorned a hook to deceive a fish—in Wales or anywhere else.

But in Wales we have a fly/fish reference from our literature in the

Middle Ages which so pre-dates others as to make it worth a mention here. The greatest of Welsh poets—without fear of contradiction—was Dafydd ap Gwilym, a lusty Cardiganshire squire who was also probably a divine. He flourished between 1320 and 1380 and his artistic genius is matched by his precise observation of nature. In a poem attributed to him, called 'The Salmon', he despatches the salmon as his love-messenger to the bed where his mistress lies with her husband. He refers to the fish as 'gylionwr', 'catcher of flies'

> Gwylia yno, gylionwr,
> Galw o'r gwely'r gwr.'

From it we can deduce that this fly-taking propensity in the salmon was common knowledge in Wales in the fourteenth century and would undoubtedly have been put to use by anglers.

Not until Dame Juliana Berner's *A Treatyse of Fysshyng wyth an Angle*, in 1496, a hundred years later, do we for certain know that fly-dressing and fly-fishing were established arts in the British Isles and that the approach to angling entomology was reasonably scientific.

'Fishermen get the better of the fish by their fisherman's craft. They fasten red wool round a hook, and fix on to the wool two feathers which grow under a cock's wattles, and which in colour are like wax. Their rod is six feet long, and their line is the same length. They throw their snare, and the fish—attracted and maddened by the colour—come straight at it'.

It was the monks in the great network of priories throughout the country who disseminated knowledge by word of mouth and by copying and circulating manuscripts. Tintern, Valle Crucis, Strata Florida and others would know as soon as anyone about a treatise on angling from the quill of a distinguished Abbess. The monks all had a vested interest in fish!

Printed books on matters relating to Wales and aspects of Welsh life, other than the spiritual, are scarce in the sixteenth and seventeenth centuries. One searches in vain for evidence of angling activity through such sources as the material collected by that greatest of Welsh scholars, the scientist and antiquary Edward Lhuyd, keeper of the Ashmolean Museum, Oxford. Lhuyd, in the mid-seventeenth century, circulated a questionaire to every squire, parson and literate person he knew in the Principality, requesting detailed information towards his projected *Natural History of Wales*. It was, alas, never realised, as he died at 38. Replies that he *did* receive were published under the title *Parochialia* where there are references to fish but none to fishing.

Delightfully, almost as a marginalium to his great devotional poetry, Lhuyd's Oxford contemporary, Henry Vaughan 'the Silurist', writing from his home at Newton-on-Usk near Crickhowell, in a

Latin sonnet addressed to his friend Thomas Powell D.D., of Cantref, to accompany the gift of a salmon offers us a brilliant description of an Usk salmon fly c.1655.

To the best of men, and his most particular friend,
Mr Thomas Powell of Cantref, Doctor of Divinity.

Accept this salmon caught in the rushing weir,
When he had battled up from the bottom to the topmost waters.
The false attraction of a simulated insect deceived him:
A fly made of feathers, painted with colourful markings.
As he seizes it, he is seized; heedless he swallows,
And is himself doomed to be swallowed,
And the catcher of the fatal morsel
Is made a welcome catch in his turn.
Blessed rest! the richest reward of this miserable life!
How safely he could have lain hidden in those still pools!
As he seeks the roar and tumult of the foaming torrent
He is swiftly made a prey to my hooked bait.
What a pregnant emblem of great matters these trifles form!
The weir is the world; the salmon, man; and the feather, deceit.

Elsewhere Vaughan gives us a glimpse of the idyllic life of the 17th century fly-fishing physician in a humorous vignette from a poem composed in 1651 that vies for high honours in terms of the obscurity of its title:

Thus feasted, to the flowrie Groves,
Or pleasant rivers he removes
Where neare some fair oke hung with Mast
He shuns the South's infectious blast,
On shadie banks sometimes he lyes
Where with his line and feather'd flye
He sports and takes the Scaly frie.

(*'The Praise of a Religious Life' by Mathias Casuirus. In answer to that ode of Horace Beautus, ille qui procul negotiis &c.*)

This is, incidentally, a reference to the sport of samlet i.e. salmon peel fishing enjoyed until the present century in ignorance of the consequences in terms of conservation: though in those far-off happy days fish were so abundant in our rivers, that it scarcely mattered.

It is not until the era of the great travellers of the eighteenth and nineteenth century, men who passed through Wales, staying at inadequate inns and lodgings, commissioning engravings and recording their observations in printed books, that we have a graphic record of fish and fishing. The picture is one of rivers teeming with fish and of wholesale slaughter by any method available. Angling activity was

Fishing the Rondda fawr. From 'The Principle & Practice of sketching Landscape and Scenery from Nature, systematically arranged etc.' (4 vols.) by John G. Wood, F.S.A., London 1823.

restricted mainly to the leisured classes—people like Rice Mansel, Sir Watkyn Williams Wynn—and early industrial barons such as Crawshay and Guest who owned stretches of the Usk and Wye for their leisure.

Sportsmen in the early nineteenth century complained of being 'glutted with sport'. Thomas Medwin returned from a day on the Teify with his 'shoulders aching with the weight of six dozen trout'. In a previous record in his book, *The Angler in Wales or days and nights of Sportsmen*, 1834, he and three fellow-anglers took 500 trout in five days from Tal-y-llyn. George Agar Hansard, author of *Trout and Salmon Fishing in Wales*, also published in 1834, apparently commonly took thirty or forty pounds of trout in a day's angling on Tal-y-llyn and he observes that three or four pound trout were commonly caught above Lampeter where thirty or forty pounds (weight) of trout could be taken on the fly in a day's fishing.

Apart from the depredations of these 'foreigners', a few professional men and a handful of dedicated locals, the fish had it all to themselves. There existed in Wales a certain ethic which identified the huntin', shootin', fishin' element with idleness: call it 'the Nonconformist work ethic'. Fish were there for the taking as food—or as a way of getting your own back on the squire or his keeper —but to spend idle hours angling for them was somewhat to be despised! This attitude undoubtedly has held out in some *cefn gwlad* 'back of the country' places until well into the twentieth century. A casual survey before 1950 would have revealed a higher proportion of 'church' men as opposed to 'chapel' on the river-bank (in season and in daylight). And it must be said that the romantisisation of the local poacher which survives is, in angling terms, the greatest anomaly in Wales and a real menace in fishery management. .

This social aspect, and its divisioning, is curiously important in this study of the fly patterns in use in Wales. The two important elements, as far as the scientific and creative advancement in styles of dressing is concerned, are the keepers and the dedicated locals. The monied classes in the past, as even today, tended to buy their flies and tackle from English and Scottish city stockists who catered principally for the gentry who fished such rivers as the great rivers of Scotland and the chalk-streams of the South Downs.

Locals could not afford luxury tackle and very few would have known how to order from Farlow's or Hardy's. To an extent they admired expensive tackle—but also held it in contempt. They themselves held secrets that the gentry and their keepers would not know about, but they would not fail to take note of innovations arriving from London, Redditch, Alnwick or Aberdeen, using ready-to-hand materials to copy them and experimenting, adapting Scottish, Irish and Southern English patterns for their own purposes. In this fusion of knowledge, obviously, the keepers and ghillies played a key role.

Many of these keepers were imported from Scotland and Yorkshire by the aristocracy and landowning classes in order to impose an alien, disciplined policing on a rural society that was steeped in tribal loyalties and prejudices in favour of a common right to the fruits of nature. Such men as Alexander Miller on the Wye or William Law on the Usk and the Barnes family on the Towy maintained an aloofness from the locals which, though always courteous and businesslike, was akin to that social demarcation which exists between Sergeants and senior Warrant Officers and private soldiers and civilians in army life. Indeed, many of these keepers were ex-military men with just such a background.

Rapidly, things have changed. The large estates have, since the Second World War especially, broken up and waters have been sold to syndicates, pension funds and clubs. The old social divisioning has largely disappeared to be replaced by another evil—money. The highest bidder is most unlikely, in Wales, to be a local person—though clubs such as Llandysul Anglers have out-bid all-comers—but club membership itself tends to be far-ranging. The danger is that local knowledge will disperse and be lost: it is long overdue for some record to be made.

Local knowledge is what counts in fly-fishing. A pattern that proves deadly one year will not raise even a laugh the following. A fly that kills consistently on the lower reaches is like a racquet without strings higher up. And a fly that catches for one person will not necessarily catch for another. Such is the fascination of fly fishing.

To lose track of some of the traditional local patterns is a loss to angling and to the cultural life of a nation. Hundreds of patterns are, undoubtedly lost—since flies are perishable objects—and so many anglers were, and still are, jealously secretive of their individual successful patterns. It is to be hoped that, as a result of this publication, more will come to light as the importance of recording every aspect of the art and science of fly-dressing is appreciated.

Some of the details of patterns included in the text will, without doubt, be found wanting for lack of steady recollection on someone's part, or the author's misunderstanding. These, we apologise for in advance. Dr Samuel Johnson in his famous *Dictionary* entry for the word 'correct' anticipates human error with the illustration 'as correct as a Second Edition'!

The patterns that follow are ones that have been tied and tried from recent information. There is nearly always room for improvement—as a living part of the art. There will always be variations on variations.

It is to be hoped that, apart from breaking the long silence that has followed Scotcher's delightful book, this publication will be seen as a move in the right direction to encourage others to record some more unknown patterns, by coming forward or by opening up the secrets of their fathers' or grandfathers' fly-cases—before any more is lost to this largely unrecognised art-form.

There is far greater enjoyment in anticipation to be gained from fishing with a pattern that is known to be a fly that has proven itself on a particular water, than to use one bought from a cataglogue or a distant shop, which by chance takes a fish. The more so if the fly is the product of one's own workmanship on the bench or tied in the old Welsh method—in the hand.

Lynn Hughes   November 1984

Note: Throughout the text, fly-patterns are printed with initial capitals—as in Stone Fly. The natural insect, stone fly, is in small type. The exceptions are, of course, February red, March brown etc. though the artificials appear as February Red, March Brown . . . and it is important to emphasise that in *this* book the illustrations of fly-patterns, both in line-drawing at the head-line with each pattern and in the colour plates, are based on examples of patterns, tied by the originators in many cases, that have been in use catching fish. They are not the usual exhibition specimens designed to catch anglers.

Plate I (Historic selection)
Flies from the wallets of the masters: Lewi Davies, T. L. Harries, Wil Harry, Dan Jones,
Dai Lewis, Molly Sweet, Pryce Tannat and Tom Tom.

Materials

Fly-dressers today are very fortunate in that they have a wide range of specialist firms eager to supply them with dressing materials and who issue comprehensive catalogues for them to study, ensuring that they get the best materials at the right price. It was not always so. Even the most casual survey of fishing tackle catalogues of 40 years ago will show that interest was more concentrated on ready-tied patterns and the colour-plates of popular patterns were much prized and, no doubt, influential. Prior to that, those 'amateurs' who tied their own flies had to use ready-to-hand materials or scratch around for anything unusual.

There are some excellent yarns about the lengths to which some of the old tyers went to to obtain the materials they wanted, none nicer than the one which claims to be the true account of the origin of the Bethesda fly 'Cochen-lady' where a quarry worker-fisherman saw the exact dubbing wool he needed seated opposite him on a train. When they entered a tunnel he made a dive at her shawl, amidst considerable protest and confusion!

Some materials readily available forty years ago are no longer obtainable because of changing times and man's depredations. The introduction of mechanised hay-mowers has meant the extinction of a once common summer bird in Wales, the corncrake. The lack of need for self-sufficiency has meant that for the most part, few Welsh farmers bother with cereal crops and so those lovely birds, the partidges, have disappeared together with the bitterns, nightjars, wrynecks and others—not to mention the otter and the red squirrel.

Let it be noted well from the outset that many of these birds and animals mentioned in the text are referred to strictly as historical illuminations. It is *not*, and this cannot be stressed too strongly, for anyone to even *think* of trying to obtain any of these feathers, in the vain hope that it might improve their chances of taking fish. The substitutes suggested are equally good in every case and the penalties for taking, or even disturbing, some of these protected species are severe. Apart from this, it would be an act of the gravest irresponsibility, even to contemplate.

Most traditional Welsh patterns used hackles from either a hen or a cock. Traditionally hen hackle was used to dress wet flies and cock hackle for dry flies. Some cock hackles are becoming difficult to obtain as the old farm rooster has become something of an endangered species himself. Many believe that it is essential for the cock to be three years old before his hackle is of the correct texture for the dry fly. This is not so. Many of the old lads who bred fighting cocks in the valleys could produce a fully mature cock from the point of view of hackle and strength in a matter of eighteen months.

Often it is difficult to obtain hackle of the exact right colour: natural colours such as coch-a-bon-ddu and various honey dun requirements are very scarce. Fortunately, great strides have been made in the dyeing of feathers and even the most delicate of shades can be achieved—with a little care.

As a beginner the fly dresser will find it difficult to recognise the various hackles. The following is a simple glossary description of the more commonly used hackles:

Coch-a-bon-ddu Black centre with red outer fibres with black tips.
Furnace Black centre with red outer fibres.
Badger Black centre with white outer fibres.
Grizzle A feather from a Plymouth Rock bird with bars of black and white alternately.
Cree A feather with ginger added to the normal Plymouth Rock colour.
Greenwell Black centre with ginger outer fibres.
Blue Dun The colour of an old Welsh slate.
Iron Blue Dun A dark shade of blue dun.
Dun A mousey grey colour.
Honey or Rusty Dun A dun feather with rusty or honey coloured tips.

Modern dressers have resorted to the use of felt pens to help them with patterns requiring coch-a-bon-ddu and furnace hackle; the use of photo-dyeing has provided blue duns of astounding quality. Thus, despite modern dressers lacking the genuine article, there are modern devices to help them out. Many birds other than domestic poultry can supply out-moded hackle. The partridge and snipe are valuable in this respect even though these birds may be better known for providing the material for winging flies.

Wild Duck

An extremely useful bird and plentiful. The bronze mallard feather —from the small of the back—is much in demand for dressing the Mallard series of flies. The best bronze feathers are obtainable in the early months of the year as the mallard drake comes into mating plumage.

Those secondary feathers on a mallard duck and drake's wing that have a bright blue sheen on them are essential for the Butcher series flies.

Grouse

The tail and secondary feathers are used for wings in the Grouse series. The feathers from the small of the back can be used as hackles for flies such as Dai Lewis's Alder.

Partridge

The wing of the partridge is used on a great number of patterns in the Bethesda area. Partridge tail feathers are used to make the wing of the March Brown. The hackle from the small of the back are used for all the Partridge series of flies that require the dark brown hackle, such as the Partridge Red and Partridge Purple. The grey partridge breast feather is used for the lighter coloured members of the Partridge series like the Partridge & Yellow. This feather dyes well for the Mayfly patterns.

Of all the feathers used in fly dressing the partridge was by far the most popular: it respresented the warm affection that the old country folk had for a bird that was formerly to be found on every farm.

Snipe

An ideal feather for smaller flies requiring grey or dun wings. A feather from the rump of the snipe is a good hackle for the Snipe and Purple.

Starling

An extremely useful bird in that the secondaries and the primaries are used for all the smaller dun wings. Starling wing fibre is of a good texture to work with. Some body feathers are used for the Black Quill.

Pheasant

The secondaries and primaries of the hen pheasant are used for March Brown and Invicta. Some of the neck feathers of the hen are also used for the Grannom. The neck feathers of the cock are used as hackle for Haul a Gwynt.

Jay

The large primaries, although of a slightly coarse texture, are good dun wings for big flies dressed on a number eight hook. The blue covert feathers are used as hackle for the Haslam and the Invicta.

Teal

The primaries and secondaries are used for dun wings. The barred flank feathers are used extensively on wings of the Teal series of flies. It is also used for the Peter Ross. Some fly dressers use a wigeon flank feather in preference to a teal, because it is often better marked and of better texture. Wigeon feathers do not have the tendency to splay out when tied in.

Peacock

The herls from the long tail are wound around the hook to form a body such as the Coch-a-bon-ddu. The sword feathers are used for wings of the Alexandra and the Marchog Coch.

Body Materials

Fly-dressers who often go to great pains to find the correct hackle for a fly often ignore the importance of the body. Of the two, the body texture and shade is by far the more important.

Many of the old traditional patterns used the fur of the hare. The colours obtainable from hare fur are quite extensive. The hare's ear provides the olive fur which is required for many Olive flies. The body fur of a hare gives fur ranging in colour from light ginger to a very dark brown. The Water Rat and the Grey Squirrel also provide good body fur for flies.

Rabbit fur, although similar in texture to that of the hare, is not quite so widely used. The blue fur provides the body of the Grey Duster and the fawn back fur is used for the Sun Fly. The mole's fur, while being of excellent texture to work with, does not have so many patterns that require its limited colour of dark dun. When dyed in Picric acid it gives a very prominent shade of olive.

The best body material for flies is seal's fur. It has the advantage of being shiny and bright even in its wet stage. It dyes well and, although quite hard to work with for beginners, it is well worth taking the trouble to learn how to dub it correctly.

Some fifty years ago dubbing, by and large, was made of wool. The choice was limited in those days and an odd garment seen being worn that took the eye of a fly dresser was in grave danger of disappearing, or at least of being shorn. That was the fate of one very attractive scarf in the Ffestiniog area. Even today one pattern bears the name of Egarych sgarff Huw Nain, which was a small Sedge tied with the body made from the scarf of some Huw who was named after his grandmother.

Many novice dressers experience some difficulty with making dubbing bodies. There is a simple way of attaching fur to silk, but, as with all other crafts, there are distinct advantages in doing it the correct way.

Some fly dressers wax the silk before applying the dubbing. If cobbler's wax is used, then the fur will stick to the silk and tend to form rather a lifeless lump of material—like so much putty. Other dressers will just roll the dubbing around the silk and let the fur stand upright and away from the silk. A body formed by such a method allows light to penetrate through the fibres. Experienced dressers only use a small pinch of fur at a time.

When applying the fur to the silk, the fur should be on the first finger and thumb of the working hand. The silk should be held taut from the hook with the other hand. The fur is then placed on the silk —and the thumb and finger should press hard together and twist— twisting the fur and silk together in one direction. Never twist in both directions, as this will unwind the dubbing. Rolling the silk and fur one way will make it into a long thin cylinder.

Some of the old dressers had another method of making a dubbing body. They would take a pinch of fur and roll it for quite some time between their thumb and first finger, making it into a small ball. They would then tie in this ball with the tying silk. Many would claim that this method, now seldom practised, provided a better body than that made by other methods.

Key to the Illustrations

The head-line drawings which illustrate many of the fly patterns described in the text are by Ian Rolls and his associates at the Wildlife Department of the Dyfed College of Art, Carmarthen. Some ten late commissions were drawn by Valerie Ganz. The photographs in the text are by the author—except, of course, for the majority of the portrait 'snaps' which are kindly loaned by the subjects or their families.

Sewin Flies

The sewin flies used by Welsh anglers at the beginning of the nineteenth century were very similar to those used for trout fishing. The reason for this thinking was the belief that the sewin was biologically similar to the brown trout. George Agar Hansard writing about his fishing in different parts of Wales in the year 1834 noted that the best fly for sewin was a Red Fly which was also used for trout fishing. This Red Fly was probably used as an imitation of the February red. His advice on the make-up of the Red Fly was:

'Take a weak light and yellowish brown dun hen feather, either from the neck or any part of the body; wind two or three times close together, a little below the shank of the hook, and make the body clear below it, of a mixture of ruddy black sheep wool, mingled with orange; use yellow silk to rib up the body with it'.

It was to be dressed on a big hook, preferably Number 5. The fly to be used as a dropper for sewin fishing was made thus:

'A light blue hen or cock hackle with two or three turns round the top of the shank of the hook, with a body below of a mixture of light orange wool and a little dark fur with yellow tips from a hare's ear ribbed with gold thread'.

If the water ran heavy it was further recommended to put on wings made of spotted galino fowl or a grouse speckled feather. Even in those early days Hansard underlines the quality of the Welsh sewin and advises:

'. . . use good sound gut for your bottom, for they are very strong and yield noble sport'.

This principle of using overgrown trout flies for sewin has persisted in Wales from those early days until the last couple of decades. Flies like the colourful Dunkeld, Alexandra, Zulu, Butcher and Peter Ross dressed on number eight hooks were the accepted sewin flies.

Fortunately, Hugh Falkus in his seminal book, *Sea-trout Fishing*, 1962, challenged this principle and brought about a necessary change. Thereafter, sewin flies have undoubtedly taken on a new look.

Unlike most other fish, the sewin's reaction to the artificial fly depends a lot on the length of time that particular sewin being fished for has been in the river. The longer the sewin remains in the river, the more difficult it becomes to catch it. The big colourful lures are not necessarily effective for these fish. It is noticeable that, unlike salmon or brown trout flies, some sewin flies are effective in one section of a river but conspicuously not in another.

Sewin fly fishing can be divided into two distinct categories:
Daylight fishing with water levels varying from high to low.
Night fishing when the water level is medium to low.

Daytime fishing for sewin demands use of smaller flies and, on the whole, fairly sober colours. If the water is running down after a flood with a little bit of colour in it, then silver-bodied, colourful flies can be effective. Bigger flies can also be used when the water flow is above normal. Many fly patterns have been specifically developed in Wales to fish for sewin during the day and most of them are made of dubbing bodies with blue dun hackle.

Night fly fishing for sewin demands a different approach from the point of view of the fly. Most night-time flies have silver bodies or marked colour patterns and they are often of bigger dimensions. Night fishing has become extremely popular in Wales and is probably more widely practised here than anywhere else in Britain. There are some rivers in the Principality which offer some of the very finest sewin fishing, and the Welsh approach to the sport is becoming a very professional one.

Many trends in seatrout fishing have been started in Wales: in the last couple of seasons, the use of hair wings. Wings composed of hair give a far better colour pattern and more life in the deep, still pools and glides. The latest trend on several Welsh rivers is to construct flies of far longer dimensions: tandem, terror and tube flies of three and four inches long are not uncommon. These long flies, in many respects similar to reservoir lures, require special fishing methods. Slow and fast stripping, varying the movement of the lure, are all being used on dark summer nights.

It is also of interest to learn that the use of surface flies is on the increase on Welsh rivers and that some of the old traditional floating patterns are regaining favour. Why the big sewin that has ignored all kinds of flies and lures that have been swimming past its nose for hours will suddenly rise from the deep to take a fly moving on the surface is beyond one's comprehension. It is such imponderables that make dressing flies for sewin and fishing them so fascinating.

Alexandra

Hook 6, 8 and 10, tandem and as tube;
Black tying silk.
Body Flat silver, ribbed with silver wire.
Hackle Black hen.
Wing Green herl from sword tail of peacock.
A thin strip of red swan feather along
each side.
Cheeks Small jungle cock each side.

Location Reservoir and sewin rivers.
Time Early season on reservoir and summer
time for sewin.
Conditions All conditions.
Method On point of wet fly cast, fished deep in
stillwaters and at night on sewin rivers.

This is a Jekyll and Hyde pattern: anglers either love it or hate it. There was a time when it was outlawed from lakes because of its killing powers. No such reputation surrounds it today. Yet in the jungle cock form it is a good lure for early season rainbows. On some Welsh stillwaters it has a reputation for taking black, out-of-condition fish.

It is gaining stature yearly as a sewin fly and has taken well to its metamorphosis as a tube fly. The green peacock sword feathers give it a very attractive action and the silver body and black feathers with a red stripe give it a good colour pattern.

The Alexandra is often used in the smaller sizes as a trout fly on rivers. It is mainly effective when the water is coloured, and is often accused of taking undersized trout and parr. Very few of our still waters today are not subjected to artificial stocking from hatcheries and a truly wild brown trout fishery is becoming a rarity. Such a wild trout fishery is Claerwen and often a small Alexandra can be most effective even on days when the coch-a-bon-ddu is hatching in its thousands.

This royal fly, named after the Princess Alexandra, was reputedly created by a Dr Burton—although some maintain that W. G. Turle of Stockbridge was responsible for it. It is at least one hundred and twenty years old. It is effective in most of its different roles but in Wales it is primarily a sewin fly, especially when a little jungle cock is added to it and it is tied as a tandem or a tube fly.

5

Allrounder

Hook *6 & 8 Black tying silk.*
Tail *Golden pheasant toppings.*
Body *Black seal's fur.*
Rib *Silver thread.*
Hackle *Black cock.*
Wing *Black squirrel with overlay of red squirrel.*
Topping *Peacock sword feathers.*
Cheeks *Jungle cock.*

Location *River Rheidol and Towy.*
Time *Night time July onwards.*
Conditions *Low water.*
Method *Downstream wet fly.*

This fly has all the ingredients of all the traditional sewin flies rolled into one and is the basic tool of a night session for sewin. On occasions when sewin are maddeningly active but refuse to respond to any offerings, it is often best to stick to one's guns with a standard pattern rather than waste time continually changing flies. Though sometimes, of course, the completely unorthodox will work.

Illtyd Griffiths after the white-trout on Lough Bartra in Ireland where the Allrounder proved its worth!

6

The river Rheidol has a run of very big sewin in late May and early June and this pattern has proved effective on many a night. Although the popular sizes are *six* and *eight* it has been discovered that the big sewin, after being in the river for a long time, favour the smaller sizes. Illtyd Griffiths, its creator, spends more time than most after the big sewin, and his faith in the Allrounder is justified. An identical pattern—but minus the red squirrel section of the wing—has been used for a long time on the river Taf in Carmarthenshire/Pembrokeshire. The Taf compares favourably with any other river in Wales for sewin and on the Gynin, a major tributary of the Taf, the Allrounder has produced an impressive record for one particular angler.

In the dawn. Some evidence of the Allrounder's work on the Towy in June 1984, christening a new reel fitted with intermediate line.

An useful variant of the Allrounder, developed with success on the Towy in the summer of 1983, a particularly difficult season with high temperatures and low-water conditions prevailing throughout the prime months of July and August, was as follows: the tying as outlined above, with the exception of the Jungle cock cheeks. For these substitute a dark muddler (deer-hair) head and fish as a surface-lure or in the surface film. After some use the fly will tend to sink out of the surface levels; when this occurs, and takes are observed to fall-off, a little floatant should be applied—to a dry specimen—to assist buoyancy.

Blackie

> Hook   *Tandem, two number 4 or 6. A number 4 plus a number 6 double.*
> Rib   *Silver wire.*
> Body   *Black seal's fur or black floss.*
> Hackle   *Black cock.*
> Wing   *Black squirrel.*
> Cheek   *Jungle cock.*
>
> Location   *River Ystwyth.*
> Time   *Night time, from June-September.*
> Conditions   *Low water.*
> Method   *As point fly on a quick-sinking line.*

The Blackie is a lure that has transferred from reservoir to river fishing in recent times. (See p. 97).

This big lure is used when the sewin are lying deep, hugging the river bed. Sinking lines should be employed to take it down to secure that eye-level confrontation with the quarry. It works well deep down during the post-midnight period.

A survey of recent progress in sewin fishing reveals that the tendency is to use bigger and bigger lures on sunken lines. As in other forms of fly-fishing, black seems to be the colour most often productive of results, especially in dark and cold circumstances.

The fact that many regular reservoir anglers come to Wales annually to fish for sewin has meant that they bring with them reservoir techniques and tackle. The casting out of long lines and stripping lures back in double quick time has been one technique adopted that has proved successful with sewin on Welsh rivers. The Blackie in its tandem form or on a number six hook with a flying treble has proved very successful in this adopted way.

Two anglers who regularly fish Draycote reservoir near Rugby have employed this approach on the Dwyfawr and, the Blackie has not only done well when stripped quickly on a fast-sinking line, but also when stripped quickly just under the surface of the water on a slow-sinking or intermediate line. This method is especially productive in the early part of the season.

Blue, Black & Silver variants

Hook 4, 6, 8 & 10 Black silk.
Rib Silver wire.
Body Silver tinsel.
Hackle Blue or black.
Wing Black, Blue and natural squirrel hair.

Location All Welsh rivers.
Time Night time.
Conditions Low water.
Method Normal wet fly.

These flies are the pack-horses of sewin fishing in Wales. The silver body is the basic requirement and the variations follow the choice of dark and light coloured wings. The Blue, Black & Silver used in Wales are similar to the basic patterns suggested by Hugh Falkus in his book, *Sea-trout Fishing*. The hair wing has replaced the fibre wings recommended by Falkus because the hair wing is instantly responsive to the slightest whim of water current as the fly is worked through a pool. A hair wing also produces far more colour patterns when moved by the current.

Although variations of colour are largely a matter of personal fancy, the fish do sometimes respond better to a darker or a lighter pattern. It would seem that the black wing works better in those rivers which tend to have dark, peat-stained water: the Teifi and the Conway. The light wing works better on rivers with clearer waters like the Aeron and the Ystwyth. The light factor on particular nights also plays an important part.

These variants can either be tied on tube or treble hooks. John Mercer, a seasoned angler on the river Towy, has cut it so fine as to be seen using just the silver body and black squirrel wing. So long as the resulting over-all fly, including the treble, is an inch and a half in length and fished mainly on a sink-tip line, colour of wings is immaterial. Another angler, Gwyndaf Evans, on the river Rheidol, a dedicated man who certainly seems to spend more time on the river bank than he does in bed during the sewin season, uses a similar fly—but adds two jungle cock eyes in refinement. These anglers, and many others, have impressive results to testify to the excellence of this Black, Blue & Silver combination.

Blue, Black & Silver Squirrel

Hook 6 & 8 *Black tying silk.*
Tail *Tippets or toppings.*
Rib *Silver thread.*
Body *Black floss.*
Hackle *Blue.*
Wing *Grey squirrel.*

This version of the Blue, Black & Silver variant is known as the Squirrel in some areas while in others it is just used as another variation on the same colour theme of silver and blue. The grey squirrel wing makes for a much lighter colour pattern and this sometimes triggers off a response from the sewin on difficult nights, those nights that really test a fly pattern; the simple change of colour of the wing is often enough to give success.

The wing is tied on at a very flat angle over the blue hackle, some even putting the wing under the hackle. The hackle then is tied rather heavily which results in more movement of the hair fibres as the fly is worked through the water. This version worked well in the dry summer of 1975, and on those clear nights with an uncomfortable. amount of moonlight it was by far the best fly on the river Rheidiol and the Aeron.

Brown Bomber

Hook *6 & 8 Brown silk.*
Tag *Silver thread.*
Body *Peacock quill.*
Hackle *Woodcock: (hen blackbird subst.)*

Location *River Towy.*
Time *Mid summer to end of season, evening and night.*
Conditions *Low water.*
Method *Downstream wet fly. Point fly.*

Some flies have a killer look about them—this is certainly true of the Brown Bomber, named after heavyweight boxer Joe Louis who, in 1935, packed a similar punch to this deadly sewin fly. The Brown Bomber is another creation from the work-bench of a carpenter on the Dynevor Estate in Llandeilo, the colourful Wil Harry. Folklore has it that at one time Lord Dynevor had a stuffed bittern in a glass case in the library at Dynevor Castle, where Will Harry, during one of his Lordship's absences in London, was doing some maintenance work. Always interested in birds, especially dead

ones, Will Harry immediately took a fancy to the bittern. A small secret door was ingeniously constructed near the base of the glass case, through which *one* feather was taken to tie a particular pattern. The pattern proved so successful that another and another, then another feather disappeared out through the trap door. Eventually a half-bald bird revealed a mysterious affliction, and the butler had the bird thrown out before his Lordship discovered the grand larceny.

Fly dressers like Will Harry went to great lengths to secure the correct materials, and the original wing for the Brown Bomber was

Wil Harry in his young days as a member of Llandeilo Town band. His rough and ready approach to fly-tying almost belied his deep knowledge and real expertise as an angler.

11

said to be, not a bittern, but the wing of a hen blackbird taken in the third week of January. This piece of technical information comes from Major T. E. Hughes of Llandeilo, one of the most experienced Towy anglers, who claims to have baptised the fly which his old friend Wil Harry concocted.

Night fishing for sewin is a branch of angling widely practised in West Wales, especially on the river Towy. Some of these patterns, created by local artisans given the privilege of fishing, gratis, the Dynevor estate waters where the rule was 'fly only', are very resourceful and worthy of closer study.

This pattern, tied in tube and long-shank versions with 'flying trebles' built into the head, is recommended by Raymond Harris from Oxford—a keen, experienced and expert night fisher on Llangadog waters. He believes that a treble at the head can solve the nip-and-away phenomenon quite substantially.

Bomber

Hook *6 or 8 L.S.*
Tail *Deer hair or calf's tail.*
Body *Clipped deer hair to cigar shape.*
Rib *Brown or red hackle.*

Location *Conway.*
Time *After dark.*
Conditions *Low water.*
Method *On surface, downriver.*

This pattern came originally from America where it was used as a salmon fly. Here it has been used mainly as a surface lure for sewin. It is cast across the river and allowed to swing around in its own time without inducing the retrieve. Being made of deer hair, it floats well and can be swung on the surface across the pools and glides. It is effective in fishing for sewin that have been in the river quite a long time, fish, which, for some reason, will ignore the traditional wet fly cast across their path but will come up to hit the Bomber patrolling across the surface.

The Orvis Pennell reel.

Brown and Yellow Mole

Hook   *4 & 5 Black silk.*
Tag   *Yellow wool.*
Rib   *Gold wire.*
Body   *Rear ⅓, yellow. Front ⅔, mole.*
Hackle   *Ginger.*
Wing   *Brown hen or turkey.*

Location   *River Towy.*
Time   *Early summer until autumn.*
Conditions   *Low water for night fishing.*
Method   *Wet fly downriver.*

This represents a very sober pattern, by some standards, from one of the most colourful fly dressers of the river Towy. Wil Harry's aim with this fly, in all probability, was a pattern calculated to take fish from his favourite runs on the river Towy when the water was down to summer level and success was only to be achieved by subtle but, at the same time, unconventional means. One can understand the dark bulky body with the yellow rear and tag being dressed to persuade playful and indifferent fish to go for the business-end of the shank rather than tweak the head—as they will do time after time on summer nights. In recent times, the addition of a small treble with a bright yellow tag attempts the same objective.

It is worth noting with regard to some of these mid-Towy dressings that their appearance seems to spell a rough and unfinished approach to suggest, perhaps, the effect of a wounded or struggling creature. Lazy fish will often go for what they consider 'easy pickings' when oxygen levels are low.

This is not to deny or forget that often these flies were tied on the river bank in difficult light conditions with ready-to-hand materials —a heron feather, a bit of sheeps' wool and part of the dressing off an old fly. The light dressing suited rivers like the Towy which normally run clear and shallow in mid summer which is the height of the sewin season.

Closs Special

Hook 8 & 10 Black silk.
Tail Golden pheasant tippets.
Body Rear half: white tinsel; Front half:
      gold tinsel.
Hackle Orange.
Wing Bronze mallard.

Location Elwy & Clwyd.
Time Night time in mid summer.
Conditions Low water.
Method Wet fly method downriver.

Norman Closs-Parry, an angler of considerable all-round ability, devised this fly for use on the river Elwy in Clwyd. Norman is an angler who sometimes adds a maggot to the fly, which helps him to take sewin. This practice is prohibited on the rivers of south and west Wales while it is practised legally and extensively on the rivers of North Wales. It is difficult to quantify how much the fly accounts for the success of the effort and how much the maggot. Some flies do seem to work better with the maggot than do others, and this, apparently, is one of them.

Some sewin anglers on North Wales rivers who would never dream of fishing for sewin without a maggot on the fly, believe fervently in the creed that a maggot converts all the nips and pulls felt on 'fly only' terminal tackle into firm pulls. This is not always so and, even *with* the use of maggots, sewin will often just 'tweak' the maggot—much as a trout will do with a worm. The use of a flying, small-size fourteen, double or treble hook is then advised.

Conway Badger

Hook *6 & 8 Black tying silk.*
Rib *Three turns of flat red tinsel.*
Body *Black floss.*
Wing *Twelve hairs from badger back.*

Location *Originally river Conway*
Time *Summer night-time.*
Conditions *Low water.*
Method *Downriver wet fly.*

This old pattern, originating from the river Conway, is very similar to the Conway Red which is more widely used. The three specific turns of red tinsel make for a predominantly black body and this is the tellingly attractive feature of the pattern according to Roy Jones, the Head Keeper on the Gwydir Hotel water on the river Conway. Roy also is adamant about the number of hairs used to make the wing. The number twelve is both puzzling and surprising. It allows for the body to be clearly visible—veiled, as it were, by the few hairs which are more active and attractive for their sparseness.

Roy also maintains that the correct procedure in tying the wing is important. The hair is tied out over the eye and then folded back and tied again so that it rests back over the body. This makes for a rather more bulky head, which is believed to give the fly the required action in the water. The fly has no hackle: and is somewhat unusual in this respect. The folding-over of the wing ensures that there is no danger of the hairs being lost, as sometimes happens with poorly tied flies.

Roy Jones, Blaenau Ffestiniog, head-keeper on the Gwydir Hotel water on the Conway, specialist in Conway flies, here with his winning catch in Welsh Fly-fishing Championships on Llandegfedd.

16

Conway Red

Hook *6 & 8 Black tying silk.*
 Rib *Thin flat red tinsel.*
Body *Black floss.*
Wing *Hairs from badger back.*

This is a more common version of the Conway Badger without the meticulous restrictions on materials. This variant has travelled well and finds favour with anglers in other parts of the Principality. During warm weather when the sewin tend to be in the more quick-flowing parts of the river, the Conway Red, fished on a floating line, does very well. It is a far more bulky creation than the Conway Badger making more disturbance when fished in the surface film—thereby attracting more attention to itself.

The Conway Creel.

Cooke's Bogey

Hook   8 & 9 Black tying silk.
Tag   Silver tinsel.
Body   Black ostrich herl.
Rib   Silver thread.
Wing   White hen secondary quill.
Hackle   Badger cock.

Location   Originally river of mid Wales.
Conditions   Normal river flows.
Time   Dusk and evening time.
Method   Normal wet fly tactics.

Pryce Tannatt produced some excellent fly patterns which are masterpieces of the art of fly dressing. This pattern has achieved considerable success as a late evening sedge and also as a sewin fly. When used in the late evening, it is advisable to use a floating line to 'skit' the fly across the surface of the water. Often the fly will be ignored completely until the angler begins to move it. It has the added advantage of being highly visible as darkness approaches.

In its role as a sewin fly, many anglers find it successful for the first hour after darkness when fished on a floating line. The aim then is to have it fishing just under the surface and a short, sink-tip or, better still, slow-sink, line does this job rather well.

It is a pity that this pattern is not better known and more widely used—as it certainly can be a great help. Yet it is often the case that one particular angler can stumble across a pattern which will work well for him but always disappoint the next man. On the river Taf at Saint Clears the fishing for sewin at night can be exceptionally good where sewin of up to twenty pounds are seen every year. Cooke's Bogey is a pattern for the smaller sewin which move upriver after the big sewin have moved on to the higher reaches. These smaller sewin provide good sport though there are arguments for not making serious depredations of them. Bag limits of two or three brace should be observed by responsible anglers. It often pays to move the fly rather quickly as these smaller sewin are extremely active and playful and will chase anything fished near the surface. Unfortunately this active period is all too short and the angler must be ready to react quickly at such times.

Dai Ben

> Hook   *6, 8 & 10 Black silk.*
> Tail   *Honey dun fibres.*
> Rib   *Flat silver tinsel.*
> Body   *Rabbit fur.*
> Hackle   *Honey dun.*

> Location   *River Towy.*
> Time   *Daytime at normal water levels.*
> Conditions   *Medium to low water.*
> Method   *Wet fly—point*

This fly in the fifties and sixties reigned supreme on the river Towy where it took over from and displaced the Silver Invicta and Teal, Black & Silver. Today it is not so widely used. It was a fly designed for day as well as night fishing and achieved quite a record on the tidal reaches—especially as the tide ran out.

It was baptised by David Benjamin Glyn Davies, a great fly fisherman from Abergwili, near Carmarthen, on the river Towy. He maintains he received the pattern from Lord Dynevor's coachman. As Mr Davies did not tie his own flies he sent the pattern off to the Cummings Fishing Tackle firm and ordered a couple of dozen. For reference purposes he was asked to name it; he used his own first names, 'Dai' being short for David and 'Ben' for Benjamin. Hence the name Dai Ben.

It is an easy fly to tie, but the designer insisted that the hackle be of good quality. It would seem that, as the season progresses, a darker hackle is preferable. The fly is tied rather full with plenty of guard fibres sticking out to give the whole fly an animated effect when drawn through the water. The rabbit fur to be used is best taken from the back of a rabbit, taking only the top layer of fur—not the mid and lower—where the colour is of a more blueish hue and the texture is of a more woolly nature. Fly bodies made of that woolly dubbing will not give the life and sparkle required.

When the normal three-fly cast for sewin is used, the Dai Ben should generally go on the point position. The modern tendency is to use a two-fly cast with just the one dropper which invariably is a fly of a smaller size. Dai Ben has the reputation of being a good day-time fly particularly on rivers like the Towy which is controlled by a reservoir in its upper reaches. These rivers, of which there are many in Wales, often have high water without much colour. Under such conditions the Dai Ben fishes well.

19

This is basically a Towy pattern and it must be accepted that it does not work well on many other rivers. Prolonged trials have revealed that it does not meet with much success on the rivers Teifi, Taf, Dovey or Conway while it has accounted for some fish on the Dwyfawr, Dwyryd, Rheidiol and Cleddau.

Probably the most surprising success achieved by the Dai Ben has been on the Towy Estuary. Some anglers do rather well by fishing the tail of the tide. This is quite good fishing and the Dai Ben seems to be the kind of pattern to offer the sewin that hang back in the pools as the tide drains away.

David Benjamin Glyn Davies, alias 'Dai Ben', of Abergwili, who gave his name to a most effective sewin fly on the Towy.

Doctor's Special

Hooks   9 & 12. Brown silk.
Tail   Ginger cock strands.
Rib   Fine gold wire.
Body   Fawn or cinnamon fur from base of
  hare's ear.
Hackle   Coch-a-bon-ddu.
Wing   Bronze mallard.

Location   Dwyfach.
Time   Summer.
Conditions   Water thinning down.
Method   Downriver wet fly.

Dr Shelton Roberts, who fished many of the Lleyn rivers in North Wales, favoured drab-coloured flies in his approach to sewin fishing which was close to that of the trout angler. Fifty years ago the fancy-coloured flies—with their sparkling tinsel—were not as popular as they are today; and flies were generally far smaller. The doctor used the bigger fly dressed on a size nine hook for high water conditions and the smaller version dressed on a size twelve hook for very low water conditions.

When fishing the Dwyfach, a very small river, in low water conditions the wet-fly cast used was often no longer than four feet —yet it supported two or three wet flies which were no more than nine to twelve inches apart!

21

Dovey Black & Orange

        Hook *4, 6 & 8 Salmon doubles: 6. Black silk.*
        Tail *Red swan.*
         Rib *Silver thread.*
        Body *Black floss.*
      Hackle *Orange.*
        Wing *Black squirrel.*
      Cheeks *Jungle cock.*

    Location *River Dovey*
        Time *Day and night time.*
  Conditions *All conditions other than high water.*
      Method *Normal wet fly.*

Another excellent pattern from one of the premier sewin rivers in Wales. Most examples are tied on number six doubles which give the pattern extra hooking capability.

This pattern has the advantage of being an excellent taker of sewin irrespective of the level of water in which it is being fished. As on most rivers, the Dovey sewin also give anglers a couple of hours of near-surface activity before midnight when the Black & Orange serves well. Fished then on a floating or a short sink-tip line the fly provides a good colour pattern and visibility in all conditions.

Sewin anglers in Wales tend to try out each other's patterns on different rivers. Some patterns travel well and are effective on all rivers, others fail to produce the same magic away from their own home patch. The Dovey Black & Orange has scored successes on the Glaslyn, Dwyfawr and Conway. Sewin anglers today look for good colour contrast in their sewin flies and the drab and sober colours of years gone by are tending to give way to more vivid combinations. Emyr Lloyd, a river keeper on the river Dovey, recommends this pattern and believes that it is a *must* on the Dovey.

Dovey Bumble

Hook 6, 8 & 10 Black silk.
Rib Silver thread.
Tag Silver thread.
Body Green peacock herl tied full.
Hackle Barred Plymouth Rock.

Location River Dovey
Time Daytime, July onwards.
Conditions Normal river flow.
Method Downriver wet fly. On point & dropper.

It is only fitting that the river Dovey, one of the most prolific sewin rivers in the Principality should have its own special pattern. The Dovey Bumble is not so popular today as it was. As a pattern it bears little resemblance to the Bumble series from Derbyshire; although, after an initial success, Bumble bodies of different materials and colours were used on the Dovey.

The Dovey Bumble is tied with two hackles; the smaller of the two being used to palmer the body down. Some dressers, in the interest of better hooking, add a small amount of hackle down along the body. The river Dovey is normally a clear river when not in flood, and the Dovey Bumble looks well when fished in the runs. At night this pattern can be used as a dropper with a bigger point fly. In recent years some anglers have been using the Dovey Bumble in a tandem form.

During the thirties many different Bumble patterns were tried on the Dovey for sewin. It would appear that none of the variations were as successful as the original—although occasional success did come their way.

Yellow Bumble

Tail Golden Pheasant toppings.
Rib Gold thread.
Body Golden olive seal's fur.
Hackle Yellow (Palmered).
Front hackle Blue jay

This pattern gained much favour with anglers fishing in water just clearing after a flood.

Fiery Brown Bumble

Tail　Golden pheasant toppings.
Rib　Gold thread.
Body　Fiery brown seal's fur.
Hackle　Red and fiery brown mixed.
Front hackle　Grouse hackle.

This pattern was used in fast-flowing water when the river level was down to low summer flow.

Claret Bumble

Tail　Golden pheasant tippets.
Rib　Gold thread.
Body　Claret seal's fur.
Hackle　Claret and black hackles mixed.
Front hackle　Jay.

The Claret Bumble was used mostly at dusk and was fished on the bob position during that time when moths were hovering near the water.

Earley's Fancy (No 1)

Hook No. 10 or 11 (Salmon size). Brown silk.
Tail Toppings.
Rib Gold twist.
Body Rusty red-brown fur.
Hackle Same colour (or lighter) than body.
Wing Cock Pheasant.

Location Rivers Ogmore & Ewenny.
Conditions Fairly low water.
Time Day or evening.
Method Wet fly downriver.

Earley's Fancy (No 2)

Hook 10 or 11. (Two sizes smaller than for
number 1). Brown tying silk.
Tail A few springs of tippets.
Rib Gold tinsel.
Body Dark claret fur.
Hackle Coch-a-bon-ddu stained claret.
Wing Cock pheasant.

Francis Francis in his *'A Book on Angling'*, published in 1880, notes four popular 'sewin flies' which he received from 'a Mr Berrington' who was a respected angler on the rivers Ogmore and Ewenny. Those rivers then enjoyed the reputation of being excellent sewin rivers; some anglers even considering them to be the best in Wales. George Agar Hansard who, in 1835, listed some of the catches made on the Ogmore was one who maintained that it was without equal as a sewin river. Ominously though, there were already some problems in respect of pollution.

These two Earley's Fancy flies were used for sewin in low and high water and were useful as salmon flies as well. Two other flies that were received by Francis from the same source were the Polly Perkins and the White Owl, the former, presumably recalling the popular Music-hall song of the day:

'She was as beautiful as a butterfly,
And as proud as a Queen
Was pretty little Polly Perkins
Of Paddington Green'

Polly Perkins

      Hook *12. (Salmon size). Brown tying silk.*
       Tag *Gold twist.*
       Tail *Sprigs of tippet.*
      Body *Peacock herl.*
       Rib *Fine gold wire.*
   Hackle *Coch-a-bon-ddu.*
     Wing *Two small tippet feathers.*
   Cheek *Small kingfishers.*
     Ribs *Blue macaw.*

The Wasp Fly

     Hook *12. (Salmon size). Brown tying silk.*
      Tail *Three mauve fibres.*
     Butt *Black ostrich.*
    Body *Peacock herl.*
      Rib *Yellow orange floss.*
    Wing *Rich brown speckled hen.*

The White Owl

Francis also describes a fly called the 'White Owl' which was literally white all over like a barn owl. It was a fly to be used all night for, with the coming of dawn, he observes, the fish 'cease biting'.

Fiery Brown

Hook *8 & 10 Brown silk.*
Tail *Golden pheasant tail.*
Rib *Gold wire.*
Body *Brown seal's fur.*
Hackle *Brown.*
Wing *Bronze mallard.*

Location *On North Wales rivers.*
Time *Day time.*
Conditions *Normal river level.*
Method *Normal wet fly downstream.*
First dropper.

The Fiery Brown is a comparatively little-known sewin fly, despite the fact that it was voted as the best seatrout fly in Ireland in 1905, where, in an Exhibition of Fishing, by inviting each area to nominate their favourite fly, it swept the board. It is still a good general pattern to use for sewin fishing during the day, especially with stale fish.

Much of the sewin fishing done in Wales is on angling club or association water and the approach, therefore, has to be different to that for fishing private, undisturbed water. Some anglers may, on occasion, have to share a pool with as many as eight or ten other rods —and many of those using different baits and methods. Under such circumstances the angler is well advised to modify his approach and consider flies of smaller dimensions and more refined colours. The Fiery Brown fits this bill admirably and it is a good fly for taking shy sewin. Fished on a floating line and worked slowly down and around the pool at dusk it will take the odd reluctant sewin by surprise.

In size ten, used during daylight hours, the Fiery Brown, despite its foreign origin, has the appearance of a typical Welsh fly for sewin. Fished then in the runs and the necks of pools it will take sewin in the early hours of the morning before the arrival of disturbance on the river banks.

Grey Goose
(Llwyd yr Wydd)

Hook *7, 9 & 12. Brown silk.*
Tail *3 or 4 strands of mallard.*
Body *Hare's ear (Dark).*
Rib *Silver tinsel.*
Hackle *Dark red cock.*
Wing *Saddle feather from goose.*
Time *Summer.*

Location *Rivers Dwyfawr and Dwyfach.*
Conditions *River thinning after flood.*
Method *Downriver wet fly.*

This is one of a series of flies that Dr Shelton Roberts, a G.P. in Penygroes, near Caernarvon in North Wales, used some fifty years ago. Gwilym Owen of Bangor was good enough to preserve this tying and pass on the information after his friend, the late Dr Alun Roberts of the University College of North Wales, Bangor.

A very well-known broadcaster on natural history, Alun Roberts was a member of the panel of the BBC Wales radio feature, 'Y Byd Natur' (The World of Nature). Both Dr Alun and Dr Shelton, it appears, were deacons at the same Methodist Chapel in Penygroes. Sometimes after lengthy and wearisome 'Sessions' they would go fishing together—to unwind, and in a letter to his friend one said 'Wel, dyna ni wedi setlo'r Sasiwn a'r rasus milgwn, cawn fyned at bethau sydd eli i lesg galon'! (Well, there we've settled the 'Sasiwn' (sessional meeting) and the greyhound races, now let's go at the things which raise heavy hearts!)

Dr Shelton Roberts was of the opinion that Llwyd yr Wydd was the very best sewin fly for the rivers Dwyfawr and Dwyfach. These rivers today hold some very big sewin, up to ten pounds and more in weight, which normally respond better to big lures. Smaller flies like the Llwyd yr Wydd can often rouse them though, when they are bored with being shown big tubes and Terrors.

Harry Tom

> Hook 8 & 10 Brown silk.
> Tail Honey dun fibres.
> Rib Silver wire.
> Body Rabbit fur.
> Hackle Honey dun.
> Wing Bronze mallard.
>
> Location River Ogwen and other rivers in North
> Wales.
> Time Day and night time.
> Conditions Medium flow to low water.
> Method Normal wet fly downriver.

The Harry Tom fly, from the Ogwen valley in North Wales, is somewhat similar to the Dai Ben from the Towy Valley, in south west Wales. The texture of the rabbit fur used in both patterns must be of the top layer from a rabbit's back.

As with many sewin flies, this pattern is drab in appearance and suitable for both day and night fishing. In North Wales it is customary to impale a maggot onto the fly hook—a practice deemed to improve its attractiveness (though it is debatable if it is then true fly fishing) and the Harry Tom seems to do this job.

The tendency today is to use bigger and silver bodied lures for night fishing and many of the traditional patterns like the Harry Tom tend to be used as droppers. This technique often pays, as the smaller and lighter coloured fly, fishing nearer the surface is often made more attractive by its dance in and on the surface of the water.

In recent years, use of the sink-tip line has become more widespread. The development in line technology facilitates, among other things, the drawing up of the flies as they fish up and around the bend of the cast. The presence of a smaller fly enables the angler to present his offering, which is of a different shape, just below the surface. With increasing use of quick-sink lines to fish these huge lures, there is a danger of ousting the traditional sewin fly method. But, for work with floating—slow-sink and sink-tip lines—it is still wise to remember to use these old established flies that have long proved their value to anglers, and can still do good work in a secondary role when the star attraction fails.

Huw Nain

Hook *6 & 8.*
Tail *Tippets.*
Rib *Silver wire.*
Body *Rear half: Golden olive.*
Front half: Grey seal's fur.
Wing *Hen Pheasant.*
Hackle *Partridge.*

Location *Conway & Lledr.*
Time *Day and night time in summer.*
Conditions *Normal river level.*
Method *Wet fly downriver.*

This is a good fly from the Dolwyddelan area. Dressed by Eirwyn Roberts, it pleases anglers on the Conway and its tributaries very well. This pattern has a long tradition in North Wales, being popular also in the Dwyryd and Dwyfawr. It is used both during the day and at night and has the reputation of being very successful in the taking of big sewin.

The name 'Huw Nain' suggests that a certain Huw (the Welsh spelling of Hugh) was involved in the creation of this pattern. The word 'Nain' means Grandmother in Welsh, which is interesting—as it dates the pattern to an earlier era when boys with over-common names aquired nicknames. It sounds as if in his youth this fisherman was reared by his grandmother.

The fly works well on other rivers in Wales when fished in quick runs during the daytime. In the early days of sewin fishing the all-though-the-night sessions were not so common. Many of the ordinary workmen in North Wales in those days had very little time to fish. They often worked a twelve hour day. They would go out at dusk and fish until midnight, and their flies were designed to take the smaller sewin. The big sewin that are generally the post-midnight takers did not figure prominently in the workmen's bags. Yet Huw Nain achieved the reputation of being good at taking *big* sewin— which points something of a contradiction.

Are the past reputations of such flies a safe guide to their present potential? One angler who visits the river Dyfi just once a year will never be without his Huw Nain on the cast, 'just in case there's a big one about!'

Those anglers who fish for rainbow trout can do much worse than try Huw Nain on them; it has been known to do well on Eglwys Nunydd Reservoir at Port Talbot.

Kingsmill

Hook *6 & 8 Black tying silk.*
Tail *Golden pheasant tippet.*
Rib *Silver wire.*
Body *Black ostrich herl.*
Hackle *Black cock.*
Wing *Rook wing quill rolled and tied low.*
Cheeks *Jungle cock.*
Topping *As roof over all golden pheasant toppings.*

Location *Used on middle Teifi.*
Time *Night time.*
Conditions *Low water.*
Method *Downriver wet fly.*

The Kingsmill of Hugh Kingsmill Moore, is a good point fly on a three-fly cast fished downriver. It works best used on a floating line or a sink tip. The fly should be kept in the surface layer of the water and is effective when it swings round—fishing 'round the bend'. It works well when the sewin have been in the river for some time. The dressing should be very light and the body rather thick.

It is a stalwart during the hours of darkness but it is also useful during the day and is even known to take a few salmon at the tail end of the season. Although the Kingsmill is an old and well established pattern in other parts of the country, it is a comparative stranger to Welsh waters. A visiting angler from the Midlands some four seasons ago used it extensively on the river Rheidol during his ten-day visit to the area. His results were most impressive.

The Rheidol, being a river subject to periodic sudden increased flows, due to the requirements of the electricity generating scheme, is a most difficult fishery to master. The Midlander's method was to travel light and fish quickly extensive lengths of the river: thus trying his luck successively in different locations. This way the angler can experiment in fishing a variety of pools which are affected differently by increased or decreased water flows and levels. All his fish were taken on the Kingsmill tied in size six for high flows and eight and ten as the water dropped when the generating stopped.

It is highly probable that the fluctuations in water temperature are an important factor on such a fishery, and the preference for the black and silver colours in low temperatures could also have been significant.

31

Lewi's Killer

Hook 6 *Black silk.*
Tail *Black fibres*
Body *Black wool.*
Rib *Two distinct bands of gold thread.*
Hackle *Long black hen drawn below the body.*

Location *River Towy.*
Time *All season. Day and night.*
Conditions *All water levels.*
Method *Low deep and slow.*

Today the Black Lure is the top reservoir lure. It is more than interesting now to appreciate that Lewi Davies of Llandeilo devised this pattern sometime in the thirties. The success gained by black fly patterns for still water trout is well known in all parts of Wales, but it was thought that the Black Lure has only become widely used in sewin fishing after the evidence of its success in reservoir fishing.

Few Welsh anglers between the wars would ever have thought of using a black lure for night sewin fishing, but Lewi Davies evidently did; and had success with it. The Black Lure is always fished deep and slow and has the deserved reputation of taking big fish. It is best fished in high water—and it is well to watch for salmon being interested in it in all water conditions!

That the Black Lure was being used on the river Towy in the thirties in a manner identical to the latest reservoir approach is very intriguing. Why did Lewi in those early days employ only an apron of hackle as opposed to the normal method of winding the hackle around the hook? It is that some of the old Welsh fly dressers working in isolation were really gifted, and that some of them lived out of their time.

Lewi Davies of Llandeilo whose innovative approach to fly technology on the Towy was ahead of its time. His quiet unassuming manner belied his other prowess, apparently!

Emrys Evans of Blaenau Ffestiniog, who has made a detailed study of the old fly dressers of his area, maintains that these men were gifted with an 'eye' for colour and colour patterns. Lewi had this 'eye' for patterns which means he was an artist of a sort. Lesser mortals can only be astounded, on chance discovery like this, that such advanced designs for fly patterns were being created by the unlettered and unurbane.

Lewi's Killer has a gold band around the middle, another unusual feature of his bold approach to fly dressing. Could this have been an attempt at getting the sewin to hit the centre of the lure as opposed to tweaking its head or bottom? This principle—attaching a band of (fluorescent) material around the centre of the body material—was tried a few years ago, and it was thought then to be an innovation.

Lewi did not always give his flies names. He gave examples of his successes to particular friends and, when asked what it was, he would blink and nudge, 'Never mind, take it, use it. It's a *killer*, mind!' So we named this after the inventor, 'Lewi's Killer'.

Mallard & Silver

Hook   *8 & 10. Black silk.*
Tail   *Golden Pheasant Tippets.*
Rib   *Silver wire.*
Body   *Flat silver tinsel.*
Hackle   *Black hen.*
Wing   *Bronze Mallard.*
Time   *Night time in Summer.*

Location   *River Dovey.*
Conditions   *Low water.*
Method   *Downriver wet fly.*

This fly was very popular in the fifties and sixties and was a great favourite with Peter Vaughan, the well-known fishing tackle dealer at Machynlleth, who recommended an alternative double-hook tying where conditions demanded a rapid and deeper-sinking attractor.

In those days the three-wet-fly team fished downriver was the normal method of fishing for sewin. One angler who, according to his diaries, fished the Dovey at that time some four nights every week, invariably used the same three-fly cast combination throughout the sewin season. His point fly was the Haslam; and his bob fly always Dovey Bumble. In the early years he had used various flies in the middle dropper position until Peter Vaughan persuaded him to try the **Silver Mallard**. He never changed the *dramatis personae* of his cast thereafter.

Dovey record sea-trout, 20¾ lbs. Caught by Arthur Humphreys, 1959.

34

Marchog Coch
(Red Knight)

Butt	Red Silk.
Body	Flat gold tinsel ribbed with fine silver wire.
Wing	Paired red tail feathers from golden pheasant.
Cheeks	Inner: Red body feather from golden pheasant.
	Outer: Yellow body feathers from golden pheasant.
Topping	Four strands of peacock sword.
Location	Dovey and other sewin rivers.
Time	Night time.
Conditions	Low water and running-off after a spate.
Method	Normal wet fly method of across and down. Can also be effective when stripped quickly either high or low in the water.

To make the flying treble mount:
Three strands of 20 lb black nylon looped around treble, then platted. Attach platted nylon to shank of main hook—whip firmly and trim.

A colourful sewin pattern which has many excellent qualities. The stiff tail feathers of the golden pheasant ride well in the water and will not wrap around the hooks—as is the tendency with softer hackle fibres.

The flying treble, some two or three inches behind the hook, is made of black plaited 20 lb nylon which is an excellent link. The weight of the fly can be increased or decreased by judicious use of heavier and lighter hooks. If the angler wishes to gain maximum depth the use of a double hook for the body is recommended.

This lure is the brainchild of Dr Graeme Harris of the Welsh Water Authority, who does much of his fishing on the river Dovey. The Marchog series is primarily designed to take the big sewin for which the river Dovey is rightly famed.

Marchog Glas
(Blue Knight)

Butt   *Red fluorescent wool.*
Body   *Silver tinsel ribbed with gold.*
Hackle *Golden pheasant red body hackle.*
Wing   *Two pairs of blue feathers.*
Cheeks *A Plymouth Rock feather.*
Topping *Four strands of peacock herl.*

Location *River Dovey and other sewin rivers.*
Time   *Night time.*
Conditions *Low water. Spate running off.*
Method *Normal wet fly downstream method.*
       Can also be effective when moved
       quickly high or low in the water.

In many respects the Marchog Glas is similar to its brother the Red Knight and also has a reputation for taking really big fish. When the sewin become dour, the Marchog Glas fished on a quick-sinking line is really effective. The flying treble—especially when of the outpoint variety—is an excellent hooker. Often, sewin anglers lose these big sewin when only lightly hooked. Trebles can help to eliminate this problem.

The Marchog series, soundly based as they are in the traditional mainstream of sewin attractors, also have that look about them which signifies an advance. They are the fly of the late twentieth century—for sewin or stillwater trout.

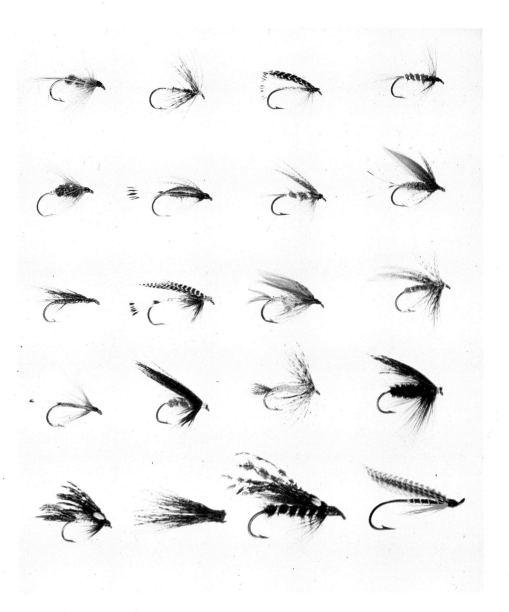

Plate II   Sewin Flies

Twm Twll	Brown Bomber	Closs Special	Dai Ben
Dyfi Bumble	Fiery Brown	Harry Tom	Huw Nain
Red Mackerel	Silver Grey	Torby Coch	T. L. Harries's Sedge
Towy Topper	Tom Tom	Yellow Plasterer	Will Harry's Green
Jungle Alexandra	Black & Silver	Allrounder	Woodcock
	tube		Teal Black &
			Silver

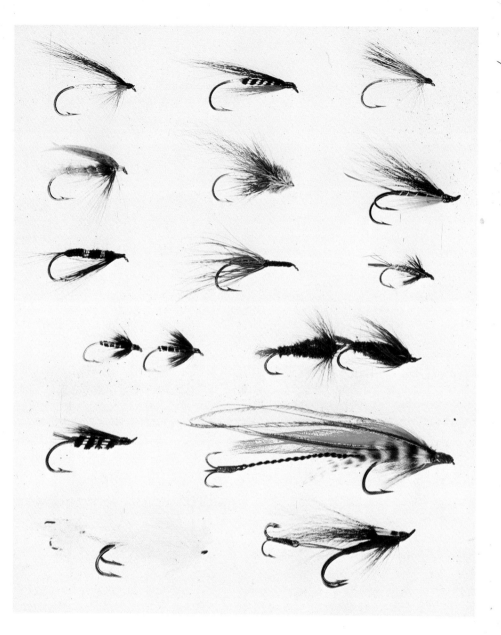

Plate III Sewin Flies

Blue Black & Silver Variants 1, 2 & 3

Brown & Yellow Mole	Blue Muddler	Dovey Black & Orange
Lewi's Killer	Night Heron	Pry-copyn
Teifi Terror		Sewin Worm-fly
Conway Red		Marchog Glas
Mouse		Blackie

The Mouse
Surface Lure

Hook *6 with flying treble. White tying silk.*
Body *White deer hair clipped.*
Wing *Deer hair and marabou.*

Location *Ystwyth, Rheidol and Towy.*
Time *Dark nights.*
Conditions *Calm and sultry.*
Method *Cast across river and allow to swing back across.*

The purpose of the Surface Lure is, by skating it across the surface of the water, **to create a wake.** The wake is the attraction more than the fly itself. Years ago, sewin anglers used a huge cork-based lure known as The Mouse constructed from half a wine-cork cut lengthways and shaped, with a 4/0 salmon hook protruding—eye-uppermost—through the cork, which was adorned with bushy, colourful feathers. The Mouse was cast onto the surface of the water and allowed to drift around. So effective was it on some rivers that it was actually banned.

Not all pools are suited to this method of fishing: it is essential that there is a firm flow to enable the lure to be swung around and across the river. A long rod allows for greater control of the lure. The Mouse will sometimes take sewin, fishing in a semi-submerged state, in the manner of a bob fly.

There is no doubt that there is a period during most warm nights when it is worth trying a short spell with the Surface Lure. Even if it fails to hook, it has the distinct advantage of showing the angler where the sewin are holding up because it often moves fish which otherwise do not show—even though they are not in a taking mood. One very successful angler on the river Towy does not use any other lure for his sewin fishing and his results are impressive—especially with big fish.

While the surface lure is designed to skate across the surface, it is possible to use this same lure in another way. This demands that the lure sink just a few inches below the surface—and is then stripped quickly, really quickly, across the pool. This tactic is best used with a short, sink-tip or an intermediate line. The surface lure is one of the most neglected devices in sewin fishing and, whether drifted across the river, or stripped quickly in, or fished just under the surface, it represents a most exciting method.

Some anglers also recommend holding the surface lure in a run and moving it slowly by carefully raising the rod: this is known as 'dibbing' or 'dibbling', which can also do the trick in bringing up very good fish. Needless to add, with such tactics, very many fish are missed: yet on some nights every one will be fast on the flying treble.

The Hardy Wake Lure.

Wake Lure No. 1

Wake Lure No. 2

Night Heron

Hook   *6 Black silk.*
Tag   *Silver wire.*
Body   *Black wool, ribbed with silver.*
Front Half   *Black silk, varnished.*
Hackle   *Mid body, heron.*

Location   *River Towy.*
Time   *Summer months, nightfishing.*
Conditions   *Low water.*
Method   *On point of a one-fly cast fished downriver.*

This fly, dressed by Lewi Davies of Llandeilo, was a complete innovation in the late forties when it was first used. He must have decided to attach the hackle mid-way down the body in order to try and combat the tendency to nip the fly which can be so infuriating when fish are somewhat stale and in shoals in low water conditions, and at other times when this unaccountable behaviour is observable. Lewi, though not the world's neatest fly dresser, was remarkably scientific in his approach.

Today we think of the Dog Nobbler (Page 248), as the newest reservoir lure which has adopted the same principle. The modern material used with such flies is marabou feather whith its long fluffy fibres, but Lewi Davies, by utilising the soft heron feathers had achieved the same effect by 1950.

The heron herl used by Lewi as centre hackle for this pattern is ideal material for this sewin fly. Modern fly dressers use marabou for the same purpose, but it is doubtful if it is as effective. Most sewin anglers in the days of Lewi Davies retrieved their flies by the simple figure-of-eight action of the hand. This works the flies in a slow, jerky action which activates the long hackle. One could claim that the Night Heron is of a superior design to the modern Dog Nobbler, using as it does, subtler ready-to-hand and more resilient material. The Dog Nobbler was the top reservoir lure of 1982 and 1983 and is well set for repeating that feat in 1984.

Old Favourite

Hook *9 & 12. Claret silk.*
Rib *Yellow silk thread.*
Body *Wine coloured wool and dark hare's ear.*
Hackle *Partridge.*

Location *River of Lleyn in North Wales.*
Time *Summer.*
Conditions *After flood.*
Method *Wet fly downriver.*

This fly was described by Dr Shelton Roberts as his favourite sewin fly and, as in most of his patterns, the hook sizes are numbers nine and twelve: somewhat unusual. The Doctor's patterns form a valuable contribution to the history of fly dressing in North Wales.

This pattern closely resembles the Tom Tom from the Cwmystwyth area of mid Wales, the identical body being used as a wet fly when the alder is on the water; though the hackle used by Thomas Thomas for the Tom Tom varied from partridge to grouse. It seems that the Tom Tom sported the partridge hackle early in the season and the darker grouse hackle later on.

Pry-copyn

Hook *6, 8 & 10 Black silk.*
Tag *Red ibis or red wool.*
Rib *Thin silver wire.*
Body *Grey seal's fur.*
Hackle *Well-marked badger.*

Location *North Wales sewin rivers.*
Time *July & August.*
Conditions *Low water.*
Method *Normal downriver wet fly.*

This is an old Welsh pattern which was used for sewin fishing on the rivers Glaslyn and Dwyryd with considerable success. It is not so widely used today, except by a few of the older generation of sewin anglers. Some find it especially effective when used with a maggot, a method which is illegal in south and west Wales.

The badger hackle has been a favourite in Wales on many rivers and for many years. The tendency is to use it in hot, bright conditions. It is a highly visible feather which accounts for its being used when the river is just losing its colour after a flood. Some anglers also use the Pry-copyn in smaller sizes for day-time sewin fishing when the water is low. Sewin *can* be taken during the day, but the angler is well advised to guard his approach and it is necessary to work up-river. There is also an advantage in adding a little weight to the dressing so that the fly, when fished up-river, sinks immediately and can be drifted at the level at which the sewin are lying. Remember that it is most necessary to sink the fly down to that eye-ball to eye-ball level when fishing for sewin during the day. They will seldom rise and take a fly on the surface like trout.

Rancid Racoon

Hook	6 or 8. Black tying silk.
Tail	Golden Pheasant toppings.
Body	Gold lurex.
Rib	Gold wire.
Hackle	Black cock palmered.
Throat hackle	Natural gallina.
Wing	Grey squirrel.
Cheeks	Jungle cock.
Location	Eastern Cleddau.
Conditions	Low water for night fishing.
	High water for day fishing.
Time	(See above)
Method	Wet fly downriver.

This fly was devised by Winston Oliver, known as 'Scruff Oliver', who fishes the Red House beats on the Eastern Cleddau in the county of Pembrokeshire. It was designed as a night fly, but it has proved successful during the day as well. It is tied generally on a number six hook with the squirrel tail extending out beyond the bend about half the length of the iron. The whole tying should be done with the maximum economy of materials.

Scruff Oliver, when he set about devising this pattern, was looking for something unnatural, something spooky: for sewin fishing is conducted during the dark, and he wanted a fly somewhat suggestive of a witch moving on her broom across the moon! The outline of the fly is important, though only Old Nick himself knows what the fish see when the R.R. haunts their lairs! Yet Rancid Racoon has taken large numbers of sewin on the Cleddau.

When required to fish low in the water it is tied on a number ten double salmon hook. In this guise Rancid Racoon has also accounted for a number of salmon on the Eastern Cleddau and it will be interesting to discover what successes will be credited to this unusual pattern on other waters.

The Red Mackerel

Hook *6 & 8 Red tying silk.*
Tail *Bronze mallard.*
Body *Red lurex.*
Hackle *Blood red hackle.*
Wing *Bronze Mallard.*

Location *The sewin rivers of North Wales.*
Time *Summer months.*
Conditions *Low water for night fishing. High water for day fishing.*
Method *Point fly on a two- or three-fly cast.*

This fly originated in North Wales, but its fame spread quickly to other parts of the principality. In this expansion of its territory, the pattern suffered a debasement of its original dressing. In some areas patterns masquerading under the title Red Mackerel bear little or no resemblance to the authentic dressing given above.

Of bigger sewin rivers like the Dovey and the Towy, the Red Mackerel does quite well when the river is running down and losing its colour. The modern tendency in such conditions is for anglers to resort to the use of spinning equipment. Use of the colourful Red Mackerel or similarly visible attractor fly can be equally effective, particularly in taking stale fish that have been in the river for some time and are rather wise to the ironmongery that is hurled at them across the pools.

Many night-time sewin anglers develop a fondness for some particular fly and, no doubt, do better for that faith in their particular favourite pattern. On the river Cleddau, when the main run of smaller sewin comes in during late July, one particular angler does well by sticking with the Red Mackerel. When it was permissible to use a maggot in that part of Wales, this was the fly that was always used to fish the maggot.

Silver Grey

Hook *6 & 8.*
Tail *Golden pheasant tippets.*
Body *Silver tinsel.*
Rib *Silver wire.*
Hackle *Badger hackle.*
Wing *Teal.*

Location *Llanrwst area of the river Conway.*
Time *Night time.*
Conditions *Low water.*
Method *Normal wet fly downriver.*

The Conway river is considered one of the finest sewin rivers in the Principality. A sewin angler of repute in the sixties was J. O. Jones who was renowned for his expertise in matters piscatorial. The Silver Grey was his brainchild and, while there were many who tied the pattern, few scored the same success with it as 'J. O.' He tied his flies very lightly and the teal flank feather was tied very short, often not reaching back more than to half the hook. This Conway sewin fly is not to be confused with the classic salmon pattern.

One old angler who used to fish with J. O. relates that two or three of them would follow each other down a long glide or a pool at night. It implied a friendly rivalry, with each angler trying hard to do better than his partners. Although using identical flies and fishing down the same stretch of river, their results could never be compared. J. O. would invariably do better than his friends with his Silver Grey

somewhere on the cast of two or three flies. The combination of J. O. and his Silver Grey was unbeatable!

Some anglers formerly used a wigeon feather instead of the teal flank feather—because of its better marking and closer webb. The tendency today is to use grey squirrel as wing. Many believe that hair wings are a decided improvement.

J. O. Jones, of the Conway, sometime member of the Welsh fly-fishing team who was responsible for many enduring patterns.

44

Teifi Terror

Hook *10 & 8 Black silk.*
Rib *Gold wire.*
Tail *Furnace fibres.*
Body *Black floss.*
Hackle *Furnace.*

Location *River Teifi.*
Time *Day time and night time after July.*
Conditions *Medium and low water flow.*
Method *Normal wet fly fishing, good dropper.*

The Teifi Terror, once a traditional sewin fly, is more often than not these days tied on a tandem principle. This enables the angler to present to the fish a bigger lure and a lure with added hooking potential. The trend today is towards maximum hooking power, with double and treble hooks being increasingly used.

In its original form, tied solo on size 10 or 8 hook, in the middle reaches of the Teifi, the Teifi Terror is still capable of doing well, fished in the traditional manner with a more gentle approach. It is a fly that can be fished with either a floating or a sink-tip line.

The river Teifi, being often peat-stained when running down after a flood, needs a flashy solution to the problem of attracting the fish; the Teifi Terror is then, in daylight, particularly effective.

In its tandem form the Teifi Terror is a late-night or near-dawn lure. Generally, big lures are fished on quick-sinking lines and are stripped along the bottom of the pool. This is a recent technique in river fishing, derived from reservoir methods. Big sewin often lie close to the bottom of the river bed and these big lures can sometimes tempt them to take. Tactics like these are worth trying on heavily-fished rivers.

Tom Tom

Hook 8 Yellow tying silk.
Rib Silver thread.
Body Pig's hair.
Hackle Greenwell.
Wing Bronze mallard.

Location Middle reaches of Glaslyn.
Time July and August.
Conditions After flood.
Method Wet fly downriver.

This was rather an unusual pattern taken from the box of Thomas Thomas who lived the latter part of his life in the Cwmystwyth area, having lived prior to that in Llangurig and in Maentwrog. He was an accomplished fly dresser—all his patterns being dressed on eye-less hooks. Most of his patterns were dressed in the North Wales manner —except this particular one. The Tom Tom was liberally hackled and was somewhat in the tradition of the 'shaving brush', over-hackled flies, sometimes known as 'Loch Maree style'.

Pig's hair, although easily available in the days when practically every household kept a pig at the end of the garden, was a material not often used by fly dressers. The pig's soft bristle gave the fly a yellowish tinge and this resulted in a highly visible fly—even in the most dirty water. The body material being of pig's hair also made for a very buoyant fly which would be quite active when moved through the water.

It is interesting to note that it was often the custom in Wales to have the same christian and surname, and Thomas Thomas was invariable known as Tom Tom—just as Morgan Morgan is known as Moc Morgan!

(See Old Favourite p. 40).

T. L. Harries's Sedge

Hook *8 Brown silk.*
Body *Peacock herl.*
Hackle *Three or four ginger cock hackles.*
Wing *Partridge hackle.*
Location *River Towy/Teifi.*
Time *Mid Summer evening & night.*
Conditions *Low water.*
Method *On a floating line with the sedge allowed to skate across the surface.*

This sedge was dressed very full, with four strands of peacock herl twisted into a rope and put around the iron. Three or four ginger hackles are tied in to form a very bushy hackle. The line and cast were kept off the surface of the water, bringing the fly around to form a big wake. The wake was just as important as the fly itself. Hugh Falkus in his book, *Sea-trout Fishing*, refers to this method in a more sophisticated form in the section on the surface lure.

In fishing a pattern like this, the line was greased and, with the rod held high, the T. L. Harries Sedge was fished in the surface film and lifted up now and then just as one would with a bob fly. The action of lifting the fly up from the water can prove to be decisive—and will often move fish that have been indifferent to any other offerings.

There are certain conditions—such as prolonged periods of low water and hot weather—when, at dusk, and again at dawn, this surface fishing for sewin is the only productive method. T. L.'s Sedge, like the modern Muddler Minnow, is then just the right tool for the job.

T. L. Harries was not himself an enthusiastic fly-dresser. He was, however, a great innovator—responsible for cross-pollinating ideas from differing rivers like the Towy and the Teify, the Usk and the Cothi. It is thought that patterns like T.L.'s Sedge were probably tied by that great Lampeter fly tier, Fred Atkins. Many of Wil Harry's creations also were in his well-worn leather and parchment fly-wallet when he died in 1951.

47

Torby Coch

Hook   *6 & 8 Yellow silk.*
Rib   *Flat tinsel.*
Tail   *Red Ibis.*
Body   *Light coloured hare's ear.*
Hackle   *Brown hen.*
Wing   *Plain brown hen.*

Location   *River Conway.*
Time   *Daytime.*
Conditions   *Low water.*
Method   *Wet fly downriver.*

Another fly from the Conway stable which came to prominence some thirty years ago is the Torby Coch. It has many big sewin to its credit and is a favourite with anglers in the Dolwyddelan area.

Despite the modern swing towards sewin flies with silver tinsel bodies, the old fur and fibre bodied flies remain supreme for daytime fishing when the water is low.

A number of traditional sewin flies have fur bodies: this light fawn has undoubtedly proved itself attractive. It is puzzling why some patterns are effective on certain rivers and then fail miserably on others. The Torby Coch has proved its value on the Dwyfawr, Glaslyn and the Ystwyth. One angler who has done rather well with the Torby Coch ties it well up on the cast as a dropper.

The St. George reel.

Towy Topper

Hook *8 & 10 Black tying silk.*
Tail *Golden pheasant tippets.*
Rib *Thin silver wire.*
Body *Well marked quill.*
Hackle *Blue dun or rusty dun.*

Location *River Towy.*
Time *Day time after July.*
Conditions *Normal river flow.*
Method *Normal wet fly down stream.*

The river Towy is a wonderful sewin river and it is not surprising that so many seatrout patterns have been developed and perfected there. The Towy Topper is not so well known any longer as other patterns, but it has its admirers, especially amongst daytime anglers.

With sensitivity, the day angler can fish the Towy Topper in the runs and shadows of trees and take sewin even during low water conditions. Sewin will, in summer levels, tend to move into the more oxygenated runs and the Towy Topper is at its best when fished at times like these, fished small and fine. Fished as a dry-fly, especially for sewin that have been in the river for some time, the Towy Topper tied on a size twelve hook has proved successful. This method, especially just as dawn is breaking, can be very rewarding.

Twm Twll

Hook 8 & 10 Yellow silk.
Tail A blue hackle tip.
Rib Gold wire thread.
Body Hare's ear and orange wool mixed.
Hackle Rusty Andulusian cock.

Location River Towy.
Time Mid summer. Day/evening.
Conditions Low water in runs.
Method Wet fly downriver.

This fly was dressed very lightly with the minimum of materials. It was created by T. L. Harries, an auctioneer who hailed from Lampeter and who founded a firm of auctioneers in Llandeilo in the 1920-1940 era. 'T. L.' was a great trout angler who, no doubt, brought his restrained, upper-Teifi approach to sewin fishing. The Twm Twll is a very delicate fly, similar to the Dai Ben—except that the Twm Twll has a much darker tone to it, such that it could be used effectively in conjunction with the Dai Ben. The Dai Ben, with its lighter tone and thick silver rib, is recommended for use in the early part of the season, and the Twm Twll, then, should be used later on.

It is an accepted principle in fly fishing that, with the use of dun-coloured hackle, a darker dun is required for the later period of the season. Dai Ben, with its silver band and dun hackle, is more visible and would be more attractive to the comparatively fresh sewin. The more delicate colour tones of Twm Twll are more effective with sewin that have been longer in the river.

T. L. Harries, Teify and Towy angler of renown.

Water Rat & Red

Hook   *9 & 12. Black silk.*
Tail   *Dark red cock.*
Rib   *Silver wire.*
Body   *Water rat fur.*
Hackle   *Dark red cock.*
Wing   *Corncrake—sub Speckled hen.*
Time   *Summer.*

Location   *Rivers of Lleyn in North Wales.*
Conditions   *Low water.*
Method   *Wet fly downriver.*

Another fly from the box of Dr Shelton Roberts which has stood the test of time over the last half century, as a daytime fly in low water. Walton's advice in *The Complete Angler* 'to fish fine and far off' is operative with the Water Rat & Red. The bigger version tied on a number nine hook has a wider silver band on it; the number twelve hook was preferred when the water was very low.

North Wales sewin flies bear close relationships to those used for trout fishing on lakes and rivers. This pattern is the exception, being a modification of an established Irish pattern. There is a long history in angling, of coming-and-going between Ireland and North Wales—due to proximity and the similarity of conditions in peaty waters, which do not apply in the south west and south east of Wales.

51

Wil Harry's Green Woodcock

Hook *8 & 10 Green silk.*
Tail *Golden pheasant tippets.*
Rib *Gold wire.*
Body *Light olive green seal's fur.*
Hackle *Woodcock.*
Wing *Woodcock.*

Location *River Towy, middle reaches.*
Time *May onwards. Day and late evening.*
Conditions *River dropping after high water.*
Method *Normal wet fly downriver.*
A good dropper fly.

This fly was dressed very much in sedge form with bulky body and a heavy hackle and wing. Its body was a distinctive green shade, identical to that used in Ireland for the great Green Peter which is a 'must' on the bob position with most of the Irish lough fishers.

Sedge fishing for sewin is often practised when the water is running high. Under such conditions night fishing is not productive and anglers fish to the lip of the evening—just before the daylight is lost.

This pattern, which was used exclusively for sewin fishing on the river Towy, has the added ingredient of being an exceptional sedge pattern. It has numerous similarities with the G & H Sedge (Messrs Goddard and Henry) and deserves a fair trial purely as a Sedge trout fly.

Another sewin angler on the river Towy who fishes a pattern similar to Wil Harry's Green Woodcock, is Sid Gardner from Cardiff. He also dresses his patterns very full with plenty of hackle in order to enable the Sedge pattern to fish right in the surface of the water. The disturbance caused by the Sedge in and on the surface is the important quality—and the trigger point of the fly.

Worm-fly

Hook *Two number 6 or 8.*
Tail *Red wool.*
Rib *Gold wire.*
Body *Peacock herl.*
Hackle *Coch-a-bon-ddu.*

Location *Rheidiol & Teifi.*
Time *Night time.*
Conditions *Low water.*
Method *On quick-sinking line fished deep.*

The idea of joining two Coch-a-bon-ddu is a comparatively new one as a reservoir lure but it has been around a long time as a 'poacher's fly'. There is a modern tendency to use most reservoir lures right on the bottom. The Worm Fly, however, is quite often used as a bob fly. The two-hook principle was intended to help with hooking, as bob flies are notorious for their poor hooking capability.

Bob flies are not entirely to be recommended for sewin, as they are liable to cause problems with snagging in certain waters where there are rocks or other obstacles in the river. Still-water fishing for sewin is not much practised, certainly not to the same extent in Wales as in Scotland and Ireland. Sewin flies used in lakes are very much the same as the standard lakes flies. It is feasible that the Worm Fly used as a bob would be useful for experimental purposes on Irish loughs and Scottish lochs as a sea trout attractor.

An interesting development in the use of the Worm Fly has been its use on an intermediate line. This could well be the most important role for the Worm Fly. The intermediate fly line is of neutral density and keeps fishing just below the surface film. The Worm Fly in the smaller sizes dressed on two number ten hooks has proved very effective at dawn. The new line enables the fly to be fished slowly just under the surface and the Worm Fly is certainly at its best when fished slowly.

The origin of the Worm Fly is still something of a mystery, but as it is made of two Coch-a-bon-ddu flies it is reasonable to suppose that it could have been developed somewhere in the Principality.

Yellow Plasterer

Hook *8 & 10 Yellow tying silk.*
Tail *Red fibres.*
Body *Yellow plastic.*
Hackle *Woodcock.*

Location *River Towy.*
Time *Summer months, night time.*
Conditions *Low water.*
Method *Downriver, fished deep and on the point.*

A very colourful fly which, being used around 1950, reveals considerable science and inventiveness on the part of Lewi Davies who was in business as a plasterer in the Llandeilo area—and a good fisherman. The plastic strips gave a very useful impression of a segmented body. This is evidence of inclination towards the yellow end of the colour spectrum in the materials chosen for a fly pattern aimed to achieve the quality of high visibility when used on rivers such as the Towy. As the plastic used on the fly was rather heavy, there is little doubt that it was intended to sink rapidly to fish deeply, and would be well suited to fishing the deep glides characteristic of the middle reaches of the Llandeilo Association and old Dynevor Estate waters where Lewi fished.

William Davies, 'Teilo Fardd', writing in *Llandeilo Past and Present* in 1858, has some illuminating remarks to make on fish and fishing in the locality. The 'yellow fly' for sewin and trout was recommended. No scientist, the bard thought that sunlight oxygenated the water, he adds that 'The flies best adapted throughout the season in the Towy for trout (and sewin) fishing are dark blues with light yellow bodies.' A clear reference to the tradition in yellow bodies and blue-winged or hackled flies which was once practised on the Towy and elsewhere in evening fishing for sewin.

Use of the modern swanandaze for the body gives a smoother effect for the body segmentation than Lewi attempted to achieve with his yellow plastic strips. This modern refinement could prove counterproductive—as Lewi's rough-and-ready approach contained method in its seeming madness. It is often these roughly-tied flies that prove, as he would say, 'killers': just as flies that have been knocked almost to pieces with catching fish are often more effective than newly-tied 'exhibition' examples.

Salmon

It is now commonly accepted that the salmon does not feed in fresh water and therefore he takes the 'fly' either out of curiosity, anger or memory. As to what the salmon fly is supposed to represent to him and whether the 'fly' has any resemblance to items of food is anyone's guess and actually immaterial. A great number of traditional feather flies are tied merely as an aesthetic exercise and their dressers would not think of fishing with them. The correctly dressed salmon fly is a work of art.

The earliest reference to the salmon fly appears in *The Booke of St Albans*. In that collection of manuscripts by various hands, Dame Juliana Berners in her *Treatyse of Fysshing wyth an Angle* observes that when a salmon leaps it is possible to take him with a fly. In the mid-seventeenth century Thomas Barker, who caught salmon in the Thames, outlined the construction of the salmon fly, which, according to his authority, had four wings. It was not until the early nineteenth century that fly fishing became the socially accepted way of fishing for the salmon and the flies then in use for their pursuit were still inclined to be of a sombre hue.

George Agar Hansard writing in 1834 about Welsh salmon flies tells us: 'The flies used by the native Welsh angler are very sober in colour and few in number. The hooks they prefer are also large and the execution altogether exceedingly coarse'!

'A Spring Fly:
Wings, the dark mottled feathers of the bittern body orange silk or worsted with broad gold twist and a smokey dun hackle for legs.'

'A Summer Fly:
Wings, the brown mottled feather of a turkey cock's wing with a few of the green strands selected from the eye of a peacock tail feather. Body of yellow silk, and gold twist, with deep blood-red hackle for legs.'

At the same time, so-called 'Irish flies' were being sold in the shops of the seaports of Wales. These imported flies, with their colourful feathers, within twenty years, had been responsible for the capture of many hundreds of Welsh salmon. Hansard gives one dressing of an Irish salmon fly:

'The wings were made of the feathers of a guineafowl; the body of a blood red ostrich feather and the Hackle of yellow and blood red feathers.'

In 1845 the most famous salmon fly of all time was tied—the Jock Scott. It was first dressed by a Scottish ghillie on board ship on the North Sea—bound for Scandinavia. It was tied for a Scottish gentleman named Scott. It is not known for certain if the first Jock Scott was dressed on a metal-eyed hook even though the first all metal eyed-hook was produced in that same year.

Plate IV   Wye Salmon Flies

A selection of salmon flies that were used on the upper Wye between 1880 and 1910.
The gut eye was still being used despite the fact that the eyed hook had been in
existence for over fifty years.

Following the advent of the Jock Scott, salmon flies changed their garb completely. It meant an end to the dull, sombre colours and into fashion came the exotic colours of tropical birds. The blue and green parrot, blue and yellow macaw, red and gold of the golden pheasant and the black, yellow and white of the Jungle cock became the rage. Ireland, too, played a prominent part in this revolution and the 'Irish flies' were being widely sold in tackle shops at the seaports—the name of Rogan of Ballyshannon becoming familiar on Welsh rivers.

Despite the invention of the metal-eyed hook in 1845, Welsh anglers were observed still to be using the gut eye on their salmon flies as late as the eighteen nineties. An interesting collection of salmon flies of that period is now housed in Llanllyr Mansion in the Vale of Aeron. Captain Hext Lewes has a fly-book which was used by both his father and grandfather containing the flies in use during their two lifetimes in the last century on the upper stretches of the river Wye—with very comprehensive notes attached. Most of the flies in the collection are seen to have vivid yellow bodies and the notes reveal that most of the flies were reckoned effective during the months of September and October. The late John Lewes records the capture of six salmon in one morning on a visit to the Highmead Beat on the river Teifi. All was not well, even in those days, with salmon stocks—as an entry in the accompanying notes says that in the year 1898 the fishing was so poor that it was not worth the price paid for the licence!

A page in the old wallet reveals that all the salmon flies dressed for the Wye were dressed on bigger hooks, for use on the Nantgwyllt estate on the Upper Wye. The whole estate was later sold to the Birmingham Corporation to set up a reservoir complex.

Since the first decade of this century, the dressing of salmon flies in Wales has been moving back towards its earlier form. In 1920 A. E. H. Wood convinced many anglers of the necessity of using smaller and more sparsely dressed flies near the surface of the water. In the forties and fifties it was becoming acknowledged that hair-wing flies were steadily growing in usefulness so as to displace the feathered, fully-dressed, traditional varieties. The influence was largely from the United States.

These American hairwinged flies, tied with limited materials and skills, were rather crude. Yet they proved effective. They were made from deer hair, fox fur and squirrel tails. Success with patterns such as the Stoat's Tail hastened the end of the fully-dressed salmon fly, added to which there was the increasing difficulty of getting the correct feathers for some of the Scottish and Irish patterns. So, the salmon fly has gone the complete circle, and modern anglers are almost back to where it all started nearly four hundred years ago.

Yellows, reds and blues were the dominant shades of the Ballyshannon flies illustrated in William Blacker's *Art of Fly-making Angling & Dyeing*, 1855.

Black Doctor

Tag   Round silver tinsel and lemon floss.
Tail   Topping and Indian crow.
Butt   Scarlet wool.
Body   Black floss.
Rib   Oval tinsel.
Hackle   Dark claret hackle.
Throat   Speckled guinea fowl.
Wings   Mixed—Tippet in strands with golden pheasant tail over married strands of scarlet, blue and yellow goose, florican bustard, peacock wing and light mottled turkey tail, married narrow strips of teal and barred summer duck, narrow strips of brown mallard over and topping over all.
Head   Scarlet wool.

Location   Wye, Cleddau, Towy and Usk.
Time   Late season.
Conditions   Good river flows.
Method   Down river with sinking line.

The Doctor series of salmon flies was formerly much in use on many Welsh rivers such as the Towy and the Usk. In the early nineteenth century, even on the Cothi, a tributary of the Towy, the Black Doctor was considered to be the right medicine for the Autumn running salmon.

Early examples of Doctor salmon flies were tied with gut eyes, despite the fact that after 1845 metal eyed hooks were available. Salmon anglers were rather conservative in their approach and distrusted innovation feeling that the gut-to-gut tyings fished better.

Blue Doctor

Hook 6 & 8 Black tying silk.

Tag Round silver thread and golden yellow floss.

Tail A topping and a tippet.

Butt Scarlet wool.

Body Pale blue floss.

Ribs Oval silver tinsel.

Hackle Pale blue hackle.

Throat Pale blue hackle.

Throat Blue jay.

Wings Mixed—Tippets in strands with strip of golden pheasant tail over married strands of scarlet blue and yellow swan, florican bustard, peacock wing and light mottled turkey tail, married narrow strips of teal and barred summer duck, narrow strips of brown mallard over, a topping over all.

Head Scarlet wool.

Location Rivers Teify, Towy and Dee.

Times All season.

Conditions Good river level.

Method Normal downriver salmon fly fishing.

The Blue Doctor did not gain quite such a reputation on Welsh rivers as did the Black and Silver Doctors, but when it was discovered that it was also a good sewin fly the situation changed dramatically. The Blue Doctor became extremely active on the lower Teify at the turn of the century but it was to give way to the Silver Doctor in later years.

Plate V

Masterpieces in the art of fly-dressing. A selection of Salmon flies by Pryce Tannat.

Thurso Canary		Beauly Peacock
Flash Light	Iris	William Rufus
Delfur's Fancy	Benchill	Gordon

Silver Doctor

Hook 6 & 8 *Black tying silk.*
Tag *Round silver tinsel and golden yellow floss.*
Tail *A topping and blue chatterer.*
Butt *Scarlet wool.*
Body *Flat silver tinsel.*
Ribs *Fine oval silver thread.*
Throat *A pale blue hackle and wigeon.*
Wings *Mixed—tippet in strands with strips of golden pheasant tail over married strands of scarlet, blue and yellow swan or goose, florican, bustard, peacock wing and light mottled turkey tail, married narrow strips of teal and barred summer duck, narrow strips of brown mallard over, a topping over all.*
Head *Scarlet wool.*

Location *Wye, Dee, Cleddau, Teify, Towy and Usk.*
Time *All season.*
Conditions *Normal water flows.*
Method *Wet fly with sinking line.*

The Silver Doctor was considered, in the upper Usk, as a good early season fly, dressed in bigger sizes. The three members of the Doctor series, Black, Silver and Blue, were standbys for many anglers and, when the change came from the complicated Scottish built-wing patterns, these three patterns were quickly seen in their simple, hair-wing, modern garb.

Conway Blue

Tag Round silver thread and golden yellow floss.
Tail Golden pheasant crest.
Butt Black ostrich herl.
Rib Oval silver tinsel.
Body Royal blue seal's fur.
Hackles Black hackle, dyed blue cock.
Front hackle: Blue jay.
Wing Two golden pheasant tippet feathers tied back-to-back.
Roof Bronze mallard with golden pheasant topping over it.

Location River Conway.
Time Mid season onwards.
Conditions Water clearing after flood.
Method Normal wet fly salmon method of across and down river using a sinking line.

The Conway Blue is a highly colourful pattern which only works well on the rivers Conway, Dee and Dovey. The importance of visibility is largely historical—recalling a time in the salmon's life as a predator in flashing Arctic waters, and times in angling history before the fixed spool reel made life difficult for the salmon if easier for the unimaginative angler.

J. O. Jones of Llanrwst was one of the leading anglers in North Wales during the thirties and forties of this century and he was fortunate enough to have fished for salmon on the river Conway when it held really good stocks of salmon. His tackle was designed to fish the salmon fly on a silk line at about mid-way level in the water. Most salmon fishing was done in those days immediately after a flood and salmon flies were used in conditions which are now reserved for the spinning minnow and it ferrous relatives.

J. O. Jones was quite fond of this pattern and he maintained that it would also do well at the tail end of the season when the smaller sewin came upriver. Another prominent salmon angler in North Wales, R. H. Hughes who was an enthusiast for the Conway Blue, gave the pattern to Tom Stewart for his book, *Two Hundred Popular Fly Patterns*. Hughes dressed most of his flies on the slim side and was most economical with his materials. His slim version was naturally, at its most effective in the low water conditions of high summer.

Dwyryd Red & Yellow

Hook 6 & 8 Black tying silk.
Tail Golden pheasant topping.
Body Rear third Yellow wool, Middle third Red wool,
      Front third Black wool.
Hackle Guinea fowl.
Wing Dark brown turkey.

Location River Dwyryd.
Time Summer.
Conditions High river flow.
Method Wet fly cast downriver.

This was an attempt to follow the trend towards bright colourings that overtook salmon fly-dressers at the end of the last century. Most of their materials were home-produced and the overall attempt of the fly design was to imitate Scottish and Irish patterns. Salmon fishing was not widely practised by the locals during the 19th century and so salmon fly patterns were not subject to as much experimentation as were trout flies.

The Dwyryd river has a fair run of summer salmon and in the Maentwrog area it lends itself well to fly fishing. Most fly fishing activity took place when the river was running down after a flood and the brightly coloured body was ideal in the brown-stained water.

Some reports of quite astounding catches—five or six fish to one rod in an hour—are recorded on the Dwyryd river and there is little doubt that when the river was at the correct level, the fly was as deadly a method as any.

Haslam

Tag *Flat silver tinsel.*
Butt *White wool or floss.*
Tail *Small golden pheasant crest.*
Body *Flat silver tinsel.*
Body *Oval silver wire.*
Throat hackle *Blue jay, or guinea fowl dyed blue.*
Horns *Blue macaw, curving along the wings
and crossing over the tail.*
Wing *Hen pheasant tail.*
Head *Black varnish.*

Location *Originally on the Dovey.*
Time *Day time for salmon also at night for
sewin.*
Conditions *Best on clearing water.*
Method *Normal wet fly for salmon and in smaller
sizes as greased line.*

Old examples of the Haslam fly tied on gut-loop eyes are still in existence. Origination of this good-looking and killing pattern is attributed to Sam Haslam of Uppingham, now famed for founding the fishery at the excellent Rutland reservoir. It is doubtful if Sam Haslam is accountable for introducing the pattern to Wales, and to the river Dovey in particular, which is acknowledged as its home.

Peter Vaughan, a local tackle dealer at Machynlleth, on the river Dovey, was the man largely responsible for spreading the fame of the Haslam of which he sold literally thousands in a season. Peter Vaughan claimed that it was by far the best fly to use for salmon on the Dovey and that it worked equally well in low or high water conditions. Such was its effectiveness that it was known also as 'The Universal Provider'.

The Haslam could be effective also, in small sizes as a sewin fly. In the Dovey area anglers call all sea-trout up to one pound 'sewin' and anything over that weight 'sea-trout'. This distinction is not made in any other part of Wales.

Somehow over the years the Haslam pattern developed body hackle. Most samples sold by Peter Vaughan in the forties had white body hackles. There is no doubt that this did add to the attractiveness of the fly. Some examples of patterns with blue andalusian body hackle have appeared from time to time but have not endured very long.

The Haslam is a very typical example of a Welsh fly pattern which has undergone too many alterations with the result that it has been subjected to criticism for dressings far removed from the original. This has meant a loss of attractiveness and performance when incorrectly dressed.

Often tackle shop owners and assistants have a good knowledge of local fly patterns. A good instance was Paddy Aylward, former proprietor of the Wynstay Hotel at Machynlleth. On his retirement, he took over a tackle shop in the main street where he maintained a profound interest in flies and in fishing. Not surprisingly, the Haslam was a speciality of his and copies of the many variants which he collected before his death are still to be seen in his tackle shop. The business is now run by his widow, Pat, who is always pleased to show the display patterns of the Haslam to serious customers and students of the fly dressing art.

The pattern tied by George Roberts, doyen of Dovey anglers, has hackle right through the body. The variation tied by Amos had a much darker hue. The variations attributed to George Forrest, Billy Mitchell and Jim Dulson, all expert Dovey anglers, also show slight bias towards the darker end of the spectrum. The pattern sold by Mrs Aylward in the shop today has a false blue jay hackle and an orange tag. The popular sizes are six and eight.

Emyr Lewis, a keeper on the river Dovey, himself an excellent angler, speaks of a Captain Wilson, in the thirties, who tied a yellow body to the fly which had red horns instead of the blue macaw. This variation was known locally as The Empress.

That same tackle shop at Machynlleth today sells more Baby Dolls than it does Haslams.

Irt Fly

Hook   4 & 5 Black silk.
Tag   Flat silver.
Tail   Golden pheasant toppings.
Rib   Silver thread.
Body   Two turns of red silk, rest of blue tinsel.
Hackle   Black & Orange.
Wing   Squirrel tail dyed red & Orange.

Location   River Lledr & Conway.
Time   July onwards.
Conditions   Normal and high water levels.
Method   Normal salmon wet fly method.

This fly has an excellent reputation on the river Lledr which is a tributary of the Conway. It is extremely colourful and does well when there is some spate-colouration in the river. Eirwyn Roberts of Dolwyddelan, a fine dresser of salmon flies, dresses the Irt fly for some of his friends. It would seem that the success it scores on the Lledr river is not general. Extensive trials on the Usk and Severn by a number of anglers have not brought many results.

The Irt fly was, however, quite successful on the river Rheidol on a few occasions, with fresh sewin just off the tidal stretch of the river; and it would seem that further trials under such conditions might reveal it to have an important secondary role as a sewin fly.

Jenny Wren (Pluen y Dryw)

Hook   *7. Brown silk.*
Tail   *Golden pheasant topping and mallard.*
Rib   *Silver tinsel.*
Body   *Dark Hare's ear.*
Hackle   *Dark red cock and brown partridge.*
Wing   *Medium mallard over grey goose feather.*
Time   *Daytime in summer.*

Location   *Rivers of North Wales.*
Conditions   *River thinning down after spate.*
Method   *Wet fly downriver.*

This modestly-dressed little fly, used by Dr Shelton Roberts some fifty years ago, was effective on the rivers of North Wales— especially the Dwyfawr. It shows the bias in North Wales was towards browns and greys as opposed to the colourful creations used on the Rivers Dee, Wye and Usk.

The normal method of fishing the Dwyfawr was the downriver wet fly for salmon which ran strongly even in mid summer. The salmon clearly went for the smaller and more drab fly which they would often take just below the surface: the rather bulky body tending to hold the Jenny Wren high in the water.

The name given to the fly, Pluen y Dryw (Jenny Wren Fly) would appear to apply equally to its colour as to its diminutive size.

67

Jock Scott

Hook   *4 & 6 Black tying silk.*
Butt   *Black herl.*
Body   *In two equal halves—first half golden yellow floss butted with black herl and veiled above and below with six or more toucan feathers; second half black floss.*
Rib   *Fine oval silver tinsel over golden yellow floss, broader oval silver tinsel or flat silver tinsel and twist over black floss.*
Hackle   *A black hackle over black floss.*
Throat   *Speckled gallina.*
Wings   *A pair of black white-tipped turkey tail strips, over these, but not entirely covering them, a mixed sheath of married strands of peacock wing, yellow, scarlet and blue swan, bustard, florican and golden pheasant tail; two strands of peacock sword feathers above the married narrow strips of teal and barred summer duck at the sides, brown mallard over.*
Sides   *Jungle cock.*
Cheeks   *Blue chatterer.*
Horns   *Blue and yellow macaw.*
   A topping over all.

Location   *All rivers especially Wye and Usk.*
Time   *Early season.*
Conditions   *Good water levels.*
Method   *Downriver wet fly.*

This is without doubt one of the best known salmon fly patterns of all times. Little did the gamekeeper who first devised this complicated pattern realise that he was to achieve immortality with it. The year of its birth was around 1850 when it was designed to fish the river Tweed. It proved to be an excellent pattern in Scotland and its fame spread quickly to other rivers. In Wales it has scored well on the Dee, Wye and Usk.

The reason for the demise of the fully-dressed fly is the scarcity of many of the component parts as some of the basic feathers are no longer available—as there is a ban on import of capes and live

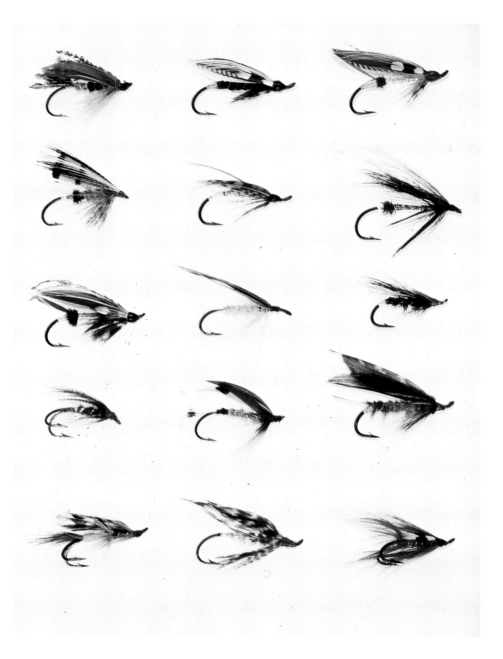

Plate VI   Salmon Flies

Will Harry	Black Doctor	Silver Doctor
Conway Blue	Haslam	Irt Fly
Jock Scott	Leslie Peters' Fly	Pry Llwyd a Choch
Pluen Y Dryw	Penybont	Twrci Coch
Welsh Shrimp-	Dwyryd Red & Yellow	Usk Grub
Variant		

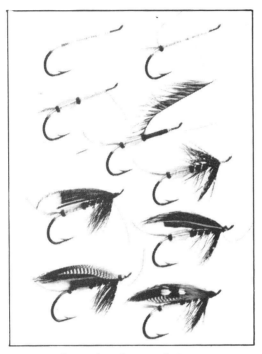

Stages in tying a Jock Scott

species. Under these circumstances, the fly dresser is obliged to use substitutes. In tying a Jock Scott it is the joining of feathers from different birds to make a composite wing that presents the dresser with problems. It is always important to remember that the fresher the feathers the easier it is to manage them. Feathers stored for a long time—especially in central heating—dry out and lose their natural oils—so becoming very difficult to keep in well-knit units. All individual strands of feathers are joined together by a miniature system of hooks, these hooks lose their joining power as they dry out. It is essential, in the dressing of the Jock Scott, that the very best materials are used.

The Jock Scott is one of the most difficult patterns to dress—even the modern version of it with hair wings which is equally as effective.

It will be a sad day for the art of fly dressing when the old patterns like the Jock Scott are no longer being tied anywhere—even as an exercise in dexterity and craftsmanship.

69

Leslie Peters's Salmon Fly

Hook *6 & 8 Yellow silk.*
Tail *Golden pheasant toppings. Black silk.*
Rib *Golden wire.*
Body *Yellow seal's fur.*
Hackle *Yellow hackle.*
Wing *Grey squirrel dyed brown or off-black.*

Location *River Usk in the Brecon area late season.*
Time *Late season.*
Conditions *Good river level.*
Method *Downriver normal wet fly.*

In recent years most salmon fly patterns have been simplified and the former Jock Scott that needed twenty six different items for its original tying, now in its hair-wing form, only requires nine. This simplification of patterns has also been in evidence on Welsh rivers and hair-winged salmon flies are now used extensively.

Leslie Peters of Brecon, who has fished the river Usk for over fifty years, has developed a hair-wing salmon fly which he now uses in preference to the old fully-built winged salmon flies. The highly-visible yellow seal's fur body is in keeping with the traditional salmon flies used on the Usk in Brecon around 1850 which can be seen in a case at Brecon Museum today. The wing for the fly is dyed squirrel tail and the whole pattern is simple to tie and not expensive to make.

The Usk basket

Penybont

Hook 6 & 8. Yellow tying silk.
Tail Golden pheasant tippets.
Rib Silver thread.
Body Well waxed (Cobbler's wax) yellow silk.
Hackle Brown hen.
Wing Grey heron wing, encasing golden
 pheasant tippets.

Location River Dovey.
Time Mid and late season.
Conditions Normal river flow.
Method Wet fly downriver.

This is rather a sober-coloured fly which some anglers on the upper Dovey would use as a dropper with the more colourful Haslam on the point. The choice of size would be governed by the flow of the river. The river Dovey has a big catchment area and is subject to quite big, and at one time, prolonged flood conditions. The Penybont proved effective in the period when the water was thinning down.

One somewhat unusual method of fishing the Penybont is to use it as a point fly. After tying it on in the normal manner, loop the nylon back around its throat. This is then cast across the river and the eye of the hook is kept in the surface film of the water, just like a miniature periscope. Salmon hooked by fishing this method are always fast by the top of the mouth. The fly is best tied on a double hook if it is intended to fish this way, and well worth a try using other patterns, in pools of slow to medium flow and when the water temperatures are up to summer level.

Some versions of this fly are tied (minus the golden tippets) in smaller sizes for summer fishing. Sometimes the body is made of dirty yellow seal's fur and the brown hackle is palmered down the body. In this guise it also proves to be quite attractive to sewin.

Pry llwyd a choch

(Badger hair and Red)

Hook *6 & 8 Black silk.*
Tag *Flat silver.*
Tail *Golden pheasant toppings.*
Rib *Red tinsel.*
Body *Black seal's fur.*
Hackle *Badger.*
Wing *Badger hair.*

Location *Rivers of North Wales.*
Time *Summer months.*
Conditions *Normal river flows.*
Method *Normal wet fly down-river.*

This fly, although primarily listed as a salmon fly, is also used extensively for sewin fishing.

As with many fly patterns, the amount of dressing used can influence the method of fishing the fly. When dressed fully, it is best used as a normal wet fly on a sinking line or sink-tip line. Used in this fashion on the quick-flowing rivers of North Wales it takes fish that have just moved into the river or are on the move from pool to pool.

A slimmer version can be fished using the semi-greased line method, fishing the fly in or very near the surface. This method, which lately has been compared to nymph fishing in a reservoir, is effective with salmon that have been in the river for some time where they represent a greater challenge to the angler.

Richards's Fancy

Hook *8 & 10 Single or double Limerick.*
Tail *Golden Pheasant topping.*
Body *Black floss.*
Rib *Flat gold tinsel.*
Hackle *Blue dun.*
Wing *Bronze mallard.*

Location *Middle Towy.*
Time *Late June-September.*
Conditions *Down to low.*
Method *Middle depth on slow sink.*

Dilwyn Richards is the natural successor to Wil Harry Richards and Lewi Davies in as much as he learned at an early age the art of innovation derived from his observations while fishing the fly-only Dynevor and Cawdor waters on the Towy at Llandeilo. The incidence of an insect with a particular blue wing which rose several salmon on one occasion sent him back to his work-bench one day in the mid-seventies. Within a couple of hours he was back, and soon had a brace of fish on the bank. This is an answer in defiance of the many pundits who have written about salmon fishing where they maintain that it is pure reflex to some deep-sea memory that makes a salmon move to a fly. Those who have observed, as closely as Dilwyn Richards has, will know that salmon will sometimes rise like a trout and can even sometimes be seen in slack water with their backs out of the water as if nymphing.

The Salmon's formative year is lived as a trout and with trout in brooks and rivers where they take small flies all-too avidly. This youthful memory must remain with them when they return to their native streams on migration, and they will sometimes come up to a dry fly.

Stoat's Tail

Hook   *6 Black tying silk.*
Tail   *Golden pheasant topping.*
Rib   *Silver thread.*
Body   *Black seal's fur.*
Hackle   *Black hen.*
Wing   *Black tip of stoat's tail or black bucktail.*

Location   *River Dee.*
Time   *All season.*
Conditions   *Normal river flow.*
Method   *Downriver wet fly.*

This is now one of the most commonly used salmon flies and has for some time been used to good effect on the Usk and the Wye and to a leser extent on the river Dee. There are minor variations observable in the dressing from river to river depending on local availability of materials. In recent years the Stoat's Tail wing has given way to buck-tail wing which, according to some, appears to be more effective.

This fly is generally tied as a tube fly or a Waddington these days—the reason for this being the alleged greater hooking power of the treble. A number of anglers on the rivers of mid Wales use stainless wire to build the body upon and then attach a treble hook to the end to make a nice loop at the other end to which they attach the nylon. These home-made traces are very effective and very cheap. The great advantage of making one's own trace is that it is possible to add different weights to it—enabling the fly to fish at the required depth.

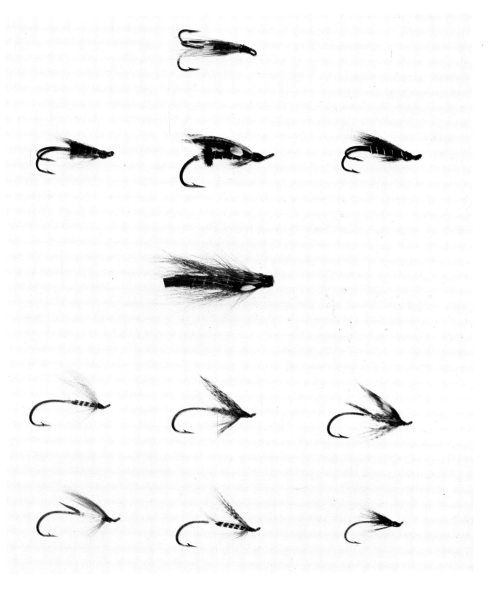

Plate VII   Salmon Flies

Variations on the Thunder and Lightning fly

Thunder & Lightning on Long shanked treble
Thunder & Lightning on Double hook   Hair Wing Thunder & Lightning
Standard Thunder & Lightning
Thunder & Lightning on Tube

Low Water versions of some traditional flies

Red Gauntlet   Invicta   March Brown
Green & Gold   Teal Blue & Black   Black Mini

Thunder & Lightning

Hook 6 Black silk.
Tag Round gold tinsel, yellow floss silk.
Tail Golden pheasant topping.
Butt Black ostrich herl.
Body Black floss tinsel.
Hackle Orange
Throat hackle Blue jay
Wings Bronze mallard and golden pheasant
    toppings.
Cheeks Jungle cock.

Location Usk and Wye.
Time Throughout the season.
Conditions Normal water.
Method Wet fly downriver.

This is one of the most frequent salmon flies used on Welsh rivers and its dark hues suit the peat-stained waters of Wales. Of all the popular salmon flies this is one of the easiest to dress, and it bears quite a close relationship to the old Welsh 'Turkey' flies. It is also one pattern that can be dressed in various forms without losing any of its effectiveness. The demand in recent years for the use of the treble hook in preference to the single has seen this pattern dressed as a tube fly, Waddington and on Esmond Drury hooks. Some anglers on the lower Teifi use Thunder & Lightning as a low water pattern and it is a style of dressing that does well towards the evening of a warm day in summer when the small summer salmon or grisle have started running.

On the principle of a bright fly for a bright day, this dark pattern does better than most others in water that is heavily stained after flood. Some Welsh rivers that run out of peaty moors tend to give anglers a couple of days sport in beer-coloured water, not the best of water for success; but this is the very type of water that favours this particular pattern.

In tying this simple salmon fly, it is probably advisable to use a matched pair of mallard feathers for the wing. Many dressers use double matched pairs, which makes for a more solidly-built dressing. Some insist that it is imperative to make a red head with varnish.

This pattern was created by that excellent salmon fly dresser from Sprouston on the Tweed, James Wright. It was first tied around the 1850's when fully-dressed salmon flies were at the height of vogue.

75

Coracle fishing on the Dee!

Twrci Coch
(Red Turkey)

> Hook 6 Black silk.
> Tag Silver thread and yellow silk.
> Tail Golden pheasant toppings with red
> feather.
> Rib Gold thread.
> Body Hare's fur.
> Hackle Ginger cock.
> Throat hackle Blue jay.
> Wing Brown turkey.
>
> Location The rivers of North Wales.
> Time Mid-summer.
> Conditions Medium water.
> Method Downriver wet fly.

This salmon fly is a native of North Wales and has accounted for a good number of salmon on the river Conway. It first saw light of day in the forties and, curiously, it has not proved its effectiveness in other areas.

In its original form it was dressed rather heavily, although some have tended to dress a slimmer and smaller version in the last decade. It was formerly considered to be an especially good grilse fly, and, as grisle runs have tended to diminish in recent years, so the reputation of the fly has suffered accordingly. The Twrci Coch was also a favourite fly on the river Dee, but in a darker version which evidenced itself in the late twenties.

Twrci Du
(Black Turkey)

> Body Black wool & black seal's fur.

Some anglers who fished between Bala and Corwen found this fly a better pattern than the original. The sole variation is the black wool and black seal's fur for the body. G. O. Jones of Llanrwst was of the opinion that black was a good colour to use on summer salmon. He likened this pattern to the better-known Thunder & Lightning and considered the salmon angler who did not have either the Twrci Du or Thunder & Lightning on him to be improperly dressed!

Usk Grub

Hook	4 & 6 Black silk.
Tag	Silver thread.
Rear hackle	Golden pheasant red plumage.
Body	Rear half, dull orange.
Hackle	(Halfway down hook) White and orange.
Body	Front half, black seal's fur.
Rib	Silver thread.
Front hackle	Pair of jungle cock.

Location	River Usk.
Time	All season.
Conditions	Normal river flows.
Method	Downriver wet fly.

Many inexperienced anglers confuse this pattern with the Welsh Shrimp Fly which is rather similar. This confusion seldom takes place on the river Usk where the Usk Grub has long been a firm favourite. The fully-dressed version has been somewhat trimmed down and it appears that the simpler modern version is equally effective when the salmon are in the river in good numbers.

This pattern was a speciality of the late Molly Sweet who used to dress salmon and trout flies for local and visiting anglers fishing the river Usk. It was a joy to watch her create a very neat fly beside what can often look a very bedraggled specimen when dressed by fly dressers of lesser ability. Her square-headed vice was especially well suited to dress this pattern particularly when tied on a double hook. The version tied by Molly Sweet was a much fuller and more bulky fly than that dressed by Captain Coombe Richards whose version of the Usk Grub was far more slim-line and bordering on a low-water version.

The Sweet family of Usk were the ideal fishing couple in that Molly dressed the very killing patterns for both trout and salmon and Lionel, her husband, used them with great precision and delicacy to take fish from the nearby river.

Lionel Sweet on the Usk near his home

Welsh Shrimp Fly

Hook 6 & 8 Yellow silk.
Tag Yellow floss.
Tail Golden pheasant crest feather.
Butt Black ostrich herl.
Body Yellow floss.
Rib Oval silver tinsel.
Wing Tip of a red golden pheasant body feather tied over body of fly with jungle cock each side.
Hackle White cock wound as a collar.
Head Black varnish.

Location Most Welsh rivers.
Time Daytime throughout the season.
Conditions All levels of water.
Method Normal wet fly method for salmon.

The late J. O. Jones, Llanrwst, a noted angler on the lower reaches of the river Conway, was responsible for this pattern, which grew up and developed on the river Conway, becoming widely known and adopted on the salmon rivers that flow into what is now called the Celtic Sea.

'J. O.', as he was known to his friends, used the sinking line for most of his salmon fishing and he would favour this pattern dressed rather full on a size six hook. Many anglers now use the Welsh Shrimp Fly in much smaller sizes and find it effective as a low-water pattern.

Salmon fishing on the Conway was at its best when the river was thinning down after a flood. In the days when J. O. operated, the river took the best part of a week to thin down—which resulted in long periods of ideal all-round wet-fly fishing conditions. The fact that this is a colourful pattern was of help when fresh-run salmon moved in the wake of a flood.

In recent years, a variation on the Welsh Shrimp has come into being and is probably now more widely used than its predecessor.

Welsh Shrimp Fly—variant

> Hook 8 Yellow silk.
> Tail Reddish golden pheasant body fibres.
> Rib Silver thread.
> Body Rear two thirds, yellow floss.
>   Front third, black floss.
> Hackle Body hackle at joint of body, badger
>   cock.
> Front Orange.
> Wing Two short jungle cock tied back to back.

The variation is used in identical conditions and like manner. It is often tied on double hooks and has gained favour with salmon anglers on the river Dwyryd.

Wil Harry

Hook *4 & 6 Black silk.*
Tag *Silver thread.*
Tail *Peacock sword feather.*
Rib *Silver wire.*
Body *Rear third Orange wool. Front Black silk.*
Hackle *Olive cock.*
Wing *Blue and Red swan with peacock herl.*

Location *River Towy and Dwyryd.*
Time *All seasons.*
Conditions *Normal river flow.*
Method *Normal wet fly.*

This interesting Towy salmon fly, which was the creation of William Henry Richards of Llandeilo, is as good an example of a local pattern as one would wish to find. Wil Harry, who worked as a carpenter on the Dynevor estate, was an immensely personable character who breathed and lived fishing. It appears that even in the most heated moments of the Battle of the Somme, when Wil served with the Royal Engineers, he found time to go fishing behind the lines. He claimed, as a boy, to have been inveigled into Sunday School attendance but twice, on the first occasion when he saw the feathers in the teacher's hat, and on the second occasion when he got them. Could this have been the imaginative birth-place of this irridescent fly?

The Wil Harry is a colourful pattern which ensures that it is highly visible under difficult light conditions and attractive in fast-moving water. It deserves tying on double and treble hooks and being more widely used: it has a pleasing simplicity about it and the 'lethal' appearance of a really good salmon fly.

Trout—Wet Fly

Were we to rely on printed book sources, there is no really reliable evidence of fly-fishing activity in Wales before 1820, at which time it is seen to have become developed, on the authority of George Scotcher's *The Fly Fishers Legacy*, published in Chepstow, into being a highly exacting pursuit. There are a number of references to angling in general sporting publications such as Lascelles's *Letters on Sporting*, which, as it were, venture into Wales, but do not deal specificaly with the subject 'from the inside'. Early engravings and poetical citings, dating from the beginning of the 18th century and depicting angling, are not really specific about the *method*. Typical of these, and exceptionally graphic, is this passage from 'A Country Walk' written around 1715:

> 'And there behold a bloomy mead,
> A silver stream, a willow shade,
> Beneath the shade a fisher stand,
> Who, with the angle in his hand,
> Swings the nibbling fry to land.'

It is tempting to think that the 16-year-old John Dyer, later to become famous for another poem, 'Grongar Hill', which describes a feature near his home in Carmarthenshire on the river Towy, is depicting the sport of 'samlet' fishing which, according to Scotcher, was the pursuit of a species caught on two flies with a well-scoured maggot on each hook. 'When they are once hooked get them speedily out, as they are a nimble fish . . . and you may take from ten to twenty dozen in a day.' This was before anyone realised that these little finger-marked trout were not a separate species from the salmon and sewin they were destined to become.

SAMLET.

Copper engraving of a samlet by Moses Griffith: the species considered for centuries as a most diminutive salmonid

Plate VIII

Original selection of flies from the wallets of Tom Tom, tied at the turn of the century.

marlow buzz. They were designed to imitate drowning and drowned insects and those that descend into the water to lay their eggs on plant life and the mud or gravel on the bottom.

Usk anglers used flies with very slender bodies and very little hackle. Their divided wings were set low over the hook with concave sides set together. These early Usk flies had dun wings and hackle, they had no tails and the body was of wool or hare's ear fur. Scotcher's 'Grey Drake, The Tilt-up, or Up-and-Down Fly' was tied as follows:

'The wings are made of mallard's feather, which may be chosen exactly to the color of them; the head either of peacock's herl, or ruddy black sheep's wool, the body of white shalloon, with a very small quantity of pale yellow with it, darkened with ruddy black sheep's wool at the extremity of the tail; the three whisks as the green drake, and an almost black hackle for legs.'

He, presumably, intended here an artificial of the oak fly, sometimes called the 'downlooker'.

Interestingly, Scotcher remarks at the conclusion of this article on the Grey Drake, 'The Green and Grey Drakes are by no means general flies, for several English rivers and most of the Welsh rivers are without them,' thus making it clear that there were, around 1800 and earlier, generally known and adopted local patterns, and other places where these were either unknown or unfruitful.

In general outline, throughout their history, Welsh wet flies have been streamlined to ensure good entry into the water. As the great Dai Lewis demonstrated, they should swim on an even keel and possess sufficient 'kick' to suggest life. This liveliness is achieved by the all-important setting of the wings and the hackle, so that they spring back against the current when released from the tension of forward movement. This facility for reaction to movement in the current is of vital importance in fast-flowing rivers such as characterise the Principality.

Plate VIII
Original selection of flies from the wallets of Tom Tom, tied at the turn of the century.

But there is every reason to assume that fly-fishing *was* practised in Wales from the Middle Ages—and when Dame Juliana Berner's *A Treatyse of Fysshynge wyth an Angle* came out in 1493—her dressing for a Dun fly, in all probability a March Brown, was as well known in fishing circles in Wales as elsewhere in the British Isles. All fly-patterns in use from this period until the early 1880s were bushy flies designed and produced to float on the surface. They were not what we now regard as dry-flies.

The distinction between wet and floating fly fishing in times past was obscure, even to those who practised it. Robert Brookes writing in 1740 suggested sinking the fly as much as six inches and Lascelles in 1811, in a letter from Wales, gives a 'tip' for bright days—'sink the fly a little'. When Charles Cotton, in an addendum to the 1676 edition of Walton's *The Compleat Angler*, refers to the technique of keeping the fly afloat in a stiff breeze, he seems to be alluding to a generally understood and the most widely-practised tenet of fly fishing—the up-stream floating fly, and not one exclusively pursued in the South of England. It can be surmised that all patterns were tied to float until they submerged and that, like the naturals they represented, they swam until they sank. George Agar Hansard in *Trout and Salmon Fishing in Wales*, 1834, says 'When you flourish your fly on the surface, be sure you gain the head of the stream.' So the up-stream floating fly, it would seem, was still being advocated for trout fishing in Wales at a time when wet fly patterns and techniques were in use elsewhere.

The number of rivers in Wales where the dry-fly fishing approach is more efficacious than the wet, is anyway limited—as the Geography of Wales dictates fast-flowing, rough waters. Thus, for the most part, Wales is, and has been since the early nineteenth century, a straightforward, up or downstream wet-fly fishing place. Stiff, hickory rods did not allow for very subtle casting or presentation until the arrival of greenheart and, later, split cane around 1860.

Wet flies, or flies that could be fished wet, were fully evolved by the beginning of the nineteenth century. Influences arrived from England. Samuel Taylor in his *Angling in all its branches reduced to a complete science: being the result of more than forty years real practice and strict observation throughout the Kingdoms of Great Britain and Ireland*, (1800), is typical of the day in assuming that the salmon and trout patterns known to him in his wide experience were equally applicable to England and Wales. The northern English flies, as earlier described by Cotton, were eminently suited to Welsh conditions. They were sparsely dressed in terms of hackle, with wings set at a very high angle. They were quick to sink and when retrieved showed a lot of life through the water. Early wet flies are imitations of stone flies, the sedges and terrestials such as the oak fly and the

85

marlow buzz. They were designed to imitate drowning and drowned insects and those that descend into the water to lay their eggs on plant life and the mud or gravel on the bottom.

Usk anglers used flies with very slender bodies and very little hackle. Their divided wings were set low over the hook with concave sides set together. These early Usk flies had dun wings and hackle, they had no tails and the body was of wool or hare's ear fur. Scotcher's 'Grey Drake, The Tilt-up, or Up-and-Down Fly' was tied as follows:

> 'The wings are made of mallard's feather, which may be chosen exactly to the color of them; the head either of peacock's herl, or ruddy black sheep's wool, the body of white shalloon, with a very small quantity of pale yellow with it, darkened with ruddy black sheep's wool at the extremity of the tail; the three whisks as the green drake, and an almost black hackle for legs.'

He, presumably, intended here an artificial of the oak fly, sometimes called the 'downlooker'.

Interestingly, Scotcher remarks at the conclusion of this article on the Grey Drake, 'The Green and Grey Drakes are by no means general flies, for several English rivers and most of the Welsh rivers are without them,' thus making it clear that there were, around 1800 and earlier, generally known and adopted local patterns, and other places where these were either unknown or unfruitful.

In general outline, throughout their history, Welsh wet flies have been streamlined to ensure good entry into the water. As the great Dai Lewis demonstrated, they should swim on an even keel and possess sufficient 'kick' to suggest life. This liveliness is achieved by the all-important setting of the wings and the hackle, so that they spring back against the current when released from the tension of forward movement. This facility for reaction to movement in the current is of vital importance in fast-flowing rivers such as characterise the Principality.

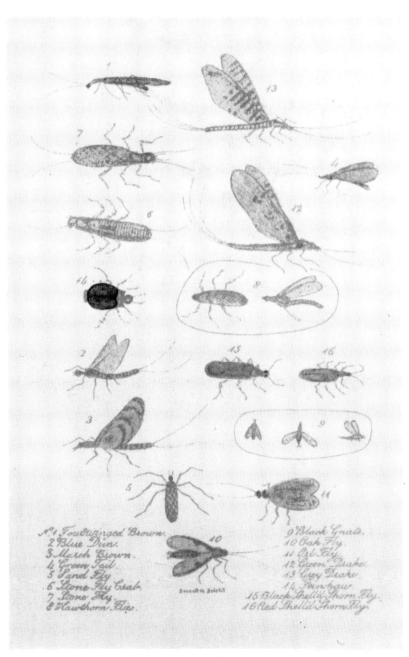

Frontispiece of George Scotcher's *The Fly Fisher's Legacy* (1820).

Alder
(Sialis lutaria)

> Hook   *12 Brown tying silk.*
> Body   *Rusty coloured wool.*
> Hackle   *Dark blue dun.*

> Location   *Rivers in Bethesda area of North Wales.*
> Time   *April and May.*
> Conditions   *Normal river flows.*
> Method   *Downriver wet fly.*

Pluen lwyd ar gorff lliw haearn. A dark blue dun hackle on rusty body.

The age-old custom of naming Welsh fly patterns by describing the material make-up of a fly has many advantages. The immediate one being that the angler never forgets the dressing of any pattern. This particular pattern appeared in the booklet, *Llawlyfr y Pysgotwr*, (*The Fisherman's Handbook*) written by William Roberts, and published in 1899. It is a representation of the alder larva.

The alder fly is well known to most anglers. It has a dark head, an even darker body and heavily-marked, rich brown, roof-shaped wings, somewhat sedge-like, but lacking the minute hair covering that is found on sedge flies' wings. It flies to and fro in rather a ponderous manner and could be likened to a helicopter as it chops about depositing its eggs on bank-side vegetation from which, in due course, the larvae fall into the river and proceed to burrow into the mud on the river bed. They spend some ten to twelve months in the river growing and shedding their skin in the process. Then each larva crawls back to the bank and, after locating a soft patch, buries itself for the period of pupation. In ten days it flies away—a fully-fledged insect—to find a mate in the bankside vegetation, before the story starts all over again.

The artificial Alder was extensively used in Wales in the early nineteenth century and the dressing used in those days is outlined in *The Fly Fisher's Legacy* by George Scotcher. In it he says:

> '*Natural*. It has four cloak wings like the green tail fly, of a yellowish smoky color, strongly paned or chequered with black; the wings rise from the ground in a ridge over the back and body, which they entirely hide. The two feelers, legs, head, and body of the fly are of a dull redish black, except the under part of the tail, which is first of a blood red and then inclining to a Seville orange color. It abounds mostly in brooks, or rivers whose sides are

wooded by orl or alder bushes, on which, during their season, they are always found, they do not hover over the water like other water flies, but being rather a full fly, are seen flying across and from bush to bush, and on rails by the river's side, running very fast, and frequently fallen on the water. You may use them any time of the day after the sun is well up till evening, and a warm blowing day which beats the bushes about is the best.

'*Artificial.* Make it with a freckled dark cock's hackle round the top of the shank of the hook, and the body either of ruddy black sheep's wool, with waxed Seville orange colored silk, or else with a coppery tinged peacock's herl, twisted round the silk and worked on together. As a winged fly, I have made it from the brown speckled feather on a wild mallard's back, a very dark hackle for legs, and the body of chocolate and orange wool well mixed, tied on with redish silk.'

Alder—variant C. F. Walker

Another representation of the larva that has been used in Wales is a pattern suggested by C. F. Walker:

Hook	*Long shank· 10. Brown silk.*
Tail	*Ginger hackle points.*
Rib	*Gold tinsel.*
Body	*Tapered brown & ginger seal's fur.*
Gills	*Sandy hen.*
Thorax & head	*Hare's ear.*
Hackle	*Brown partridge.*

Scotcher's Alder which he calls 'The Orl Fly, Lifting Fly, Orange Tawney, Orange Brown Camlet Fly, or Bastard Cadis' is an interesting representation of the natural, but today the Orl in use on reservoirs is somewhat different.

Red Ant
(Formica rufa)

Hook *16. Red tying silk.*
Body *Red tying silk built up to form two thick sections, a thorax and an abdomen with a thin waist between. Varnish the silk body.*
Hackle *Ginger cock.*
Wing *Blue dun hackle tips.*

Location *Most rivers and stillwaters.*
Time *July & August.*
Conditions *Warm still day.*
Method *As dry fly on the surface or in windy conditions in surface film.*

A fall of ants on the water on a day will always trigger off mad activity among the trout as the rush to feed on them, often ignoring all other forms of food. An angler is very fortunate if he happens to be out with the rod when the ants fall if he has, or can make up by hand, a pattern that is likely to fool the trout: it need not be too exact as, in their excitement, the trout feed with blind avidity. Many believe that trout are partial to formic acid; if so, it is always a temporary addiction, as they will only feed on ants for a short while and then lose interest completely.

Most anglers who have trout-fished for a number of years will have come across a fall of ants. Why these most organised of insects develop wings and, for no apparent reason, fly off from their nests no-one really knows. Some believe that the flight may be a nuptial one and that after the mating ritual the females return to the nest.

Black Ant
(Lasins niger)

> Hook 16 Black tying silk.
> Body Black dyed peacock quill. Butt and
>   thorax of ostrich herl.
> Hackle Cock starling.
> Wing Pale starling.

The colour of the Ant is not all that important: it is the overall impression of the body shape that matters. There are critical light conditions when perhaps more precise dressing and colour is likely to be effective.

George Scotcher writing around 1820 from Chepstow found difficulty in finding an exact feather to match the wing.

'It is needless to describe the form of these, as they are only the ants or pismires with wings, except that I think their tails are more of a bottle shape at this time.

'*Natural*. The wings of the red ant are light and yellowish, the body yellowish brown, and the legs light ginger.

'*The Artificial*, is made from the light-yellow part of a thrush's quill feather, the legs by a small ginger hackle, with the fibres taken off one side of it, and the body from a yellowish herl near the eye of a peacock's feather. I have known the hackle and herl answer better without wings.

'*Natural*. The wings may be made as the others, or from the light part of a starling's wing, for I know no feather that will match it exactly, the body of brown peacock's herl, with a brownish or almost black hackle, or, as said of the other, the hackle and herl alone.

'They come on, in a hot season and low water, about the beginning of July, and generally from mid-day till three or four o'clock, but unless well looked after, are not observed; in a wet season they are entirely lost. Towards the end of August, a smaller sort of each kind come down, but it requires great nicety either to fish with or make them, indeed it may be said of both sorts, that if not seen in great numbers, they are not worth attending to. I believe no angler ever goes purposely out to fish with the ant fly, but if in this season he should be out and observe the fish rising much, without seeing any fly on, he should then look carefully for them on the eddies, froth, or still water, and most likely will find the rise is at these flies, which he must then throw.'

August Brown
(Ecdyrrus longicuda)

> Hook 12 & 13. Pale orange tying silk.
> Tail Cock pheasant strands from tail feather.
> Body Two or three strands from cock pheasant
> tail (light shade), ribbed with gold
> wire. Two or three turns of bronze
> peacock herl at shoulder to represent
> the thorax.
> Hackle Pale honey dun cock and grey partridge
> dyed beige.
>
> Location Rivers of Mid Wales.
> Time Late Season.
> Conditions Normal river flows.
> Method Wet and dry method.

Despite the excellence of this pattern (by Pryce Tannatt) in representing the August dun, many Welsh anglers just use a smaller version of the March Brown which is similar. The August dun, as its name suggests, appears on Welsh waters in late summer, long after the March brown has gone. While the male spinners of the August dun are somewhat like red hot needles, the female spinners are almost identical to those of the March brown.

Courtney Williams gives a dressing for the August Brown attributed to Francis Walbran and, quite rightly, claims it to be a very effective fly.

> Hook 12-14. Brown tying silk.
> Rib Yellow silk.
> Tail Two rabbit whiskers.
> Hackle Cock pheasant wing feather.
> Hackle Brown hen.

In recent years there has been a tendency among anglers in Wales to concentrate on the dry fly after early May—even on fast flowing streams. Some, however, do well with the wet fly immediately after high water. The August Brown fished on the point does well in such circumstances.

Soldier Beetle
(Tolephorus rusticus)

Hook *10 & 12. Hot orange tying silk.*
Body *Golden pheasant tippets tied in, having*
      a dark bar at the extreme end, carried
      over and fastened at shoulder.
      The body of hot orange floss.
Hackle *Bright ginger cock.*

Location *Originally mid Wales rivers.*
Time *July*
Conditions *Hot weather.*
Method *Wet or dry fly.*

Pryce Tannatt, during his time in Wales, must have seen thousands of these insects in late summer. His pattern bears a close relationship to those given by Taff Price and Eric Horsfall Turner, both of whom have or had connections in mid Wales.

Soldier Beetle (Taff Price)

Hook *12. Orange tying silk.*
Body *Orange floss.*
Wing case *Brown raffene, the tail end marked with*
           a black felt pen.
Hackle *Natural red.*

Recently, in a competition on one of the mid Wales reservoirs, soldier beetles were swarming all over the place and being blown onto the water. The trout were quick to receive the manna—which does not come that often from the heavens of the mountain regions. Taff's pattern proved to be more attractive than either that of Eric H.T. or Pryce Tannatt. It was taken in both wet and dry form.

Eric's Beetle

Hook *8. Yellow tying silk.*
Body *Bronze peacock herl over yellow wool*
      with some yellow showing at tail.
Hackle *Two turns of black cock.*

The beetle family is important to the upland angler. Eric Horsfall Turner spent a lot of time fishing the uplands of the Severn valley. It is fitting to record this pattern in memory of a grand old angler.

Hugh Howells, Llanidloes on Trawsfynydd with the Blackie.

Blackie

Hook *8, 10 & 12. Black silk.*
Tail *Black fibres.*
Rib *Silver wire.*
Body *Black seal's fur.*
Hackle *Black shiny cock.*
Wing *Black squirrel tail or long hackle fibres.*
Cheeks *Small jungle cock.*

Location *All still-waters.*
Time *Early season.*
Conditions *All conditions, but very good in cold weather.*
Method *On quick sink line fished deep.*

This is a very young pattern which has become more widely known and used because of its success in fly fishing competitions. The man who was responsible for bringing it to the notice of the competition circus was Hugh Howells of Llanidloes. It is primarily a reservoir pattern for use on Llyn Clywedog, Llyn Brenig and Trawsfynydd. The success of black lures on reservoirs is well known. Blackie, fished on a sinking line, does seem to have the ability to make contact with fish lying on the bottom. Often it is used on a three- or four-fly cast and is invariably put on the point. In that position the Blackie is the fly that fishes deepest on the cast and so performs the task of scraping or bumping along the bottom of the water.

Blacke is also a very successful boat fly. Again, used on the point, it takes fish when stripped fast, as is the custom in modern reservoir fishing. Boat fishing on reservoirs that have rainbow trout often produces a situation known as 'bottom pinching' in which the trout follow for a considerable distance, just giving the fly a tweak now and again. Often by moving the fly more quickly the trout can be hurried into being hooked. The Blackie can, more than most, cure this perversion of bottom pinching!

The Blackie in tandem form too, is an excellent sewin fly for use with a quick sinking line. (See page 8).

Black & Silver

Hook 12. Black silk.
Rib Silver wire.
Body Flat silver tinsel.
Hackle Black hen.

Location River Teifi.
Time All season.
Conditions River clearing after flood.
Method Wet fly downriver. Point or bob.

The old market town of Tregaron on the river Teifi holds an important place in the development of trout fly fishing in Wales. The primary reason for this, of course, is that 'the famous' Dai Lewis lived there. Another great fly dresser too, not so well known, who lived only a hundred yards from Tanygraig, where Dai lived, was Charles Harrison, or 'Charlie' as he was known. Charlie was also a very gifted fly dresser, if not such an energetic fisher as Dai. His exquisitely dressed flies are known to decorate Angling clubs as far afield as New York.

His favourite fly was the Black & Silver which he fished with great delicacy. He would sometimes add a red tail to the pattern which helped—especially in dark water conditions. The pattern was, otherwise, dressed on a small double hook which helped with the hooking—when used as a bob fly. In recent years the pattern has been tied up in tube-fly form for sewin fishing, and larger versions on Esmond Drury, double hook and Waddington irons are effective salmon lures. In tube form the black hen hackle has been replaced by squirrel hair dyed black.

The simplicity of this pattern belies its effectiveness. Anglers using a Black & Silver tube fly of some one, to one-and-a-half inches long, as does John Mercer on the River Towy, find that it produces excellent results with sewin.

Black Gnat
(Bibio Johannis)

Hook *14 & 16. Black tying silk.*
Body *Ostrich herl (Black).*
Hackle *Black hen.*
Wing *Starling or snipe.*

Location *Rivers of mid Wales.*
Time *May, June and July.*
Conditions *Normal river flows.*
Method *Wet fly downriver or upriver dry fly.*

The Black Gnat was at one time widely used on the upper reaches of the Wye and the smaller streams of mid Wales. In a collection of top lines dressed by Tom Tom of Cwmystwyth many casts had the above dressing of the Black Gnat tied on the top dropper, while in the same collection there were a number of black flies tied with black ostrich herl and no hackle or wings.

The black gnat is quite a common fly—not unlike the ordinary house fly—but it is not really as black as many anglers may suppose. Some tend to use dun hackle—especially on the dry-fly version of the Black Gnat.

In common with a number of other flies, this artificial will take fish when the natural is nowhere near the water. When there are a lot of the naturals about the trout will feed avidly on them to the exclusion of everything else.

Scotcher, with characteristic sensitivity, gives this description of a master angler's approach with such a dainty offering:

'Natural. Like a small house fly but still much smaller, and the tail part of the body runs taper to a point; the wings are very light and the body dark. They begin to appear early or late in May, according to the mildness or warmth of the season, and are seen hovering in great numbers together generally over the tail or side of a stream, or on some particular part of a still water, where you will see the fish rise at them as they fall in couples on the water. At first they appear about two o'clock and as the cool evening draws on you lose them; after that as the weather becomes hot, they are solely an evening fly from about five or six o'clock till the edge of night, and as the wind then generally sinks in the evenings, you will perceive on the still water where they are by the fish rising at them, and by having a long rod, a light line, with the finest bottom, a small and light wired hook, a neat made fly, and keeping well off the water,

throwing gently and with great nicety in the ripple near the fish's rising, in the way you perceive he is swimming, you may succeed, and, but in a moderate way only, unless you are very skilful and use the utmost caution; towards the tail and side of streams your sport is more certain. They continue at times almost all the summer, and should only be used in calm hot evenings.

'*Artificial*. I make it on the lightest hook I can procure of No. 12, breaking the shank short, with a very light-blue dun hen's hackle, making the body of a small herl of a peacock's tail feather, the fibres of which should be very short and thinly scattered. When the fish are small, and the river free from any foul bottom, I sometimes tie it on to a fine glass coloured round hair, and of course the other part of my bottom single hair, which falls excessively light and will lie on the water, and the fly is frequently so taken, but without much practice and care you are very apt to snap it off in throwing.'

Black & Peacock Spider

Hook   *10, 12 & 14. Black silk.*
Body   *Under layer of black wool, covered by bronze peacock herl.*
Hackle   *Soft black hen.*

Location   *English reservoirs and rivers of North Wales.*
Time   *Throughout the season.*
Conditions   *Normal conditions.*
Method   *Wet fly—point fly on a three-fly cast.*

Tom Ivens's excellent book, *Still Water Angling*, was responsible in part for spreading the word about the Black & Peacock Spider. Since then, most stillwater anglers have the pattern with them as a general standby and, luckily, it is also one of the easiest of all patterns to tie. It was, however, known in North Wales for at least half a century before Tom Ivens's book.

Pluen ddu ar gorff paen
(Black feather on a peacock body)

Pluen ddu ar gorff blewyn het ddu
(Black feather on a body of a feather from a black hat. The feather from a black hat was always the ostrich herl).

Black flies were very much in vogue at the turn of the century, at a time when most Welsh rivers held amazing stocks of fish. The advice in *Llawlyfr y Pysgotwyr* (Angler's Handbook) 1899, was that wet flies on a cast should be some twelve inches apart. If this is correct, it provides another insight into methods practised some eighty years ago. It underlines the fact that much of the fishing done was on comparatively small rivers. These Welsh flies were tied extremely sparsely and were fished up-river because of the problem of keeping out of the trout's view.

The second of the two flies using a black ostrich feather was a typical example of how fly dressers at the turn of the century used readily available materials. In this instance the feather came from a lady's hat—as did indeed so many other fancy feathers.

101

Black Pennell

Hook *4 & 6 for sewin. 8 & 10 for reservoir.*
      12 & 14 for river.
Silk *Black.*
Tail *Golden pheasant tippets.*
Rib   *Silver wire.*
Body *Black floss.*
Hackle *Black.*

Location *All stillwaters and rivers of Wales.*
Time *Throughout the season.*
Conditions *All conditions.*
Method *Normal wet fly. Point or bob.*

It is generally accepted that an angler cannot go far wrong with a black fly pattern on all Welsh waters be they rivers, lakes or reservoirs. Black Pennell was a natural progression from the all-black patterns of the early years.

Black Pennell has an excellent reputation on stillwaters and is a fly that works almost everywhere in Wales—as in the rest of the United Kingdom. It can be depended upon to give the angler an even chance on most waters and is a good standby when one is unsure of what to use.

It has no favourite position on the cast, many anglers use it on the bob while others always have it on the point. On some of the bigger Welsh reservoirs like Trawsfynydd and Brenig it does well when used with a quick-sinking line and fished deep. On many natural lakes it serves well as a bob fly.

It was, some two decades ago, a very popular sewin fly—but this is not so today. On the river Conway it was formerly known to take good sewin; some do still tie it in tandem form today.

In recent years, certain modifications have been made to the Black Pennell. Some anglers add a lime-green fluorescent tag to the fly and this is said to help the pattern. Others have palmered the hackle—quite a popular variation with reservoir anglers. The palmered hackle tends to create quite a lively object from the trout's view-point as it bobs on the surface—which accounts for its effectiveness as a bob fly.

Its creator, H. Cholmondely Pennell, had other Pennell patterns of different colours, the best known of them being the Claret Pennell. Claret Pennell has its addicts on a few reservoirs in the Taff Valley. There are other Pennells with green, yellow and brown bodies, but they are not used extensively on Welsh waters.

Black Quill

Hook 14. *Red silk.*
Body *Well marked quill.*
Hackle *Short black cock.*

Location *Upper Teifi.*
Time *April and May.*
Conditions *Normal river flow.*
Method *Downriver wet fly, cast on the bob.*

This pattern, in common with many others, is the victim of poor tying. Many of the commercially tied examples of this pattern are an especial abomination. Often it is evident that little effort has been made to secure well marked quills. It does not seem to be appreciated that some of the drab quills commonly used detract greatly from the pattern. Some tyers mark the quill with a black felt pen to achieve this striped effect. Unless this is done to perfection, the contrast between the black and the white part of the quill will be seen to be lacking. On choosing material for the quills it is always wise to inspect the hind side of the peacock eye feather. If that is not registering a whiteish hue, then it should be rejected. The best method of stripping the flue from the peacock quill is still the old fashioned thumb and fore-finger method, done quickly against the grain of the flue. Flies made with quill bodies have always been popular in Wales, despite the fact that quill is not the most durable of materials. Some fly tyers would use a thin silver wire in order to protect the quill from the teeth of the trout. The red silk was intended to show both at the head and the tail.

The Black Quill has long been used both as a wet and dry fly. It has proved a favourite bob fly on a three-fly cast fished downstream. In days of old, wet fly anglers would hang their wet flies from their very long rods directly downstream—moving the bob fly in and onto the surface of the water. This technique, while it often succeeded in moving a fish, is notoriously poor at hooking them. The Black Quill used as a bob fly or dry fly was thought to be a good representation of the black gnat.

Black Spider

Hook 11, 12, 13 & 14 Purple tying silk.
Body Rear portion, flat silver tinsel;
front portion, three or four turns of
peacock sword feather.
Hackle A black cock saddle hackle.

Location Rivers of Mid Wales
Time Early season.
Conditions Low water.
Method Wet fly.

The Black Spider pattern designed by Pryce Tannatt has proved to be a more than adequate variant on Williams's Favourite. Some anglers, approving the silver tag especially, have used it to good effect when fishing the pattern during a buzzer rise. Some of these spider patterns often score better than do the more sophisticated dressings of the buzzer pupa.

The spider pattern was designed primarily to fish on the smaller rivers and streams of Wales. Often the dressing would only cover the upper half of the hook as per the style of a low-water salmon fly. The approach was to dance the wet flies on the surface of the quick flowing water with the long hackle being brought alive by the play of the current. This mobility of the long cock hackle gives the fly a semblance of life and a fascinating colour pattern where the body colour is veiled with the sparkling hackle.

Into the setting sun, waiting for the evening rise.

Black Spot

Hook   *14. Black tying silk.*
Body   *A small ball of black rabbit fur wound*
          close to base of hackle.
Hackle   *White cock dyed dark green.*

Location   *Border rivers and the Teifi.*
Time   *Evening.*
Conditions   *Low water.*
Method   *Dry fly or wet upriver.*

This pattern was devised to suggest the gnats and midges on which trout often feed on 'difficult' evenings. Anglers at such times try hard to find a pattern in the box that will attract the trout and the Black Spot often so succeeds. Some fly patterns, although not used often, are an essential reserve ingredient of an angler's equipment to be kept for especially difficult occasions.

The author employing cunning tactics on the upper Teify, near his home.

Bloody Mary

Hook   *10-12 Magenta silk.*
Tag or Tail   *Red wool or ibis.*
Body   *Peacock herl with gold at tail.*
Hackle   *Grizzle hackle dyed scarlet.*

Location   *Rivers and Lakes of Mid Wales.*
Time   *High summer.*
Conditions   *Warm day.*
Method   *Wet fly.*

A variation of the Coch-a-bon-ddu, though it is doubtful if it offers an improvement on the original. It has scored success with rainbow trout and, as it continues to do so, it could become a favourite. Most fisheries in Wales now stock with rainbow trout, and so Bloody Mary could in time, prove its worth as a bob fly.

It is one of the attractor-type flies that was used on the Elan Valley Lake complex in the forties and was offered to trout that had refused everything else thrown at them—a great test for any fly. It is a totally unusual pattern: and, perhaps, there-in lies the reason for its success!

Recently, the hatches of coch-a-bon-ddu beetle have been more pronounced, and trout in places like Claerwen have been taking them well. After a few days, however, they tend to look for something different: and then it is worth shaking them a Bloody Mary.

Bluebottle
(Cynomya mortuorum)

Hook 12 & 14. Blue silk.
Body Peacock herl, ribbed with thick blue floss.
Hackle Honey dun.

Location Originally on the upper Teifi.
Time All season.
Conditions Normal water flows.
Method Normal wet fly.

I euan Owen in his book *A Trout fisherman's Saga*, about the great Dai Lewis of the Teifi, includes a pattern tied by Dai of the Bluebottle. This was *not* really a favourite pattern of Dai's and by the diminished standards of tying and innovation apparent in this pattern it is obvious that he had lost interest towards the end of his fishing days.

According to the account given in the book, the fly was best used after a flood, both early and late in the season. The bluebottle is probably the best known of the flat-wing flies, the *diptera* family. A goodly number of newly-hatched flies from this family get blown onto the water: witness the hatches of daddy-long-legs on the rivers and lakes of Wales.

On those rich rivers where there is a plentiful food supply, members of the *diptera* family do not assume any great importance—but on the many Welsh rivers where food is always short, all tit-bits are welcomed.

Bluebottle

Hook 10 & 11. Orange tying silk.
Body Dark blue floss ribbed with black ostrich herl.
Wings Jay's secondary quill.
Hackle Black cock.

Pryce Tannatt's version of the Bluebottle proved once to be quite effective on rivers like the upper Severn, but it has lost a lot of its appeal in recent years.

Blue Hen

Hook 13. Black silk.
Body Black quill, finely dressed with two
       turns of black herl as thorax.
Hackle Underwing of moorhen.
        (Summer plumage)

Location River Teifi.
Time Early season.
Conditions Normal river flow.
Method Wet fly downriver.

This fly earned the reputation of being an excellent top dropper on a three-fly cast fished downriver. The main drawback was that the trout invariably damaged the quill body. Unfortunately the Blue Hen, like many other fly patterns tied by Dai Lewis, is in danger of being forgotten, and traditional wet-fly fishing is itself being practised less and less as other styles become the fashion.

It is therefore fortunate that some of the more successful river patterns are still being used by stillwater fishers. The Blue Hen has itself been subjected to this transference and is proving its value in its new environment. This change of location has also meant a change of position on the cast. It now operates well on the point position of a long cast. Here, the angler casts his flies out, and allows the Blue Hen time to sink some ten to fifteen inches below the surface before he brings her and the team back by means of the sink-and-draw method.

Dai Lewis tied flies commercially and there was a great demand for his productions outside the Principality. A large number of Blue Hens went to tackle shops in the North of England where they must have worked well for discriminating northern customers.

Dai Lewis, Tregaron, taking to the hills in summer drought.

Blue Ruff

Hook 14. *Green silk.*
Body *Heron fibre or green wool.*
Hackle *Pale to dark blue dun hen, or pale to dark
olive hackle.*

Location *River Usk.*
Time *Early season.*
Conditions *Normal water flows.*
Method *Wet fly downriver.*

This is another fly from the river Usk. The pattern was given to the
Editor of *The Field* by a Mr Acheson who was a keeper on the
Usk. The herl body was used on a number of flies and, with the green
silk, made a good body to represent the olives. It was generally used as
a dropper and fished when olives were hatching in the early part of the
season.

The Usk is an admirable river for fishing a wet fly in the normal
three-fly cast down-and-across method. It has a good hatch of olive
flies and the Blue Ruff fished in the surface film, as recommended by
its creator, does well. The combination of green silk and heron herl
makes for a very good olive body which is required in the early weeks
of the season when many of the *ephermidae* family hatch.

Blue-Winged Olive
(Emphemerella ignita)

> *Hook*   12 & 14. Green tying silk.
> *Rib*   Gold wire.
> *Hackle*   Greenish-blue hen hackle.
>
> *Location*   River Usk.
> *Time*   May and June.
> *Conditions*   Normal water flows.
> *Method*   Upriver or downriver wet-fly tactics.

This pattern was devised by William Law, a renowned bailiff on the Buckland Estate on the river Usk. William Law came from Scotland where he was known as the King of the Spey. He was a great caster and an expert angler. Anglers of such stature often exercise a big influence on the angling trends in an area; and if they tie flies, then those flies can acquire a reputation not always earned: this pattern falls into that category.

The Blue-Winged Olive is a difficult fly for the angler to get to terms with and there is no indication that this pattern is any more effective than are those of David Jacques (see *The Fisherman's Fly and other Studies*, 1965).

> *Hook*   14. Orange tying silk; Dark olive.
> *Body*   Dirty olive ostrich herl wrapped with olive P.V.C.
> *Hackle*   Dark olive cock.
> *Wing*   Upright coot.

In recent years the use of daylight fluorescent silk has been responsible for some very interesting body colouring. One pattern which has proved quite effective with the blue-winged olive dun on the upper Teify is as follows:

> *Hook*   12. Green tying silk.
> *Body*   Blue and lime green DFM wool very thinly applied.
> *Hackle*   Rusty blue dun.

The spinner stage of the blue-winged olive is generally catered for on many Welsh rivers by the Orange Quill.

> *Hook*   14. Orange tying silk.
> *Body*   Condor quill dyed hot orange.
> *Hackle*   Red cock.
> *Wing*   Starling or snipe.

111

Bongoch
(Red Base)

Hook 12. Black silk.
Body Black silk.
Hackle Dyed blood red.
Wings Medium dun (Starling).

Location Lakes of North Wales.
Time August and September.
Conditions Windy and rough.
Method Wet fly.

Another old Welsh pattern from the Ffestiniog area. it is somewhat similar to the modern lure, Sweeny Todd, which is a jumbo version of Bongoch used as a lure.

Bongoch is a late-season fly. Some anglers think of it as a beetle-like representation. It is recommended for use in wild and windy conditions. An old pattern, primarily designed for use on Gamallt lake in the Ffestiniog area, it has proved its value in modern times on other lakes.

Some anglers have, in the past, confused this pattern with the Cochen Las, but the hackle and the wing differ—the Bongoch being a fly of lighter hue and of more rotund form. Many anglers use it as a point fly, but it is always worth a trial on the bob. The point fly, fishing as it does, lower in the water, is the better for being thin and streamlined—while the more beetle-like flies fish better in the upper layers.

Many of the old Welsh fly patterns were meant to be fished very slowly in the water—moved in the traditional figure-of-eight retrieve. The Bongoch, dressed on bigger hooks, has produced good results when moved quite quickly on the reservoir.

Many flies, like the Bongoch, designed in Wales, up to the last decade or so, were intended to fish for brown trout. Now these flies have been put to the task of tempting rainbow trout—and brook char as well. These foreign fish—like all newcomers—have taken time to earn the respect of the locals who, experimenting with traditional Welsh flies like the Bongoch, have gradually identified their preferences.

The Bongoch, dressed very lightly, as in the original form—with just two turns of hackle, is a fair representation of a red and black buzzer pupa.

Bracken Clock
(Phyllopertha hosticoln)

                    Hook *12. Red silk.*
                    Body *Red silk.*
                     Rib *Bronze peacock herl.*
                  Hackle *Cock pheasant neck feather.*

                Location *Mountain lake.*
                    Time *June and July.*
              Conditions *Warm day.*
                  Method *Wet or dry fly.*

The quality of the cock pheasant neck hackle is often responsible for the success or failure of this pattern. It must be provided in the right size and colour. On a size 12 hook the hackle must come from about one-third of the way down the cock pheasant neck. As in the pattern Haul a Gwynt, the hackle has to stand square on the hook to get the fly to work best as a dropper. Cock pheasants vary in their shades of neck-feather colour. Some melanistic cok pheasants provide hackles in much darker hues: these are first-class.

The coch-a-bon-ddu beetles occasionally descend on Welsh lakes in great numbers and the trout quickly gorge themselves. However, after a few days, the angler will get a better response by fishing something slightly different—and this role can well be filled by the Bracken Clock. This is a fly to keep as first reserve for just such an occasion—and, as in other walks of sporting life—the reserve often scores where the first team have failed.

Brown Owl

Hook 14. Orange silk.
Body Orange silk.
Head Peacock herl.
Wings Hackled with a reddish feather from the
       outside of a brown owl's wing.

Location Mid Wales rivers.
Conditions Low water.
Time Night-time.
Method Wet fly.

The Brown Owl is used to represent small sedges in late summer. The dressing is generally tied very lightly. This is a pattern that came to Wales from the north of England and gained favour with anglers in some localities. Fished around ten o'clock on a summer night it takes good quality trout as it is moved slowly in the surface film of the water.

Black Beetle
(Coleoptera)

Hook 12. Black tying silk.
Body Ostrich herl.
Wing Black shiny crow.
Hackle Short black hen.

Location Still waters.
Time June
Conditions Warm and sunny days.
Method On wet fly cast, on the bob or second
        dropper.

The body of this pattern was tied very full and beetle-like; the black wing was tied flat on the body. This pattern was the brainchild of Tom Thomas who moved to the Llangurig area from North Wales in the early twenties. He could very well have brought the pattern with him.

Butcher

Hook 10, 12 & 14 Black tying silk.
Tail Red ibis or substitute.
Body Flat silver tinsel ribbed with silver wire.
Hackle Black hen.
Wing Blue section from mallard wing.

Location All rivers and lakes.
Time Throughout the season.
Conditions Water running down after flood.
Method Either as bob or point fly on a three wet-fly cast.

One of the best known wet flies of all time. It has been in existence since 1838 when it was first wrought by a Mr Moon and a Mr Jewhurst from Tunbridge Wells in Kent. Mr Moon was a butcher and it could be his blue bloodied apron that gave the fly its name. It is a fly that will take trout all season through, although it is especially effective in the early days.

It is difficult to understand why the fly was not included in a number of collections of flies used on Welsh rivers that were made during the nineteenth century.

In a bigger size the Butcher is used for sewin fishing and it has accounted for many sewin when used as a bob fly on the three wet-fly cast.

Bloody Butcher

Hook 10, 12 & 14 Black tying silk.
Body Flat silver ribbed with silver wire.
Hackle Dyed red hackle.
Wing Blue section of mallard wing.

A slight variation on the original Butcher is the Bloody Butcher which has a blood red hackle instead of the black one of the original.

Kingfisher Butcher

Hook 10, 12 & 14 Black tying silk.
Tail Fibres from Kingfisher's wing.
Hackle Hot orange.
Wing Blue section of a mallard wing.

Some anglers who fish from boats on stillwaters use another even more vividly colourful variation of the Butcher, known as the Kingfisher Butcher, a widely-used fly. Many will swear that the Kingfisher Butcher will raise fish from the darkness of the waters and that it is essential as a bob fly.

Trawsfynydd Becalmed.

116

Capel Celyn

Hook *12*
Tail *Two strands of mallard fibres.*
Rib *Copper wire.*
Body *Peacock quill.*
Hackle *Black*
Wing *Jay (Blue dun)*

Location *River Celyn, Usk and Wye tributaries.*
Time *Day time.*
Conditions *Normal wet fly water levels.*
Method *Upriver especially in low water.*

This was widely fished in the early days on the river Celyn and hence half the name. It was fished as a point fly on a three-fly cast. Over the years the fly seems to have lost its tail, and so present-day patterns tend to be tied tail-less.

The old river was drowned as was the Capel (Chapel) when the reservoir was constructed, and so the primary element in the fly's eponymy together with its birthplace was lost. Many anglers have tried the pattern on Llyn Celyn—which can at times be a very pleasant fishery, although it is not being developed to its full potential—without exceptional success.

Many of the older anglers keep faith with their old patterns which, naturally, occupy honoured places in their fly wallets. As anglers are far more mobile today many such patterns are found being used on other and distant waters. Capel Celyn has proved latterly quite effective on the tributaries of the Usk and the Wye.

The Chief

Hook   *12 & 14. Green silk.*
Rib   *Medium flat gold.*
Tag   *Red wool.*
Body   *Light fur from rabbit face.*
Hackle   *Brassy dun.*

Location   *River Teifi.*
Time   *Mid season.*
Conditions   *Normal river flows.*
Method   *Wet fly downriver. Point, bob or dropper.*
Also dry fly.

This fly was dressed with a very thin body, and the green tying silk was expected to show through the fur body. The rabbit fur was taken from the top layer on the face and was not to include the middle and the lower layers of fur which are very dark.

This was a pattern designed by Dai Lewis of Tregaron and is used extensively on the upper Teifi. Ieuan Owen included it in his delightful book on Dai Lewis, *A Trout Fisherman's Saga*, although it seems that it was among the flies that were marked 'Top Secret': not for general information.

The fly was christened after a certain Chief of Police; but the pattern cannot seriously be regarded as meriting the high security classification with which he endowed it. The Chief was often called upon during the 'dog days' of July, a time when most anglers eat by the sweat of their brows and fly fishing is a struggle. Any fly pattern that achieves success in difficult conditions is a far greater weapon than the average and one can understand the urge to keep quiet about it.

The Chief has proved to be more successful fished in wet form than it has as a dry fly. It is not easy to pick a good middle dropper for a three-fly cast. The bob fly, or first dropper, is often an automatic choice, as is the point fly. Doubt often exists about the middle fly. The Chief succeeds in filling this troublesome, question-mark position, and fishes well in water of light ale colour.

Tied on size 14 hooks The Chief has done quite well on lakes and reservoirs. When fished on a floating line and kept in the surface film it must be taken for a buzzer.

Chwilen Ben Glec
(Coleoptera)

>   Hook *12. Black tying silk.*
>   Body *Bronze peacock herl.*
>   Tag *Silver.*
>   Hackle *Black hen.*
>   Wing *Black hen.*
>
>   Location *Small mountain lakes with wild brown*
>   *trout.*
>   Time *Good fly in Summer.*
> Conditions *Warm windy days.*
>   Method *Fished on a floating line on a three-fly*
>   *cast.*

Chwilen Ben Glec is a beetle pattern that serves as a representation of any of those black beetles found in the grassland adjoining lakes and rivers, which inevitably get onto the water. The trout take them readily.

Some anglers have also put forward the theory that the normal Coch-a-bon-ddu pattern does not always continue to prove effective after the natural insect has been on the water for a few days. Recently, in a Welsh Championship fly fishing match held on Claerwen Reservoir, anglers fished hard for eight hours using the artificial Coch-a-bon-ddu because hordes of the naturals were about on the bank. The champion match man, however, took his winning catch of six fish with two other black patterns. Another did well with Chwilen Ben Glec—which does suggest that, under certain circumstances, black beetle approximation will serve the angler better when beetles get onto the water.

Consistent with the style of most beetle patterns, Chwilen Ben Glec is dressed with a nice full body. In windy conditions, most anglers use the pattern as a bob fly, dapped in the surface of the water. Other anglers use it as a dry fly, and in calm conditions it does take a lot of fish. One angler who, because of a physical disability leaving him unable to cast, uses the Chwilen Ben Glec as the Irish do the Daddy-long-legs. This is a method that could be further developed on Welsh waters, especially as more and more of the disabled take to fishing as a hobby.

Cinnamon Sedge
(Limnophilus lunatus)

> Hook 12. *Cinnamon tying silk.*
> Body *Cinnamon turkey feather.*
> Rib *Gold wire.*
> Hackle *Ginger cock.*
> Wing *Landrail wing feather.*
> Front hackle *Ginger cock.*

> Location *On most Welsh rivers and lakes.*
> Time *June to September.*
> Conditions *On warm evenings.*
> Method *Fished upriver as dry fly or on still-water just in the surface film.*

There seems to be some doubt as to the origin of the name, some being of the opinion that it refers to the colour, while others think it is because of the smell given off by the natural insect. If it is the latter, then one can only add that it requires a very keen nose to detect it!

The cinnamon sedge is of medium size with yellowish cinnamon wings. The body of the female is brown and that of the male green. Fished in the evening as a dry fly it has the ability to take fish well until dark. Often it will pay the angler to move the fly and cause a wake, the wake being attractive to the fish.

Cinnamon Sedge (J. T. H. Lane)

> Hook 12. *Silk, Golden olive.*
> Tail *Ginger cock hackle fibres.*
> Body *Ginger cock hackle.*
> Wing *Ginger cock hackle fibres.*
> Head hackle *Ginger cock.*

Col. J. T. H. Lane in his book, *Lake and Loch Fishing for Trout*, 1955, suggests this pattern in which he clipped the body hackle. The clipped hackle gives the impression of a hairy body and is an excellent way of achieving a good floating fly pattern. This pattern performs well in big wave conditions on stillwaters. The advent of deer hair as body material has by now surpassed the clipped hackle bodies suggested by J. T. H. Lane.

Cinnamon Sedge (W. Lunn)

>   *Hook* 14. *Hot tying silk.*
>   *Body* *Swan fibres dyed a light greeny yellow.*
>   *Body hackle* *Buff Orpington cock hackle.*
>   *Wing* *Well mottled cock pheasant wing dyed
>   cinnamon.*
>   *Front hackle* *One ginger and one bull Orpington cock.*

William Lunn was the creator of many fly patterns while he was keeper on the river Test. This particular pattern has not gained much support on Welsh rivers.

Cinnamon Sedge (Pryce Tannatt)

>   *Hook* 9 & 10. *Pale orange tying silk.*
>   *Body* *Unstripped condor quill dyed a greenish
>   yellow ribbed with fine gold gimp.*
>   *Wing* *Rhode Island Red secondary quill.*
>   *Hackle* *(In front of wing) Ginger cock hackle.*
>
>   *Location* *Most rivers and lakes.*
>   *Time* *Summer and early Autumn.*
> *Conditions* *On windy evenings.*
>   *Method* *Dry or wet.*

Another first-rate pattern from Pryce Tannatt. It is a medium-sized sedge fished mainly in the dry form—although it can be quite effective on windy days used as a bob fly on a wet-fly cast. As is common with most sedges, it does best in early and late evening.

Many sedge patterns primarily designed for river fishing have transfered to stillwaters and done well in their new environment. This is true of the Cinnamon Sedge which has earned the reputation of being able to summon the trout up from the vasty deeps. On some remote Welsh mountain lakes anglers tend to fish the Cinnamon Sedge as a normal dry fly and cast along, parallel to the bank, to take trout lying close in to the bank waiting for the tit-bits that come off the land.

The variant pattern of Cinnamon Sedge attributed to Roger Woolley is also a great favourite: (see over)

Cinnamon Sedge (Roger Woolley)

Hook   11-13. Brown silk.
Body   A strand from a cinnamon turkey tail
feather.
Rib   Gold wire.
Body hackle   Ginger cock.
Wing   Landrail wing.
Front hackle   Ginger cock.

This fly was primarily designed to entice brown trout, but it has proved effective with the more commonly stocked rainbows in still waters. It is also gaining its place as a grayling fly on the river Dee. It is probably most effective when used as a dry fly in the late evening. Good quality hackle allows the pattern to be fished in the surface film and the angler, by jerking the rod tip, makes the fly skit in the surface —thus emulating the action of a sedge caught in the surface film of the water.

Coachman

Hook   *12 & 14. Brown tying silk.*
Body   *Peacock herl.*
Hackle   *Ginger cock or hen.*
Wing   *White swan or hen.*

Location   *Most rivers and stillwaters.*
Time   *All through the season.*
Conditions   *Normal river flows.*
Method   *Wet fly as bob or second dropper.*

The Coachman is one of the best known of all artificial fancy flies, yet many anglers will not give it box-room. Any pattern that has been in existence for over a hundred and fifty years and has produced as many variants has somehow to be both favoured and effective. It bears no resemblance to any known living insect and therefore must be classed as a fancy fly, holding some mysterious general appeal for the trout.

Only a few river anglers in Wales now use the Coachman, when it can, especially in late Spring and Summer, do service as a dry fly in its hackle form in the late evening. The white hackle aids visibility on dark evenings, or when fishing against the sun-set.

The Coachman now seems to have more followers on the stillwaters where many anglers, disliking the pure white wing of bought varieties, immediately set about removing its 'whiter than whiteness'. This has led to the adoption, now pretty widespread, of the so-called 'Lead Winged Coachman'. Some also use the Coachman in the smaller sizes when trout are 'smutting' and reluctant to look at more conventional flies.

In the early fifties, interesting to look back on, the Coachman was much used for sewin fishing, the white wing being held in high esteem. Fashions change, and the Coachman went out when the *nouveau vague* sewin flies came on the scene in the early sixties. Very few sewin anglers use it today.

Some confusion obtains about the origin of this pattern. A Tom Bosworth who acted as a coachman to George II and IV has been credited as its inventor—although a certain John Hughes, a man of Kent who fished the river Gray, is also said to have first dressed the fly from bits and pieces, also has claims to the honour. So simple is the pattern that undoubtedly quite a number of people 'invented' it.

Hackle Coachman

Hook   10, 12 & 14. Brown tying silk.
Body   Peacock herl.
Hackle   White cock in front with ginger cock
supporting it.

This dry version is often used on the rough streams of Wales because of its visibility, a quality which, it has been observed, is an advantage on dark days and in the gathering darkness of evening against the western sky, particularly with the more myopic among fish and of the fishing fraternity!

Lead-winged Coachman

Hook   12. Brown tying silk.
Body   Peacock herl.
Hackle   Ginger cock.
Wing   Blue dun jay wing.

This was not, until its recent use on stillwaters, quite so well-known as the ordinary Coachman, despite the fact that, under certain conditions, it does better because of its more subdued wing. There is no doubt that the contrast of a vivid, white wing on a sober body does, under certain light conditions, put the fish off.

Royal Coachman

Hook   12. Brown tying silk.
Body   Peacock herl with a centre portion of
bright red floss.
Hackle   Ginger cock.
Wing   White swan, duck or hen.

This Americanisation of the original pattern is a very gaudy version, favoured by rainbow trout in light and water conditions seldom found in the British Isles.

Cob (Brecon)
(Rhithrogena haarupi)

Hook 12. Claret tying silk.
Rib Gold wire.
Body Dark red silk or seal's fur.
Hackle Dark partridge hackle.
Wing Hen pheasant wing.

Location River Usk at Brecon
Time Early season.
Conditions Normal river flow.
Method On wet fly cast downriver.

In the Brecon area anglers refer to the March Brown as the Cob and they have the Cob made up in a number of different colours. The notes appreciating to the March brown insect are applicable here. (see p. 188-9).

Yellow Cob

Hook 12. Yellow tying silk.
Rib Gold wire.
Body Yellow seal's fur.
Hackle Dark partridge.
Wing Hen pheasant.

Doyen of Brecon fly fishers, Leslie Peters, who has fished the river Usk at Brecon for the last fifty years, has great faith in his Cob, an early season fly.

Orange Cob

Hook 12. Orange tying silk.
Rib Gold wire.
Body Orange floss.
Hackle Dark brown partridge.
Wing Hen pheasant.

The Orange Cob is not quite so widely known and therefore is not so much used on the river Usk, yet, like many other little-known patterns, it has its day.

Leslie Peters of Brecon shows his selection of Usk flies.

Coch-a-bon-ddu

(Phyllopertha Horticicola)

      Hook *12 & 14. Crimson silk.*
      Body *Two strands of bronze peacock herl*
            tied full.
    Hackle *Coch-a-bon-ddu.*

  Location *Highland lakes of Wales.*
      Time *July.*
Conditions *Warm and windy.*
   Method *On the bob of a wet-fly cast.*

Time was when the highlands of Wales were covered in carpets of heather, and in June and July beetles would descend from on high onto the rivers and lakes in great numbers, providing a spread of banquet proportions for the fish. The trout feasted for days on these beetles, and the fly known as the Coch-a-bon-ddu was used by anglers to catch them. In recent years the heather has been replaced by sinister armies of green coniferous trees which sustain practically no insect life. Certain doubts existed originally about the identity of this beetle, with some anglers confusing it with the Marlow buzz, bracken clock, the shorn fly and the mini cockchafer. The coch-a-bon-ddu beetle has a reddish brown body with dark peacock green thorax and red-black legs. The Coch-a-bon-ddu, too, has the unique distinction of being the most mis-spelt fly name. Seldom is it correctly spelt—in any book or article—because its Welsh ancestry is either forgotten or mistaken for the Gaelic. Even Courtney Williams in his estimable *A Dictionary of Trout Flies*, makes a hash of it, and he had less excuse than many!

Expert etymologists (not entomologists) of the calibre of Bedwyr Lewis-Jones and the late Jac L. Williams, affirm that the term *coch-a-bon-ddu* in Welsh is descriptive of an insect which is red with a black base. The only other spelling admissible would be *coch-a-bonddu* which would be about as elegant as red-and-blackbase in English!

The hackle is tied rather heavily. Some add a gold tag to the dressing although this did not appear on the original. Others rib the body with gold wire and it is probably true to say that the ribbing is present as much to protect the herls as anything. A recent trend is to use red fluorescent filaments for the ribbing. It would certainly be wrong to think the Coch-a-bon-ddu artificial fly is only effective when the natural is about. On a cold March day in 1965 the late Evan Owen of Ynysbwl took twelve beauties on the Claerwen reservoir with 'the Cocky' as he called it. The dozen fell to the Coch-a-bon-ddu as it was bobbed along the surface, proving how effective it is as a bob fly.

George Agar Hansard in 1834 refers to the Drop Fly, as a dropper tied onto the cast by means of a hog's bristle! The pattern he gives of the Drop Fly is not dis-similar to the Coch-a-bon-ddu. Reference to George Scotcher's book *The Fly Fisher's Legacy* suggests the origin at least of the practice of fishing the Coch-a-bon-ddu on the bob.

The Coch-a-bon-ddu is also often used as a dry fly, especially on water thinning down after a flood. Here, in this guise, it would be wrong to think of it as a specific copy of a particular insect—but rather as a general all-rounder to fish during the summer months.

There is a tendency in Wales to fish trout flies tied on bigger hooks to catch sewin. A big bushy Coch-a-bon-ddu tied on a number six or eight hook has been the downfall of many an over-sanguine sewin. On a moonlight night in July, Cecil Jones of Llandysul took half a dozen sewin on a Coch-a-bon-ddu fished in the classical dry fly manner up-river from the Oak Pool. Most of the club anglers fished the traditional sewin wet fly method that same night and were fishless.

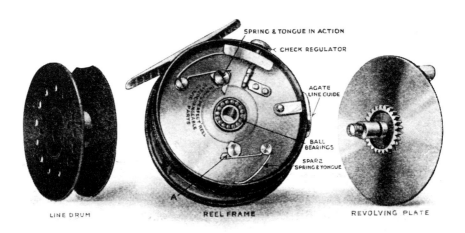

LINE DRUM   REEL FRAME   REVOLVING PLATE

The Hardy 'Perfect' reel dismantled.

Cochen-las

Hook *12 & 14. Black silk.*
Body *Black floss.*
Hackle *Coch-a-bon-ddu or black centre with single red outers.*
Wing *Dark dun, coot.*

Location *Lakes, e.g. Elan Valley in mid-Wales.*
Time *Summer months.*
Conditions *Normal summer weather and water level.*
Method *Point fly on a three-fly cast.*

A copy of the Cochen-las was received from the late Ned Hughes who, in the late fifties, was a celebrity among Rhayader anglers. The hackle on that specimen was Coch-a-bon-ddu; and Monty Powell, also from Rhayader, produced similar examples. Recently, however, a number of so-called Cochen-las have appeared where the hackle used is one with a black centre and with blood-red outers. This is obviously badger hackle dyed in blood-red dye. Another instance seen lately supported a hackle of black-orange which also is reputed to work well. Obviously, then, there are instances like this when it is not so easy to determine the authentic dressing of a vernacular fly where local opinion differs so sharply over its specification. The Ned Hughes version has always been assumed by most to be the authentic Cochen-las: though now we find that hackles with red tips are evidently proving successful.

As far as the name Cochen-las is concerned, it simply means 'red-blue-one'. The word 'las' is a mutation of the Welsh word 'glas' which means the colour blue (and sometimes green). It has nothing to do with the Scottish word 'lass' (double 's') meaning a girl—though, curiously, there is a girl skulking somewhere in the word cochen, for it means a red-head and, as 'blonde' seldom conjures a male, so the cochen is necessarily female—not impossibly a 'lass'! So Cochen-las, if you like, 'a blue red-head'. A useful fly on Claerwen (and all mountain lakes with wild brown trout) and on the upper reaches of the Wye around Rhayader where she spent her early days: since when she has grown up in beauty, stature and fascination, a winsome companion to mountain lakes.

Coch-yn-las

Hook   *14 & 15. Purple tying silk.*
Body   *Strand from brown turkey tail dyed*
        purple.
Hackle *Dark rusty dun cock.*
Wings   *Water hen secondary quill.*

Location   *Rivers and lakes of mid Wales.*
Time   *Early and late season.*
Conditions *Normal water flows.*
Method   *The middle fly on a three-fly cast.*

Pryce Tannatt confused many people with the name that he gave this pattern because they mixed it with Cochen-las (Page 129). The 'red-in-blue' of the nomenclature here clearly means a mixture of pigmentation resulting in purple. (See Snipe & purple and Usk Purple.)

This Coch-yn-las has proved to be a good trout and grayling pattern, used primarily in the early days of the season and again in September when many of the early season flies come back into their own. It became very popular on the Irfon, a tributary of the Wye, and on the Ceiriog. The 'Coch-yn-las' also gained some success on still-waters, like Claerwen, although there is some doubt as to whether all anglers questioned knew the difference between the two patterns. It could be that the success gained by one was being attributed to the other.

Cog (Sepia Dun)
(Leplophlebia marginata)

Hook   12. *Silk: Purple silk.*
Rib   *Thin gold wire.*
Body   *Chocolate coloured silk.*
Hackle   *Ginger cock.*
Wing   *Brown mallard, not too brown.*

Location   *Mountain lakes.*
Time   *Early season.*
Conditions   *Warmish days.*
Method   *Normal wet fly fishing on floating line, point fly.*

This fly, used quite extensively in the Ffestiniog area of North Wales, would be recognised as the fly to use when the sepia dun was in evidence. Quite some importance was attached to the position that the fly should occupy on the cast and the Cog was used 'next to hand' (Nesaf at law) or on the bob.

Cogyn Now'r Allt

Hook   12.
Tail   *Ginger fibres.*
Rib   *Silver wire.*
Body   *Rear half yellow silk. Front half blue silk.*
Hackle   *Black hen.*
Wing   *Light blue dun.*

Now'r Allt, 'Now (Noah?) of the woods' was one of those human curiosities, half hermit, wild man of the woods, known in Wales as 'dyn hysbys' (man with knowledge), a soothsayer. It was said that he even talked to the fish, and this, his version of the Cog is particularly interesting as it is in direct contact with angling wizadry.

The sepia dun has a very dark body and dark wings. It has three tails which generally spread well out. It is the first of the 'upwing' flies to appear and they generally show during the warmest part of the day. Many anglers rely on the Pheasant Tail pattern to serve them on the lake when the sepia dun is hatching, but the Blaenau Ffestiniog pattern, Cog, being darker, can often be more effective. Recently, some Welsh anglers have been using copper wire under the dressing of the Cog in order to get the pattern to fish deeper in the water. This is worth trying.

131

Concoction

Hook 8 & 10. Green silk.
Rib Gold wire.
Body Rear half green seal's fur. Front half red seal's fur.
Wing Light hen pheasant wing or owl.
Hackle Ginger.

Location Llyn Trawsfynydd and other stillwaters.
Time All season.
Conditions Breezy and sunny.
Method On bob or point of a three- or four-fly cast.

This fly is a variation of the old Irish pattern, Green Peter, with red seal's fur added to the body. Arthur Owen, highly respected among anglers on the Trawsfynydd fishery, devised this pattern when on a visit to Chew Valley for an International fly fishing match. Arthur, as captain of the Welsh team, produced some astounding catches with this pattern. It has proved its value on stillwaters in Wales—like Clywedog and Brenig—in addition to its home waters of Trawsfynydd.

It is generally fished on the bob, but such is the faith that some anglers have in it that they also, at the same time, place it on the point. One angler was known to have *four* on his cast on one particular day on Trawsfynydd. There's no need to ask what fly was proving effective that day!

Arthur Owen, Ganllwyd, whose Concoction has led to the downfall of countless rainbows

Cord

Hook   *12 & 14. Yellow silk.*
Body   *Hessian sack pickings.*
Hackle   *Blue andalusian.*

Location   *River Neath.*
Time   *March & April. Mid-day.*
Conditions   *Medium water level.*
Method   *Wet fly.*

This fly was one of many designed by Ernest Lewis of Glynneath. He was employed on the Rheola Estate and was an angler of exceptional ability. He was known as 'Ernie' to all the anglers in the area and his flies, great successes in their time, have guaranteed him a little share of immortality.

The Cord pattern was used mainly after the water had started to warm up. It was dressed in such a way that the dubbing was put on very lightly and the silk showed right through the dressing.

Ernie placed great importance on the blue andalusian hackle that he used for his fly patterns. The blue hackle is held in high esteem in South Wales and some anglers care little for the body of the fly as long as the quality and colour of the hackle is correct.

Often a pattern that has gained a high reputation in one locality does not reproduce the same magic on other waters. The Cord is an exception in that it is a fly that has travelled well and it has been successful in particular on sections of the upper Severn. When the fly was first dressed it was not made as a copy of any specific insect, but it would appear that it is especially effective when the olives hatch at the beginning of the season.

Corncrake Series

Egarych Cochddu
(Corncrake wing on black-red body)

Hook *10. Brown tying silk.*
Rib *Gold wire.*
Body *Wool from black ram's scrotum.*
Hackle *Brown Partridge.*
Wing *Corncrake (sandy coloured hen).*

Location *Lakes of North Wales.*
Time *Summer evenings.*
Conditions *Calm and sunny.*
Method *On the bob of a wet-fly cast.*

Many of these patterns are included as archive material and not as an encouragement for enthusiastic tyros to try and emulate the past. The corncrake has been driven to near extinction by modern farming methods. The wing of this pattern is now tied with a hen wing feather which are plentiful and make for better winging material.

This pattern is especially effective when the small brown sedge is about and will take fish when fished either wet or dry.

Egarych Corff Llygoden Ddŵr
(Corncrake wing with water rat body)

Hook *10. Brown tying silk.*
Rib *Gold wire.*
Body *Fur from water rat.*
Hackle *Ginger cock (palmered).*
Wing *Corncrake (starling sub).*

This is an important pattern for the September fisher and many anglers feel that it does better when the little red sedge is about. It will fish well during the day, taking fish that have proved difficult with other offerings.

135

Egarych Dyfrgi
(Corncrake wing on otter body)

> Hook 10. Brown tying silk.
> Rib Gold wire.
> Body Whiteish fur of otter (rabbit).
> Hackle Ginger.
> Wing Corncrake (sandy hen)

The fly dressers of old made judicious use of every material that took their eye. Many an article of clothing was shorn, regardless, in order to provide the necessary body colour and material. No doubt an otter pelt given to such a fly dresser spawned forth this pattern. Today rabbit skin provides all the fur necessary for this dressing. The light-coloured body is especially attractive to trout when used in the evening.

Egarych Clust Sgwarnog
(Corncrake wing on hare's body)

> Hook 10. Brown tying silk.
> Rib Gold wire.
> Body Hare's ear fur.
> Hackle Ginger cock.
> Wing Corncrake (sandy hen).

This pattern is equally at home on river and stillwater. It represents the little brown sedge and takes fish during the day as well as in the evening. The wings, when used in its wet form, must slope back— flat over body; while, if used dry, they can be put at a more upright angle and split into two wings separate from each other.

Egarych Corff Paun
(Corncrake on peacock herl body)

> Hook 10. Brown tying silk.
> Rib Gold wire.
> Body Peacock herl.
> Hackle Ginger.
> Wing Corncrake (sandy hen).

A Peacock Herl body was adopted and adapted for many uses with the old Welsh fly dressers. It was material that was easily available. Herl makes an ideal bulky body, characteristic of the Sedge and Beetle patterns.

Cowdung
(Scatophaga stercoraria)

Hook   *12 & 14. Brown tying silk.*
Body   *Dirty yellow wool, with pinch of brown.*
Hackle   *Pale ginger.*
Wing   *Woodcock.*

Location   *Upper reaches of most rivers.*
Time   *Early season.*
Conditions   *All weather.*
Method   *Upriver dry fly or normal wet fly
downriver.*

All anglers know this common fly well but it is not an important fly on rivers that possess a rich aquatic fly life. Its relevance is mainly to those small rivers where fly life is sparse and terrestial flies are important as food is always scarce.

The above pattern appeared as a variation of an old pattern created by Alfred Ronalds and, while its effectiveness when the cowdung insect was being blown onto the river is undeniable, it is also a good all-round pattern, successful when the natural is absent. In the early forties it was a pattern much used as a wet fly and is similar to the Woodcock & Yellow, the lake pattern. Latterly, it has been used more in its dry form and, on the smaller rivers, during low water conditions, it is important to fish it upriver.

Some fly-dressers do not put a wing on the dry version of the Cowdung fly. In addition to the normal pale ginger hackle they add a winging of cree feather which gives a sparkle to the fly. Scotcher used golden plover, or alternatively, corn-crake, starling or a pale ginger hackle. Clearly, exactness of imitation was not of high importance:

'*Natural*. It is needless to give a description of a fly so well known, as is always found on the cow-pats in the fields, from February to November; I shall only observe it is the female (which is the smallest, and of a more green cast than the male) that frequents the water the most, and the time is only in the cool windy days, from the end of February till the end of April. They are not seen in any great numbers at once on the water, but if you perceive one or two now and then, and no other fly very strong on, then is the time for the cowdung.

'*Artificial*. Take one of the dun feathers tipped with yellow, out of the wing of a golden plover, and wind it round the top of the hook, like a hackle, and under put a lumpish body of greenish yellow

137

wool; tie with brighter yellow silk. As a golden plover's feather is not always to be procured, you may use the redish dun feather from a land rail, either as a hackle or wings; or even a light ginger hackle, or starling's wing, with the above body, will answer, for being used only in rough water, the imitation need not be so very exact.'

Crane Fly (Daddy-long-legs)
(Tupulidae)

> Hook 10, 11 & 12. Pale orange tying silk.
> Body Stripped herl from moon peacock feather.
> Wings Rolled and split woodcock secondary quill.
> Hackles Rusty dun cock.
>
> Location Still-waters.
> Time Late summer.
> Conditions Windy.
> Method Wet fly cast on the point.

Of all the fly patterns that have evolved in recent years, it is the Crane Fly that has been modified with the best results. The old dressing of Pryce Tannatt (above) is now seldom used, despite its being extremely effective two decades ago. The advent of new fly tying materials has condemned many an old traditional dressing. Not that they were inadequate when they were first designed. It is simply that time has wearied them.

There has of late been a great upsurge in the interest shown in Crane Flies, due to the success they have been giving anglers on the big stillwaters. Consequently, the old art of dapping has shown something of a revival.

Although the first of the crane flies will be seen in April, it is in summer and the autumn that they really summon the trout onto the surface of the water. There exists some confusion as to how the Crane

Fly is best fished. Some tend to move it in the surface of the water, though many advocate leaving it motionless on the water—or dapping.

The daddy-long-legs, as they are generally known, are easily recognised—but many people are surprised to learn that there are nearly 300 different species of all shapes and sizes. One or two general patterns are sufficient to cover all contingencies that will confront the angler. In windy weather they are blown onto the water and will bring up even the most lethargic of trout.

In recent years more and more Welsh anglers have been trying the dapping method—especially with Crane Flies and, with the increased interest in boat fishing, it is poised to become an effective and entertaining method of fishing in the Principality.

This pattern is best fished as a dry fly and left to lie on the water without movement. A modern tying, somewhat simpler, and with greatly enhanced floatability would be:

> Hook 10. Brown tying silk.
> Body Green or brown herl or deer hair.
> Legs 6 cock pheasant centre tail fibres, knotted.
> Wings Cree hackle points.
> Hackle Ginger cock.

Crawshay's Olive

Hook *12. Yellow tying silk.*
Tail *Honey dun fibres.*
Body *Mole fur.*
Rib *Yellow silk (prominent).*
Hackle *Honey dun.*
Wing *Coot or starling.*

Location *River Usk on the Glanusk and Crawshay estate.*
Time *All season.*
Conditions *Low water.*
Method *Downriver wet fly or single wet fly upriver.*

This fly has the look of being very successful, and it is. It is rather a delicate pattern with an overall colour of olive dun; the yellow silk, the honey dun hackle and the mole fur forming the effective colour pattern. It is one of those special fly-patterns that inspires confidence.

When fished on a fine leader in the runs and glides of the river, the Crawshay's Olive is taken for a member of the olive family in one stage or other of its development. Despite its overall delicate dun shade it is an effective evening pattern, fished just under the surface of the water.

Cream

Hook *12. Yellow silk.*
Body *The fur of a Teddy Bear.*
Hackle *Light blue dun hen.*

Location *River Neath.*
Time *Mid-day onwards.*
Conditions *Normal river conditions.*
Method *Top dropper on a wet fly cast fished downriver.*

This was another pattern devised by Ernest Lewis of Glyn Neath. His very original fly patterns are still much valued: they are proving their ability to take fish on the Ystradfellte Reservoir, which is managed by the anglers of Glyn Neath.

This pattern, again, was tied using a fairly pale blue dun colour. The shade of the hackle is important, and some anglers recommend that only the 'butt' be used. Ernest Lewis was meticulous in his choice of hackle; and it seems that what we have here is a case of history repeating itself, as, in the Neath area in 1895, a Mr F. Yates developed a series of wet flies which had palish shades of hackle—hackle which he no doubt was able to produce in plenty—as he was himself apparently a breeder of game fowl for fly dressing. (See Appendix 3 pp. 316-18).

Dafydd Lloyd

> *Hook* *8 & 10. Yellow tying silk.*
> *Rib* *Flat gold tinsel.*
> *Body* *A fawny yellow floss.*
> *Hackle* *Ginger cock.*
> *Wing* *Bronze mallard.*

> *Location* *Rivers and lakes of North Wales.*
> *Time* *Evening.*
> *Conditions* *A still sultry warm night.*
> *Method* *On the bob of a wet-fly cast.*

Most of the sedge patterns devised in North Wales were of a dark hue and this particular one seems to be in sharp contrast to the general trend. It was often used in conjunction with a dark pattern, such as Y Rhwyfwr Mawr Cochddu (p. 211). Anglers felt that with two contrasting patterns they were offering the best of both ends of the colour spectrum to the trout. An useful ploy this.

Despite giving this pattern extensive trials on some waters in other parts of Wales, it has not registered much success. The fact that any pattern is still remembered after some fifty years is evidence that it must have proved successful for some anglers. It is a tragedy that often fly patterns are criticised unjustly because not sufficient knowledge is available about the correct method of fishing them. The Dafydd Lloyd pattern does work well on Clywedog Reservoir in the evenings and it proves to be most attractive when fished quickly just under the surface. Some anglers believe that it does well when the 'biga moth' hatches on the Clywedog reservoir. This curious and unique insect has a yellow body, brown legs and brown wings. It descends from the forest in June, throughout the day, and when it lands on the water the trout unanimously vote for it with their mouths.

Devonshire Doctor

> Hook   12. Black silk.
> Rib   Flat gold.
> Body   Black floss or seal's fur.
> Hackle   Coch-a-bon-ddu.

> Location   All rivers.
> Time   Late season.
> Conditions   Normal water flow.
> Method   Normal wet fly.

The Welsh pattern from North Wales.
Pluen Cochddu ar gorff du.(A coch-a-bon-ddu feather on black body.)

This fly was used in the normal down-and-across method on rivers. It would appear that it was most effective as a point fly and that it generally met with most success towards the tail-end of the season. The advice given in *Llawlyfr y Pysgotwr*, Fisherman's Handbook (1899), written by William Roberts, is that black flies worked better towards the closing months of the season on both rivers and lakes. The Welsh version of this fly was lightly dressed, in a style reminiscent of the Clyde style. Though an useful lake pattern, it is still generally fished down river on a two- or three- wet-fly cast.

The Teifi Terror, a sewin pattern, is very similar to the Devonshire Doctor.

Salmon Leap on the Teify: David Cox.

143

Diawl Bach

Hook 12. Black tying silk.
Tail Brown fibres.
Body Peacock herl.
Legs Dark brown hen.

Location Chew Valley reservoir.
Time Evenings in May and June.
Conditions Warm, calm weather.
Method On a floating line.

This pattern has gained fame outside its own native country—whereas little is known of it in many parts of Wales. Its fame runs highest in Chew Valley but it is a demonstrably good fly elsewhere.

A 'Mr Evans from Cardiff' is attributed with the invention of the pattern and, it would appear, that he used to fish the Chew fishery where, in the evenings especially, he would take many trout with this pattern. The Diawl Bach appears to be nymph-like, though it is difficult to conceive what item of food the trout take it for. The pattern is held in high esteem by notable Chew anglers like John Braithwaite and Steve Pope.

Drudwy Corff Du
(Starling wing on black body)

Hook *12. Black tying silk.*
Tail *Blue Dun hackle fibres.*
Rib *Flat silver.*
Body *Black silk.*
Wing *Starling wing.*

Location *Harlech area, small mountain lakes.*
Time *All season.*
Conditions *Normal.*
Method *Point fly on a normal wet-fly cast.*

There is little doubt that this is a variation on a number of small black flies that were used in Wales. The use of flat silver is somewhat unusual and some of the old versions had as many as six turns of silver which practically obscured much of the black body.

It was a fly used for fishing the small lakes and was considered to be something of a 'secret' pattern. The late J. O. Jones of Llanrwst was the first to publicise it in his contribution to John Veniard's book *A Further Guide to Fly Dressing*. 'J. O.' used it to good effect on Loch Leven and, when tied in the smaller sizes, especially when dressed very lightly—as was customary with many of the North Wales fly dressers—it made an excellent representation of the black midge pupa.

As is the case with many Welsh trout fly patterns, inevitably they are used to fish for sewin. Such is the fickleness of sewin and the credulity of anglers, that practically each and every pattern has its devotee. Drudwy Corff Du, although not a recognised sewin pattern, has performed offices as a sewin fly on the upper reaches of the river Aeron.

145

Dunkeld

Hook   *8, 10 & 12. Orange tying silk.*
Tail   *Golden pheasant toppings.*
Body   *Flat gold tinsel, ribbed with gold wire.*
Hackle *Hot orange cock.*
Wing   *Bronze mallard.*
Cheeks *Two small jungle cock.*

Location   *Reservoirs and sewin rivers.*
Time   *Summer.*
Conditions *After the water warms up.*
Method   *On reservoirs as a point fly on a wet-fly cast. In rivers for sewin, best in the evening.*

This is one of the best fancy flies in current use on Welsh reservoirs. There is hardly one reservoir on which this pattern does not figure in the top half a dozen favourite flies. It does seem to work better, though, after the water has warmed up. It is an attractor fly with high visibility qualities and is especially good when used on a sunken line and retrieved quickly.

So favoured is this pattern that some competition-minded anglers use as many as four on their cast at once! One effective variation on the original pattern has been the use of a green fluorescent tail.

This fly, although having become prominent again because of its powers with rainbow trout in stillwaters, is also a pattern always worthy of a try with sewin—especially just following a flood when the water still contains some traces of colour. Try fishing it in tandem form.

Some flies have the reputation of being able to attract the fish and get them to take other flies. This is a quality that has been attributed to the Dunkeld. In recent years substitutes have been used instead of the Jungle Cock which can no longer legally be imported into this country. The fly has not suffered much as a result of this importation embargo because the substitutes have done well, and jungle fowl are reared quite successfully alongside domestic fowl and fancy pheasants.

Reservoir anglers have, in recent years, been tying in hot orange hackle in palmered fashion as is the custom in Ireland. This adds to the pattern when it is fished in big wave conditions from a boat. Normally a point fly, it has proved its value in the palmered version as a bob fly. This pattern was originally designed to fish for brown trout, but today it is used mainly for rainbows in the bigger reservoirs and is at its best during those warm days when other flies tend to fail.

146

Du'r Frân
(The Crow's Black)

Hook   13. Black silk.
Rib   Thin gold wire.
Body   Black silk.
Hackle   Dyed blood red.
Wing   Dark dun (crow wing).

Location   Rivers and lakes of North Wales.
Time   Summer and autumn.
Conditions   Normal.
Method   On point of wet-fly cast.

Another black pattern from Ffestiniog. There is hardly need to underline the importance of black fly patterns in every area in Wales. Many anglers fish the season in and the season out just using black flies. They miss a great deal by this unsubtle approach, but they are seldom unrewarded.

This pattern is dressed thinly and is an ideal point fly.

The use of a blood-red hackle was much in evidence on many Welsh rivers about fifty years ago. The Welsh word used to describe this hackle was 'fflambo' and practically every area had a pattern using 'fflambo legs'. 'Du'r Frân', with its red hackle, was a break with tradition—yet it was very effective and can be thought of as the forerunner of the more colourful and fancy flies that came on to invade Welsh fisheries at a later date.

Early Brown
(Nemoura meyeri)

> Hook *12 & 13. Hot orange silk.*
> Body *Hare's ear dubbed thinly on tying silk.*
> Hackle *Under covert feather from a woodcock wing.*
>
> Location *Rivers Usk and Teifi.*
> Time *March and April (mid day).*
> Conditions *Normal water flows.*
> Method *Wet fly.*

This pattern appeared in the Pryce-Tannatt collection and it has proved to be an effective pattern when the natural is about in the early days of the season. The early brown is a minor member of the *perlidae* family, a smaller member of the order of stoneflies.

The Early Brown is best fished as a middle fly on a three-fly cast and has proved to be effective on fine days in early Spring.

Other patterns that are also effective, fished when the early brown is about, are Brown Owl and Winter Brown.

Edmondson's Welsh Fly

> Hook *10. Yellow silk.*
> Body *Dirty yellow mohair, tipped at tail with gold tinsel.*
> Hackle *Furnace.*
> Wing *Woodcock's wing.*
>
> Location *Lakes of North Wales.*
> Time *All season.*
> Conditions *All conditions of water and weather.*
> Method *Wet fly—on the point.*

Edmondson, a tackle dealer living in Liverpool, invented this fly which was used on North Wales lakes.

Primarily a lake fly, although some claim has been made for it as a late-season river fly, there is no doubt that it once enjoyed considerable status. By today this has diminished considerably in the face of the hordes of reservoir patterns that have appeared with mushroom-like suddeness. Many disappear with similar suddeness!

Edmondson's Welsh Fly has had its day on places like Claerwen and Clywedog.

February Red
(Taeniopteryx nebulosa)

Hook *Red Silk 12, 14.*
Rib *Gold wire.*
Body *Red wool.*
Hackle *Dark brown partridge.*

Location *Upper Teifi, Usk.*
Time *Early March.*
Conditions *Warm Spring day.*
Method *Downriver wet fly.*

February red is a member of the ubiquitous order of stone flies which provide that essential early bite for Spring trout in some areas. Of all the stone-flies, the February red is the most localised in distribution, being very significant, though, where it does appear. On the upper Teifi is shows in considerable numbers, and the above pattern has been in use for decades in the Tregaron area.

There is little doubt that this particular pattern is also used to good effect when the Early brown (*Prontonemoura meyeri*) is in evidence. The Early brown is similar in colour to the February red, but its wings tend to have more of a greyish tint rather than a brownish one.

Even as late as the thirties and forties anglers in the upper Teifi tended to be rather conservative in their choice of wet flies. Into March and early April the February Red was always on the cast, fished in the middle position on a three-fly cast.

A fly with a long lineage, the February red is mentioned in Dame Juliana Berner's *Treatise* in 1496, and George Scotcher—that possibly psuedonymous angler/surgeon from the Chepstow area—has a great deal to say for this fly which he obviously held in high esteem.

'*Description of the natural fly*. This is the first fly that appears on the water; in an open season I have seen it as early as January 23. It has four wings, which lie flat on the back, one over the other; they are, when open, of a light dun, with a yellowing brown cast in it, and are much veined, and are somewhat longer than the body; they are fixed far down on the back, and when it is flying or fluttering along the surface of the water, which it frequently does, you may see the four wings very distinctly, and they seem lighter than when closed on the fly, and appear to be in the middle of the body, for the head and chest are plainly perceived projecting out before them. It has two long horns or feelers, six legs, and the tail part of the body

149

is nearly of a size, and does not run taper. At its first coming, the body and legs are of a dull black, as the weather gets warmer, the under part of the tail becomes a dirty tawney, and the legs rather inclining to ash colour and towards the end of March, and in April, the body is of a brownish black, and the legs and under part of the tail of a dirty yellow; it becomes dark if a frost happens, and lighter if the weather keeps mild. The wings continue nearly the same.

'In January, February, and till near the end of March, it is on from about eleven o'clock till three; after that, till about the 24th of April, which is the latest I have seen it, it appears as early as eight o'clock, and continues till near mid-day. In February, I have seen a lump of whitish eggs on the end of the tail, and from about the middle of February to near the end of March, is the strongest time of its appearance in any numbers. After that season, I have frequently seen small ones very dark. It is stronger on those rivers or brooks whose banks are woody, than elsewhere.

'It appears to come from some cadbait, as I have found it among the stones by the river's side in a feeble state, and the wings all crumpled up, as if just come out of a case.

'*Directions for making the artificial fly*. I always make it a hackled fly, or ruff, as I do all the other four-winged flies whose wings lye along over their back, for when they fall on the water their wings make that appearance.

'The following imitation I have always found succeed, and even when the blue dun and March brown have been strong on. Take a light and yellow brownish dun hen's feather, either from the neck or any part of the body, so as it is a weak feather and all of one colour; wind it two or three times close together, a little below the top of the shank of the hook, and make the body clear below it, of a mixture of ruddy black sheep's wool, and yellow-orangy wool; use yellow silk, and rib up the body with it, and finish close to the feather, by two half-hitches. Of course make the body, by the mixture, lighter or darker, agreeable to the season, remembering that the black wool shows very powerfully when wet, and allow for it in mixing. The size of the fly will point out to you the size of the hook; you may indeed make it rather larger, as at that season of the year the water is generally pretty full, and the weather rough'.

Y Felan Fach
(The Little Yellow One)

Hook   *14. Yellow silk.*
Tail   *Golden pheasant tippets.*
Body   *Gold tinsel.*
Hackle   *Light ginger hen.*
Wing   *Snipe speckled feather.*

Location   *Rivers and lakes.*
Time   *Mid summer.*
Conditions   *Sunny and bright.*
Method   *Cast out and worked slowly back in the
surface film.*

It has always been a hard task to get a fly that will take fish in bright and sunny conditions. Often, the fish, in such weather, are down low in the water and the only way to reach them is to use a quick sinking line. Even so, in bright sunlight, the odd fish will just cruise along taking flies near the surface and the Felan Fach is designed to deceive and have him.

Designed by Gwilym Hughes of Wrexham, an angler cast in the traditional mold, who consistently stands by his conviction in very small, though not always such brightly-coloured, flies for lake and reservoir fishing, Y Felan Fach has proved its value on lakes like Trawsfynydd, Brenig and Alaw though perhaps it is more effective with rainbow trout than with the browns. It is essential to use light tackle and a very gentle approach. The Felan Fach demands good presentation and it will then help the angler to get a trout under harsh light conditions; such trout are of greater value, for they will surely be few!

Fflambo

Hook 10. *Silk.*
Body *Claret seal's fur or wool.*
Rib *Gold wire.*
Hackle *Claret hackle.*
Wing *Bronze mallard.*

Location *North Wales.*
Time *Warm nights of summer.*
Conditions *Gentle breeze.*
Method *On point or bob of wet-fly cast.*

This pattern gained a good reputation as a sedge fly in North Wales and was considered by many anglers to be the best fly to use for their night fishing.

The dressing is applied rather heavily, and is totally out of character with many of the old fly dressings from the same area. The seal's fur body is made quite thick—with the gold rib being put on tight to emphasise the segmentation. The claret hackle should have six to eight turns and the mallard wing rolled to form a heavy wing that extends well over the bend of the hook.

Sedges played an important part in the angling lives of many of the quarrymen of North Wales. Their's was a hard life, the hours of work often extending from dawn until dusk. Their angling activity was often necessarily limited to the hours of darkness. The Rhwyfwyr (Sedges) thus assumed far greater importance for them than they would have for the so-called 'gentlemen anglers'. Fflambo was a night pattern which probably was intended to suggest the grouse wing sedge (*Mysticides longicornis*). The grouse wing sedge is a medium-sized sedge with a grouse-feather-like wing and, in some cases, a reddish brown body.

Francis's Fly

Hook 12 & 10. Red Silk.
Body Copper coloured peacock herl ribbed
       distinctly with copper red silk.
Hackle Medium blue dun.
Wings Two hackle points of a grizzly blue dun
       cock's hackle set well up.

Location Mid Wales.
Time Early season.
Conditions Normal river flows.
Method Wet fly.

This is an old fly which was first mentioned in *The Angler's Register* in 1858, by Francis Francis, its creator. He gave this fly extensive trials in Wales and was convinced that it was a truly great fly. Courtney Williams for one does not agree with Francis Francis. The claims for it as a sewin fly are also hard to substantiate. One feels sorry when a fly of high reputation fails to please, but, that it is worth keeping the pattern handy, was proved on Ystradfellte reservoir recently. Rainbow trout which had been very dour all morning took a Francis Fly with confidence on the point of a two-fly cast.

The different breeds of trout respond differently to various flies, and little did Francis Francis in 1858 think that his creation would be taking fish whose forefathers then were unknown outside the United Sates.

Grannom
(Beachycentrus subnubilis)

> Hook *12. Green silk.*
> Body *Mole fur dyed in picric acid.*
> Hackle *Two biscuit coloured partridge hackles.*
>
> Location *Upper Teifi.*
> Time *April.*
> Conditions *Warm days.*
> Method *In surface film semi-wet.*

This pattern was evolved by Vicar Powell after he had discussed the grannom problem with Dai Lewis. The partridge feathers for the hackle, which *must* be of the right colour, are found mid-way between the back and the neck. The two hackles are tied in back-to-back. Many anglers have been disappointed with this pattern, but this is most probably the result of it being fished incorrectly. Vicar Powell did not fish his Grannom as a dry fly, but rather *in* the surface film.

Despite its importance in the fishers' calendar, the grannom has been neglected by Welsh anglers, and little is known of its life cycle. Records kept of grannom hatches on the river Teifi for the last twenty-five years reveal slight fluctuations—with a marked decrease in mid-seventies. Hatches in the present decade are similar to those of former years, both in density and duration.

On the upper Teifi the grannom starts hatching between the fifteenth and the twentieth of April. It will then hatch spasmodically until the seventh of May. When the grannom hatches, it may be observed that the female is slightly larger than the male and she has a greenish hue on the last few segments of her body. Many anglers think that trout only go for the female grannom and that they ignore the males. This is not conclusively proven—but most successful dressings do use green material.

On hatching, the grannom immediately takes off from the water and finds a partner. The courtship is an interesting one, interrupted only by the intrusion of a third member of the grannom family. A couple of hours after mating, the green egg-sack becomes prominent. The female then sets about getting rid of her eggs. The angler, at this time, is well advised to get ready for action on a piece of quick-running water. The female grannom flies up-river trailing her egg sack in the water—which helps her to dispose of it. It is during the time the female grannom is involved in this dipping action of her posterior in the water that the trout seize their opportunity to take them. This gives the angler the chance of taking good fish—as the broken water helps him with the deception; and it is not so demanding of the pattern. Once the eggs are in the water, they tend to stick to some underwater vegetation. The eggs are often carried down by the water for quite some distance. They hatch in about fifteen days. The larvae, after some further thirty days, are seen to construct the small cases in which they then live. The architecture of these cases is extemely interesting. As the larva grows it enlarges the case at the larger end. The materials used in the construction of the case are supposed to be cemented by a substance called *chitin* which it is able to secrete. The larva, during the month of April, closes the case by adding green vegetation to the top. Pupation then takes place, and from the larva comes the pupa which will emerge later as a winged adult.

When the adult grannom hatches, the angler who is fortunate enough to be able to fish daily—and who has the advantage of being on the spot when the hatches start—is the man who will enjoy real sport. The trout are not so selective then and the short spells during these small hatches are the best time to take fish. Later, when the hatches are very prolific, the angler's task becomes very much more difficult. Even the keenest of anglers at such times are obliged to retire to the local to alleviate their despair!

The difficulty of taking fish during a grannom hatch has resulted in many different patterns being tried. Halford's prototype is still used in Wales—especially for representation of the larva form.

Halford's Grannom

> Hook 13. Green silk.
> Body Green floss silk ribbed with green dyed
>   peacock quill.
> Hackle Rusty dun.

This is without doubt the most important trout fly for the majority of river fishers in Wales. It is so often compared with the May fly and there are many similarities. The pattern used in North Wales was known as Rhwyfwr Tinwyrdd.

Y Rhwyfwr Tinwyrdd
(Green tailed sedge)

> *Hook 12. Brown silk.*
> *Tag Gold wire.*
> *Body Wool from black sheep, with green blob*
> *on bend of hook.*
> *Wing Brown owl with partridge tail wing*
> *between the matched wing.*

It provides the trout with a veritable carnival and, at the same time, provides fishermen with a short period of exceptionally good fishing. Trout feed well during the grannom period and on many rivers it brings the trout into good condition.

To give an idea of how scientific and exact a science fly-dressing had become by 1819-20, this account in George Scotcher's *The Fly Fisher's Legacy* indicates a very precise observation of the natural and a clever tying of one of the most difficult imitations known.

'*Natural.* They have four wings which lie slopingly flat over the body, so as to entirely hide it; they are of a light and yellowish dun, with brown sandy spots; the head and body very dark, with a whitish stripe on the sides of the tail part of the body; sometimes there is on the tail a lump of green eggs, which in handling the fly will drop off; they have six legs, of a ginger cast, and two black feelers at the head. They are to be seen from the end of March to late in May, but the exact time depends entirely on the weather, for a wet season destroys them, as a fine one brings and continues them on.

'In their season, they are on in flights from 10 till 4 or 5 o'clock, and are easily known by their short returns in a zig-zag manner, in numbers together, over the water. They abound mostly in those rivers whose sides are covered with orl (i.e. alders or owler) trees, and may be seen running very fast on their leaves.

'*Artificial.* When they are flying their wings appear of a light dun, and their body dark, and for that reason I always make them with a very light yellowish dun hen's hackle, round the top of the hook; and the body of the dark fur, with yellow tips, from a hare's ear, tied on with green silk, which I take care shall be seen at the tail. Formerly I used to imitate them as follows; wings from the wings of a hen pheasant, where you perceive the color answers; two turns of a small light ginger hackle, for legs; a little mole's fur, for body; with a tail of the green silk; which mode, answered tolerably well'.

Gravel Bed
(Anisomera Burmeisteri)

> *Hook* 13 & 14. *Yellow silk.*
> *Body* *Blue rabbit under pelt.*
> *Hackle* *Blue dun with light ginger in front.*

> *Location* *Rivers Usk and Teifi.*
> *Time* *May & June.*
> *Conditions* *Low water.*
> *Method* *Upriver dry fly.*

This pattern is easy and straightforward. The body is tied rather thinly with the yellow silk just showing in the dubbed blue body. The blue dun hackle is tied behind the ginger one.

Found in abundance on Welsh rivers, gravel bed has a dark body with six long olive legs and two slate-coloured wings that lie flat along the back. Though it is a member of *tipulidae*, it is not unlike members of the crane family. It is not generally seen on Welsh rivers before early May and, when it arrives, can cause quite a furore on the water. The insect is amphibious and its metamorphasis takes place on dry land. As it moves about on the surface of the water it can occasion the trout to feed for long spells and, on some rivers, it is regarded as the 'poor man's Mayfly'. Considerable difficulty may be experienced when the hatch is at its height—because of the number of naturals around. At such times the angler's fly, no matter how well tied, or how accurate the pattern, has little chance of success. The more numerous the hatch, the more difficult it is for the angler, as the trout can become very selective in picking up natural after natural, studiously ignoring the artificial floating past their noses. There have been a good number of artificial patterns intended as representations of the gravel bed—but the one received by the author from Rev Edward Powell as a token of appreciation for a small present of coch-a-bon-ddu hackles is probably the best. The Rev Gentleman himself even admitted to pride in this above all his many patterns.

Price Tannatt, whose knowledge of the rivers of mid Wales cannot be questioned, produced a good pattern of the Gravel Bed in its dry form. His pattern is as follows: (see over)

Pryce Tannatt's Gravel Bed

> *Hook 12 & 13. Grey wool.*
> *Body Cigar-ash coloured wool, wound on and*
> *then lightly varnished with diluted*
> *Durafix.*
> *Hackle Two turns of natural black cock hackle,*
> *an over-sized hackle with a grey-ish*
> *brown feather from a partridge.*

Alfred Ronald's Gravel Bed

> *Hook 13. Lead coloured silk.*
> *Body Lead coloured silk.*
> *Hackle A long black cock, two turns only.*
> *Wing Under coverts of woodcock wing.*

A good variant also comes from the fly-tying bench of Alfred Ronalds who had a wide experience of Welsh rivers. He fished the pattern during hot bright weather and often used it when other patterns had failed.

Another Gravel Bed Variant

> *Hook 13 & 14. Purple silk.*
> *Body Peacock quill with purple silk showing*
> *at tail.*
> *Hackle Black cock.*

A friend who confines all his fishing to the dry fly on the rivers Dee and Severn received this pattern from a relation in Scotland. His confidence in the pattern is well justified.

Green Peter

Hook   10 & 12. Green silk.
Rib   Gold Wire.
Body   Green seal's fur.
Wing   Hen pheasant.
Hackle   Ginger

Location   Originally Irish lakes—today most
Welsh stillwaters.
Time   Summer
Conditions   Windy
Method   On 'bob' of normal wet fly cast.

This Irish fly has enjoyed considerable success on stillwaters in Wales. It is rather difficult to get the right shade of green for the body, as there are so many shades of green seal's fur available. The correct shade is a warm olive green, dressed rather bulkily. The ginger hackle is often palmered down the body as is the custom with many Irish fly dressers. Father Gargan, a great Irish angler, states that by using a blue hackle instead of the ginger, the Green 'Blue' Peter becomes an excellent fly for salmon; well, Irish salmon.

Greenwell's Glory

Hook   12 & 14. Yellow tying silk.
Rib   Gold wire.
Hackle   Coch-a-bon-ddu.

Location   All rivers and lakes in Wales.
Time   Early season.
Conditions   When olives are hatching.
*Method   On wet-fly cast fished down and across
river.*

Canon William Greenwell of Durham achieved piscatorial im-mortality when he invented this pattern. It appears that the first example was tied up for him by James Wright, a well known fly dresser living in Sprouston on the Tweed.

Such is the versatility of the pattern that it can serve not only as a river fly for trout—but as a reservoir and lake pattern—and also, when dressed on hooks 8 and 10, it takes sewin in daylight.

In the early days of the season the Greenwell is at its best when the dark olive is about, but most anglers regard it as a general all-round pattern which suggests a whole range of flies—mainly from the olive family. Fishing in Wales is nowadays mainly club-orientated, and it is interesting to note that, in many club handouts to visiting anglers, the Greenwell is the recommended fly 'all through the season'.

The Greenwell's reputation is equally high on still-waters where more and more anglers are deserting their colourful lures for traditional flies.

Not many fly dressers today use cobbler's wax; but it is important to note that beeswax does not give the yellow silk the same olive hue.

Greenwell (Dai's)

Hook 13. *Green silk.*
Rib *Gold wire.*
Tail *Golden pheasant tippets.*
Body *Green silk.*
Hackle *Greenwell.*

Location *River Teifi.*
Time *Early season.*
Conditions *Water running down after a flood.*
Method *On the point or the bob of a wet-fly cast.*

This fly is rather uncharacteristic of Dai Lewis's repertoire in that it is nicely colourful. Most of Dai's flies, as is well known, were inclined to be somewhat somber. From what we can gather, Dai himself considered his Greenwell best for the point position on a three-fly cast.

It is always important when evaluating some of these old flies to form an appreciation of the tackle's limitations in the conditions under which it was fished. Very few Welsh anglers, even in the thirties and forties, fished the dry fly at all. Wet-fly fishing was the norm, and that was conducted only when the river ran at a fair height. High water conditions in those days maintained for some three or four days after a spate so, in Dai's Greenwell, we should observe that it possessed the brightness to attract in semi-coloured water.

Usually it is possible to follow the development of most of Dai's flies, but this one is completely beyond the pale. It is still used by many local anglers on the upper Teifi and on its day does extremely well. Dai himself on a day took seventeen sewin, fishing the top reaches of the Camddwr—some six miles from Tregaron—all on a big version of his Greenwell.

It is distressing that so many of our fisheries are deteriorating so rapidly. It is unlikely that the sewin will ever run the Camddwr again, since man's thirst for water and the advent of a new evil, acid rain, has made these valuable nursery waters inhospitable, while the monstrous Llyn Brianne Dam prevents their migration.

So, Dai's Greenwell, in addition to being a good trout fly, has also done well with sewin. It has been tried on lakes but without the same success. Most of the Dai's Greenwells that are tied today have a long hackle; the original did not. It could be that Dai Lewis had appreciated the importance of nymph fishing long before it became standard practice.

Grenadier

Hook 12. Brown silk.
Rib Gold wire.
Body Hot orange seal's fur.
Hackle Two turns of ginger hackle.

The Grenadier, which is one of the top flies on the Chew Valley Fishery near Bristol, has proved effective on many Welsh Reservoirs. The best method is to cast it well out on a floating line and then strip it back rather quickly. This method, although somewhat unusual, seems to attract trout which are cruising just under the surface. Some dressers like to palmer the hackle in order to create more surface disturbance when fishing the fly in this quick-retrieve manner. It bears a striking relationship to the Teifi Pools Sedge.

Grouse Series

Grouse & Claret

Hook *12 & 10. Claret silk.*
Tail *Golden pheasant tippets.*
Rib *Gold wire.*
Body *Claret seal's fur.*
Hackle *Ginger.*
Wing *Mottled feather from a grouse's tail.*
Time *Late spring and summer.*

Location *Lakes and reservoirs.*
Conditions *Good stiff breeze.*
Method *Normal loch-style fishing.*

Although this pattern, as with most patterns in the Grouse series, is regarded today as a stillwater pattern, it is in fact only a slightly modified version of a fly very well known in Wales at the turn of the century. The Grouse & Claret pattern, certainly the most popular of the Grouse series in Wales is regarded by many as a 'super sub' for the Mallard & Claret. In recent years some anglers have tended to add a pinch of black seal's fur to the normal Mallard & Claret body in an attempt to darken the pattern and use a grouse wing to try to achieve this darkening of the pattern.

Grouse & Green

Hook *10 & 12. Black silk.*
Tail *Golden pheasant tippets.*
Rib *Silver wire.*
Body *Green seal's fur.*
Hackle *Black.*
Wing *Mottled feather from grouse's tail.*

Grouse & Green is a pattern that has historically been more popular than it is today. Many of the old patterns have fallen from grace since the boom in reservoir fishing, which has brought with it a new era of stillwater flies which, in the main, are inclined to employ synthetics and fluorescent materials. Some traditional anglers favoured Grouse & Green when the trout were feeding on fry. The pattern has also been tried out as a sewin fly and is worth a try as a late evening or post-dawn variant.

Grouse & Purple

Hook *10 & 12. Purple silk.*
Tail *Golden pheasant tippets.*
Rib *Silver wire.*
Body *Purple seal's fur.*
Hackle *Black.*
Wing *Mottled feather from grouse's tail.*

This pattern has a reputation for being the best of the Grouse series for early season fishing. On small mountain lakes it was used early in April; and, although most of the members of the Grouse series are fancy flies with no claim to suggest any living insect, the Grouse & Purple is used by some when olives are seen to be hatching.

The other members of the Grouse family have not gained much support in Wales although some steadfast anglers will have a Grouse & Orange, Grouse & Olive or a Grouse and Yellow in their box.

A perusual of the authoritative, *Llawlyfr y Pysgotwr* (The Angler's Handbook) will reveal that very little use was made of the grouse feather in 1899. Most dressings in the handbook favoured the partridge and the speckled hen—which is rather surprising as grouse were surely plentiful enough in North Wales in those days. It could be that as these fly-dressings were the work of ordinary working men, they had little legal access to the grouse moors.

In mid Wales, by contrast, the grouse feather figured quite prominently in many dressings. Tom Tom of Llangurig made extensive use of the grouse feather and his favourite was: Grugiar ar gorff porffor (Grouse on purple body). The dressing was simple, with only a purple wool body and a small grouse hackle. Three other similar dressings were used on the upper waters of the Wye, Severn, Rheidol and Ystwyth. Tom always used the hackle fly when fishing rivers and the winged version on the lakes.

Grugiar ar gorff lliw gwin
Grouse hackle on wine coloured body.

Grugiar ar gorff melyn budr
Grouse hackle on dirty yellow body.
Grugiar ar gorff lliw rhwd.
Grouse on rust coloured body.

It is interesting that 'Tom Tom', who dressed most of his flies on eyeless hooks, advocated fishing the wet fly upriver—having regard to the difficulty of keeping out of sight on the small mountain streams.

From accounts of fishing the mountain lakes it appears that they were full of smallish fish into the early decades of the century. They are no longer so plentiful. It was customary to use a winged fly on the lakes, and grouse patterns were very prominent in the heyday of Thomas Thomas.

Aden grugiar ar gorff porffor a thraed duon
Grouse wing on purple body with black legs.
Aden grugiar ar gorff lliw melyn budr a thraed cochion
Grouse wing on dirty yellow body with ginger legs.
Aden grugiar ar gorff lliw rhwd a thraed cochion
Grouse wing on rust coloured body with ginger legs.
Aden grugiar ar gorff lliw gwin a thraed cochion
Grouse wing on wine coloured body with ginger legs.

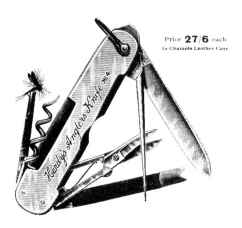

Price **27/6** each
In Chamois Leather Case

Gwybedyn Bach traed Cochion
(Red-legged gnat)

> Hook *Black tying silk.*
> Rib *Thin gold wire.*
> Body *Thin black silk.*
> Hackle *Coch-a-bon-ddu.*
> Wing *A very light coloured snipe.*
> Location *Rivers and lakes of North Wales.*
> Time *Early season.*
> Conditions *Cold weather.*
> Method *On bob of three-fly cast.*

This is a pattern used in the early days of the season in North Wales and once again the black body is favoured. This pattern has travelled well and it has proved a firm favourite with many anglers fishing the Teifi Pools—especially Llyn Egnant which is only stocked with brown trout. The rainbow trout are not quite so partial to it.

The great advantage of this pattern is that it will score when other patterns fail, a test for any pattern. Once again, it is difficult to estimate why this pattern is proving to be so successful on the very cold days of March and April when it does not appear to represent any living creature, but it is really an useful fly.

There are two variations of this pattern:

Gwybedyn Bach Llyn Manod

> Hook *12. Black tying silk.*
> Body *Black silk.*
> Hackle *Black hen.*
> Wing *White duck.*

Gwybedyn Bach Du

> Hook *14. Black tying silk.*
> Body *Black silk.*
> Rib *Thin gold wire.*
> Hackle *Black hen.*
> Wing *Starling.*

The variations are equally effective on lakes and rivers. Some find them more effective than the original.

Hare's Ear

Pluen lwyd ar flewyn clust sgwarnog.
(A dark blue dun hackle on a hare's ear body).

> *Hook* 12 & 14. Yellow tying silk.
> *Body* Hare's ear.
> *Hackle* Blue dun.

> *Location* River Ogwen.
> *Time* April and May.
> *Conditions* Normal water flows.
> *Method* Wet fly downriver.

This pattern, designed to fish the Ogwen and upper waters of the Conway, was tied with yellow silk which showed up prominently through the very sparse fur dressing. The hackle was an important part of the dressing and on some patterns it had as many as four turns. This hackle, when pulled against the current, produced life in the fly. The pattern possibly represents a nymph in the process of emerging from its shuck and on the point of hatching. This Welsh tying may not be accepted by the purists on the chalk streams of the south of England but it is the formula for 'Welsh chalk streams' like the Teifi. In all probability, on many Welsh rivers, it would be taken for the medium spring olive nymph. Many of the old Welsh dressers tended to use darker dun hackle as the season progressed.

The story of the development of the Hare's Ear is interesting. At the turn of the century it was being used as a wet fly. Gradually, as the century progressed, it grew in popularity as a dry fly until—around the nineteen fifties—the Hare's Ear could be found being used extensively on such rivers as the Usk, Teifi, Severn and the Dee. Now, in this last decade, it has become very important in its wet form as a nymph on stillwaters. Nymph fishing has given this old pattern a new lease of life and it may possibly develop into being one of the most important flies in the stillwater angler's wallet. It is to be recommended that the original Welsh pattern be used as the nymph representation of hatching olives.

To date, the Hare's Ear has proved effective when fished at all levels in stillwaters. Some add weight to the dressing in the form of lead or copper wire which lets it sink to the lower layers in the water. This is fished with a floating line and a long leader. On Clywedog reservoir in mid Wales the small Hare's ear fished in the top layer is very effective.

As an aside, when the Brianne reservoir at the headwaters of the Towy in Carmarthenshire was first constructed to obstruct the progress of that noble river, the land-locked sewin provided local anglers with superb fishing for a year or two. These stranded migratory trout, weighing around a pound and a half, moved well at dusk to a small Hare's Ear.

Scwd Gwladys

Harry Tom

Hook *12, 14 & 16. Yellow silk.*
Tail *Blue dun fibres.*
Rib *Gold wire.*
Body *Dark hare's ear.*
Hackle *Blue dun.*
Wing *Bronze mallard.*

Location *Originally from North Wales in sewin*
form, adapted for lakes of mid Wales.
Time *Early season.*
Conditions *In a good breeze on lakes.*
Method *Normal wet fly.*

This fly originated in the slate districts of North Wales where it was used by the quarrymen to fish for sewin. (See page 29). Hywel Evans of Llanfarian, a regular Dovey fisherman nowadays, gave the author the pattern in 1956. A chance success with the sewin version amongst the trout on Claerwen in wild windy conditions resulted in the development of this smaller version. In its new guise it has proved an effective stillwater pattern—especially if either pond olives or lake olives are present. It would seem that a darker dun hackle is required for early season fishing with a lighter honey dun being more effective in the summer months.

Harry Tom has proved its value on predominantly wild brown trout fisheries such as Claerwen, Nantymoch and even as far afield as Loch Leven in Scotland and Lough Conn in County Mayo in Ireland; and it is being increasingly used on Welsh rivers where it is thought that the trout might be taking it for a dark olive dun. Its distinct advantage is that it maintains effectiveness throughout the season on both rivers and stillwaters.

The tendency is to place the Harry Tom on the bob in a three- or four-fly cast. This can result in its being subjected to trout slashing at it and not being hooked. Some anglers have tied it on small double hooks, which does tend to improve the hooking capability of the pattern. Use of the Harry Tom on the point of the cast is a device to take trout from deeper water and, to this end, it is advisable to add a little lead under the dressing in order to help it to sink quickly. Fished in this manner it assumes qualities that suggest a nymph rising to the surface of the water.

Such is the all-round effectiveness of this fly that it really can be described as a 'Fly for all seasons'.

Haul a Gwynt
(Sun and Wind)

> Hook 12 & 14. Black tying silk.
> Body Black ostrich herl.
> Hackle Small cock pheasant neck feathers.
> Wing Black crow.

> Location North Wales stillwaters.
> Time All season.
> Conditions Good wave with stormy breeze.
> Method On the bob of wet-fly cast.

Haul a Gwynt is an easy fly to tie. The ostrich herl makes for a very full body. The old Welsh dressing gives the Ostrich herl as 'Blewyn het ddu' (A feather from a black hat). Many anglers have been confused by this term. The cock pheasant hackle which, in the original pattern, was in front of the black wing, has to be diminutive. The correct size of hackle is found some two thirds the way up the cock pheasant's neck. The use of too large a feather results in the black tips not forming a border around the hackle as it should.

When the late Doctor Prytherch competed on Llyn Trawsfynydd in a trial match for the Welsh Flyfishing Team he was well served by the Haul a Gwynt. He fished hard, as was his custom, in a fairly big wave but success only came his way when he used the Haul a Gwynt. The first one he tied on his cast was tied on a number twelve hook and this succeeded in getting fish to move but not to hook. When a smaller fly of hook size fourteen was tied on the cast, it proved very successful. Many anglers tend to use a bigger pattern in a big wave but it is not always wise to do so.

Haul a Gwynt—variation

Hook   12, 14 & 16. Black silk.
Body   Black chenille or black fur.
Hackle   Dark cock pheasant.
Wing   Snipe wing.
Front hackle   Two turns brown partridge.

This is a far heavier version of the Haul a Gwynt which has proved to be highly effective on Llyn Trawsfynydd. It generally occupies the bob position—but, of late, seems to work well with a Green Peter on the bob and it is itself then fished on the next dropper. This allows it to be fished in the surface film where its bulky hackle creates surface disturbance which excites fish cruising in the vicinity.

The Hawthorn Fly

Hook *12. Black silk.*
Body *Black silk.*
Thorax *Black wool.*
Trailing legs *Black nylon (knotted).*
Hackle *Black cock.*

Location *All rivers and lakes of Wales.*
Time *May.*
Conditions *Warm and windy.*
Method *Either as wet or dry.*

This big black fly makes its appearance in the countryside in May —often when the Hawthorn or May tree is in white blossom. There is no excuse for any angler failing to recognise the fly because its long legs make it look as if its 'under-carriage' were down! It only gets on the water from time to time—blown by the breeze or somehow by accident.

Scotcher, writing in the early nineteenth century, shows the modernity of his approach when he writes:

'*Natural.* It is somewhat similar in appearance to a large house fly, except that its chest is full, and the tail part of the body very small in proportion to it, the two wings too, lie flat one over the other on the back, and the legs are longer: the body and legs are of a varnished black, and withal woolly, the wings are very light, and the outside edged with black; you will now and then observe a few others whose wings are of a crow black, and the tail part of the body much thicker; there is also another sort which is like the first, only much smaller.

'In their season which is principally during May, you will see them fallen on the froth and on the dead water in warm calm days, and also flying on the sunny sheltered side of a hawthorn hedge, or ash tree; they are easily known, as their long legs hang down and make an angle with their body, the head being the point of it. They abound in rivers and brooks which run near hawthorn hedges, are only to be used when seen abundantly on, and in low water and calm days.

'*Artificial.* For the larger sort make their wings of the light part of the starling's wing, with two turns only of a long fibred black hackle, and the body of black ostrich herl. When you make the smaller sort, leave out the hackle. Your tackle must be very fine, and the hook light and proportioned to your fly.'

Corff blewyn het ddu a thraed du
(Body from black ostrich herl and black legs)

> *Hook 12. Black tying silk.*
> *Body Black ostrich herl.*
> *Hackle Black hen.*

The Welsh pattern makes no reference to its long legs. 'A black feather from a hat' is the way in which the ostrich feather was described some eighty years ago.

Aden ddu ar gorff du a choesau du
(Black wing on black body with black legs)

> *Hook 12. Black tying silk.*
> *Body Black wool or floss.*
> *Hackle Black hen.*

This pattern from the Bethesda area was used on local lakes. It was intended as a representation of the hawthorn and was generally fished in the surface film just as if a hawthorn fly has been caught by the water. The dry fly was not extensively used on the rivers of North Wales—with the exception of the Dee—until the late forties. Prior to that, most anglers practised the wet fly method fished downriver immediately after heavy water. The Hawthorn used mainly in this manner was supposed to represent the adult hawthorn fly blown onto the running water and drowned.

Hen Lambed

Hook   10, 12. Yellow tying silk.
Rib   Flat gold tinsel.
Body   Yellow rabbit flax near base of ear.
Hackle   Sooty hen.
*Wing   A thrush wing encasing bright yellow
dyed goose.*

This was used as a sedge fly and was a favourite with a number of Ffestiniog fishers. The overall impression achieved by the fly was that of a very light coloured moth, which fitted it to night fishing. The use of a wing from a thrush was later superceded by substituting a moorhen's wing which was equally effective.

While it is very important that these old patterns are not lost, it is fair to note that they are not extensively used these days. The Ffestiniog area is fortunate in that it has a fly dresser of the calibre and perception of Emrys Evans. In his evening classes on fly dressing he gives his students every assistance and the opportunity to learn to tie these old patterns. Hen Lambed is one he has kept alive. The name, meaning 'Old Lampeter' probably refers to an old character, thus nicknamed, lost to history.

Invicta—Silver

Hook 10, 12 & 14. Yellow tying silk.
Tail Golden pheasant toppings.
Rib Gold wire.
Body Seal's fur dyed yellow.
Body hackle Red cock.
Wing Hen pheasant tail.
Front hackle Blue jay.

Location Reservoirs and lakes.
Time Late spring and summer, sedge time.
Conditions Warm evenings.
Method Point or bob fly on a wet fly cast. Fished
with a floating line.

This pattern has for years been thought by anglers to be synony-
mous with sedge flies. It was the invention of James Ogden from
Cheltenham who used it in the early part of the season on lakes. On
many of the big reservoirs of Wales in recent years variations (in at
least five different colours) have been seen tied.

The tail feathers of a hen pheasant do not give a tidy wing, and so
feathers from the wing are advised. Many Welsh anglers have taken
to the Irish style, in which they palmer the Invicta with two red cock
hackles—thus giving the fly considerable 'kick' when retrieved
through the waves.

The Silver Invicta is one of the best all-round patterns for sewin, a
handy old campaigner—day, evening or night when all else fails. It is
closely related to the Dai Ben.

Invicta Black

> Hook 10. Black tying silk.
> Tail Golden pheasant toppings.
> Rib Silver wire.
> Body Black seal's fur.
> Hackle Black hen.
> Wing Hen pheasant.
> Front hackle Blue jay.

The Black Invicta is used on the Usk reservoir.

Invicta Orange

> Hook 10. Orange tying silk.
> Tail Golden pheasant toppings.
> Rib Gold wire.
> Body Orange seal's fur.
> Hackle Hot orange.
> Wing Hen pheasant.
> Front hackle Blue jay.

Orange Invicta is used on Llandegfedd reservoir.

MARTIN'S CLYDE PATTERNS (Style III.)

Tied on Adlington's Blued Round Bend Hooks, generally No. 14 size light irons. The feature of this dressing is the slight straight up wings, very sparely dressed hackles which lie nearly at right angles to the shank, together with spare and short body and usually the more sombre patterns and spiders.

This dressing, as illustrated below, is particularly successful on waters which are over-fished, where the fish are shy and discriminating, such as the Clyde, Tweed, Gryffe, Cart, etc.

Per assorted dozen, **2/6**   Per 3-yard 3-fly cast, **1/9**

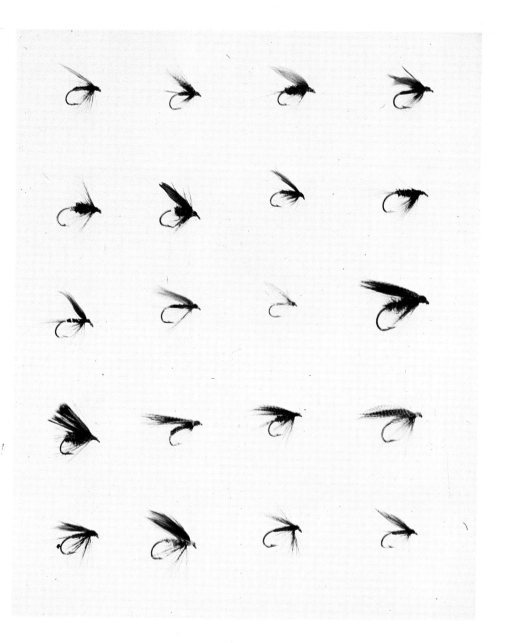

Plate IX Trout Wet-flies

Bongoch	Capel Celyn	Drudwy Ddu	Cochen Las
Coch-a-bon-ddu	Chwilen Ben Glec	Cog	Diawl Bach
Drudwy Corff Du	Du'r Frân	Felan Fach	Fflambo
Haul-a-Gwynt	Llew Bach	Harry Tom	Dafydd Lloyd
Pluen 'R Hen Law	Hen Lambed	Macrel Bach	Gwybedyn Bach
			Traed Cochion

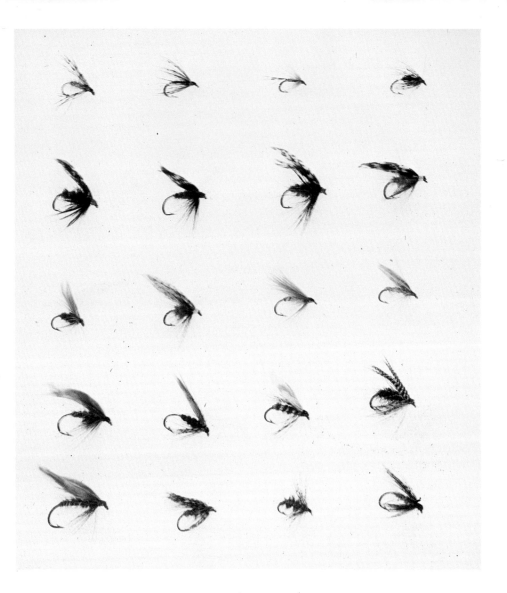

Plate X   Trout Wet-flies

Petrisen Melyn Budr	Petrisen Corff Piws	Pluen Llwyd olau ar gwilsyn paun	Petrusen liwgar ar gorff paun
Troellwr Mawr	Troellwr Bach	Troellwr Dafydd Dafis	Troellwr Llygoden Ddŵr
Egarych Gochddu	Egarych Llygoden-Ddŵr	Egarych Dyfrgi	Egarych Blew Sgwarnog
Rhwyfwr Cochddu Mawr	Rhwyfwr Cochddu Bach	Rhwyfwr Cylchau Gwyrdd	Rhwyfwr Cochddu Aden Tilsen
Rhwyfwr Ifan John Tŷ Canol	Rhwyfwr Bach 'R Hen Hafod	Rhwyfwr Petrisen ar Glust Sgwarnog	Aden Petrisen ar Gorff Snyff

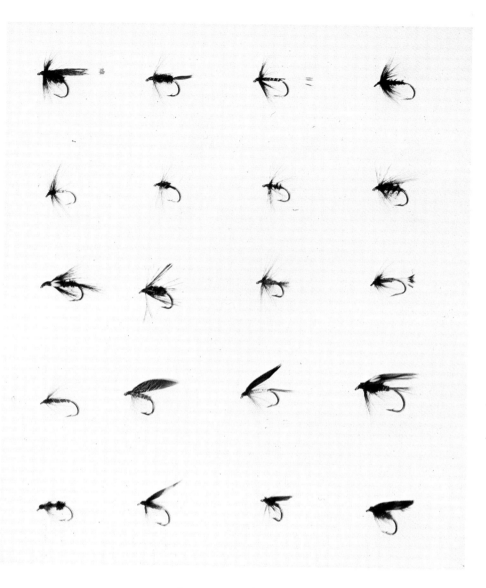

Plate XI   Trout Wet-flies

Alder	Bloody Mary	Black Pennell	Black Poeacock
Black & Silver	Black Spot	Black Quill	Blue Bottle
Blackie	Bracken Clock	Chief	Dai's Greenwell
Dai's Nailer	Cinnamon Sedge	Kingfisher Butcher	Watson's Fancy
Royal Coachman	Cyffylog ar gorff	Gwybedyn Bach	Grugiar ar Gorff
	melyn budr	Du	Piws

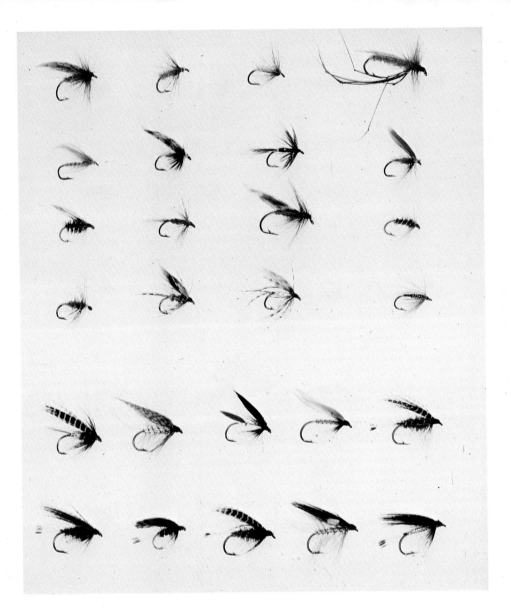

Plate XII   Trout Wet-flies

Concoction	Cord	Cream	Daddy Long Legs
Crawshay's Olive	Edmondson's Fly	Devonshire Doctor	Teifi Pool's Sedge
Francis's Fly	Dark Blue Dun	Green Peter	Grenadier
Usk Dark Blue	March Brown	Silver March Brown	Usk Nailer
Peter Ross	Invicta	Butcher	Greenwell	Teal & Red
Mallard & Claret	Grouse & Black	Teal & Green	Dunkeld	Mallard & Silver

Iron Blue Dun
(Beatis Pumilus)

> *Hook 14. Crimson silk.*
> *Tail Blue dun hackle fibres.*
> *Body Mole fur with crimson showing at tail.*
> *Hackle Dark blue dun cock hackle.*

It is probably true to say that each and every area in Wales has its own local artificial fly to represent this little chap. It is a favourite with trout and anglers alike. It is an easy fly to identify as it is small—with four wings of dark blue dun. From close inspection, it is apparent that the blue dun vary in size from river to river: they are considerably bigger on the Usk than on the upper Severn or on the Tryweryn, a tributary of the upper Dee.

Acheson's Blue Dun

> *Hook 9. Kirby. Yellow silk.*
> *Body Blue fur, with or without yellow silk*
> *rib.*
> *Hackle Blue dun hen.*

Usk flies a hundred and fifty years ago were dressed very lightly and in a manner similar to that practised on the river Clyde in Scotland. The flies that Acheson used were all dressed on a short body, utilising just half the shank, as with low-water salmon fly patterns. This style was rather unique in Wales—as, even in North Wales where fly dressing materials were used sparingly, the whole hook shank was always used to support the dressing. During the Rebecca Riots 1839-43, which were the upshot of social unrest in south west Wales —people rose in protest against such evils as excessive and unjust tolls imposed by the Turnpike companies on roads—many Welsh estates were victims of heavy poaching as an expression of social revolt. By way of defence, keepers were brought down from Scotland, and it is thought that some of these keepers may have brought with them the Clyde style of flies which, proving successful on the Usk and other South Wales rivers, were widely copied.

A number of fly patterns on the river Usk have been attributed to a Mr Acheson, a keeper on one of the beats. It was he who sent copies of the Usk Iron Blue Dun to the Editor of the Field magazine, deriving from it a certain fame.

It would appear that Acheson adopted the short body in order to facilitate quick sinking. Trout on the Usk tend to feed high up in the water at certain times. It is best with the wet fly that it penetrates the surface on landing; this way it can take the fish just below the surface. Fished in this way, it represents a hatching or a drowned dun. The short body, scant hackle and wings passing for a drowned mature fly.

William Roberts's Blue Dun

Hook   *12 & 14. Claret silk.*
Body   *Claret wool.*
Hackle   *Dark dun.*

Location   *Fast flowing rivers of North Wales.*
Time   *Spring.*
Conditions   *Normal spring weather.*
Method   *Wet fly downriver.*

This pattern was used on the fast flowing rivers of North Wales where it accounted for many a trout whenever the natural was hatching. Other patterns used in various parts of Wales when the iron blue dun is about, include Snipe & Purple, Pheasant Tail, Dark Watchet and Rusty Spinner.

One cannot improve on George Scotcher's description of what he calls the Purple, or Iron Blue Fly:

'*Natural*. In shape as blue dun, but much smaller; the wings a clear purple, the body redish dark purple, legs almost white, and the two whisks at the tail. They begin to appear early in April, but towards the end of the month, and about the middle of May, is their greatest season, they are never seen in any considerable numbers but in cloudy showery days, and when they are on the fish take them more freely than any of the other flies that may be on at the same time; from about ten to three or four o'clock is their usual appearance, and they are strongest on in the middle of the day being a small fly.

'*Artificial*. I make them with a dark blue dun hackle, and use reddish purple silk only for the body. When I made them wing'd flies, I used a hen blackbird's wing feather for the wings, and water rat's fur with purple silk for the body.'

On some rivers in the Dee valley the pattern Glas Cwta has been used to imitate the iron blue dun. The name originated in the Harlech area:

Glas Cwta

> *Hook 14. Claret silk.*
> *Body Claret quill.*
> *Hackle Almost black with brown tips.*

On the river Dee itself some anglers have evolved an interesting pattern which involves dyeing mole fur purple. It looks very attractive: a pity that it is not proving quite as attractive to the fish!

> *Hook 14. Purple silk.*
> *Body Mole fur dyed purple.*
> *Hackle Dark honey dun.*

The Gwendraeth Fach in Carmarthenshire was in the forties an excellent trout river and there were large hatches of upwing flies. On that river, considerable use was made of heron herl which produces excellent bodies for artificial flies.

> *Hook 14. Claret silk.*
> *Tail White or pale cock.*
> *Body Very dark heron herl which was liberally ribbed with gold wire.*
> *Hackle A darkish rusty dun.*

Large Whirling Dun

Hook   12. *Yellow silk.*
Body   *Blue squirrel fur and yellow marten*
         mixed, varied occasionally with
         orange mohair.
Hackle   *Brown partridge.*
Wing   *Starling.*

Location   *River Usk.*
Time   *Early season.*
Conditions   *Normal river flow.*
Method   *Wet fly downriver.*

Apattern from the river Usk. It was described in a list of flies by
Lascelles in 1789. Good reports were given about its effectiveness in the opening months of the season and it was generally placed
in the middle spot of a three-fly cast. It developed into a firm favourite
with Usk anglers fishing above the town of Brecon.

The Usk at Pont Pwll Gwyn: David Cox

Light Blue (Usk)

Hook *12 & 14. Yellow tying silk.*
Body *Yellow wool.*
Hackle *Pale blue andalusian hen.*
Wing *Starling wing.*

Location *River Usk.*
Time *Early season.*
Conditions *Normal water flows.*
Method *Downriver wet fly.*

Another good early season pattern tied by Leslie Peters of Brecon. Such is Leslie's reputation that the initials 'L.P.' are appended to his variant patterns sold in tackle shops in Brecon. The 'L.P.L.B.' pattern is designed to attract trout feeding on the numerous olives that hatch in the early days of the season on the river Usk.

The body, of vivid yellow material, is traced for its source material to the miniature ducks that are sold with Easter eggs! Just as well, the Light Blue flies are in greatest demand around Easter.

It is interesting to note from a hundred and seventy years ago that Scotcher had a similar fly about which he is unusually unforthcoming, which he calls The Blue Dun:

> '*Natural.* Like the blue dun, but smaller, the wings very light pale blue, the body and legs of a primrose colour; comes on in August and continues till October, and is succeeded by the blue dun; though so delicate a fly, it is strongest on in cool windy days, from about ten till four o'clock.
>
> '*Artificial.* Use a very pale blue hackle, with marten's yellow fur, and primrose silk.'

181

Little Chap

Hook 16 Crimson tying silk.
Body One strand of peacock herl
dyed magenta.
Hackle Hen with blue centre and ginger
points, or dark blue hen with
red points.

Location Rivers of North Wales.
Time Early season.
Conditions Normal river flows.
Method Downriver wet fly.

This fly has been extensively seen in use in North Wales—especially on the Ceiriog—in the early part of the season. It is also used on the upper Severn when the February red is about. Often, in the early part of the season, the trout are very difficult to tempt when temperatures are low. Under such conditions, the Little Chap can rouse them from their torpor.

The pattern was apparently given to G. E. M. Skues by a Welshman. There has for years been some speculation upon whether the name was a reference to the lack of stature of the donor—or a term of affection for the little fly!

Y Llew Bach
(The Little Lion)

> Hook   *13. Sneck bend. Black silk.*
> Rib   *Thin gold thread or wire.*
> Body   *Black silk.*
> Hackle   *Coch-a-bon-ddu or yellow and black*
>   *based feather.*
> Wing   *Dark bronze mallard.*
>
> Location   *Lakes and rivers of North Wales.*
> Time   *Early season.*
> Conditions   *All water levels and weather.*
> Method   *Point or centre fly on three-fly cast.*
>   *Fished in the traditional wet fly*
>   *manner on river or lake.*

This fly earned its reputation as an early season fly and was christened, if not after a diminutive angler called Llewelyn, then 'the Little Lion' because of its regal domination of other ordinary flies. (Llewelyn being a royal name in Wales recalling a line of Princes of North Wales, including 'ein Llyw Olaf', our Last Prince, killed by treachery at Cilmeri near Builth Wells.) In Welsh, comparison with the Lion = Llew denotes a hard-fighting quality and some anglers felt that their wet flies which they sent out across the waters actually fought hard for them as they searched the waters for trout. The term 'Bach' in addition to meaning the adjective 'small' is also a term of endearment. These old fishermen certainly loved their flies! Anglers in the twenties and thirties of this century had great regard for flies with black bodies and it is doubtful if a three-fly cast was ever used in Wales without one of the trio of flies being made with a black body.

There is a bigger version of the Llew Bach, which naturally is known as Y Llew Mawr (The Big Lion). It is simply the identical dressing on a much bigger hook. The Llew Mawr was used when the river water was coloured or on the lake when the wind was quite strong and the surface of the water ruffled.

Macrel Bach

Hook   12 & 14. Purple tying silk.
Body   Purple floss.
Hackle   Black hen.
Wing   Bronze mallard.

Location   Rivers of North Wales.
Time   Early season.
Conditions   Normal river flows.
Method   Downriver wet fly.

This was a very popular pattern on the rivers of North Wales where it was considered an early season fly. It bears a close resemblance to the Snipe & Purple and the Usk Purple and, no doubt, was at its most effective when the iron blue dun was hatching. Despite a tendency for the old fly dressers to use drab coloured flies, they too, like their modern counterparts, loved to have the odd colourful fly in their wallets.

While most modern dressers use floss for the bodies of many early-season flies, especially those with purple bodies, it must be remembered that their artistic ancestors invariably used wool. These wools varied considerably in shade, and some surviving examples of these old flies with supposedly purple bodies often varied in shade from lilac to black. The same dresser would be capable of producing a wool bodied fly with alarming variations as he was dependent on the availability of materials; and once a source of, say, one colour wool dried up, the next best thing in terms of colour had to do! These wide divergencies in colour have often confused students of these old classical fly paterns.

Mallard Series
Mallard & Claret

> *Hook 10, 12 & 14. Claret silk.*
> *Tail Golden pheasant tippets.*
> *Rib Gold wire.*
> *Body Claret seal's fur.*
> *Hackle Ginger or claret.*
> *Wing Bronze mallard.*

> *Location Most still-waters and rivers.*
> *Time All season.*
> *Conditions All conditions.*
> *Method Wet fly methods on stillwaters and rivers.*

This is the standard tying of the Mallard & Claret which is probably one of the best-known wet flies in use today. It is used on most Welsh lakes and reservoirs and to a lesser extent on Welsh rivers. In Wales, however, there are a host of variations which have been used from the turn of the century.

Aden ceiliog hwyaden ar gorff paun a thraed cochion.
(A mallard wing on a peacock body and ginger legs).

> *Hook 12. Brown tying silk.*
> *Body Peacock herl.*
> *Hackle Ginger.*
> *Wing Mallard.*

Bronze mallard was an important winging material for the old Welsh fly dressers. They made the distinction between well-marked bronze and a bronze feather of poor quality. Most winged patterns were used as a point fly when fishing stillwaters. Many of the old remaining specimens of this pattern had no tail and we find, too, that the peacock body was tied rather bulkily.

This pattern is not a copy of any known natural insect. The bodies used with the mallard wing may suggest the movement of some sub-aquatic creature of the shrimp/nymph/beetle variety. As a point fly it was generally used in the lower layers of the waters and the technique was to cast the fly out and give ample time for it to sink and bring it back with the traditional figure-of-eight retrieve.

Aden Ceiliog Hwyaden ar gorff lliw gwin a thraed du-flaengoch.
(A bronze mallard wing on wine coloured body with coch-a-bon-ddu legs).

```
Hooks   12. Black tying silk.
 Body   Claret wool.
Hackle   Coch-a-bon-ddu.
 Wing   Bronze mallard.
```

This is the Welsh forerunner of the modern Mallard & Claret minus a tail. Most of the flies listed in *Llawlyfr y Pysgotwr* (The Angler's Handbook) 1899, written by William Roberts, had no tails added to the dressing, and it would be safe to assume that he did not consider the tail to be important. Many flies tied in this pattern at the turn of the century *did* support tails. The late G. O. Jones from Llanrwst, who wrote a great deal about Welsh patterns, is on record as saying that he did not consider that tails added anything to the effectiveness of the Mallard series. He felt that most of the Mallard flies were nymph-like and that the pattern was at its most successful when the trout were actually feeding on nymphs. There *was* a tendency to tie this pattern on size 14 hooks and it was probably the only fly pattern to be used right through the season.

Aden Ceiliog Hwyaden ar gorff lliw cochddu a thraed duon.
(Bronze mallard wing on black/red body with black legs.)

```
 Hook   12. Black tying silk.
 Body   Red/Black wool.
Hackle   Black.
 Wing   Bronze mallard.
```

This was the favourite of the Mallard series brought into play in August and September. It was always used as a point fly and was retrieved slowly. In some of the old flies examined, the wing was tied very short and would look very much like a wing case when pulled quickly through the water. A number of present-day anglers favour this pattern above the popular Mallard & Claret on sale in tackle shops.

Aden Ceiliog Hwyaden ar gorff coch tywyll a thraed cochion.
(Bronze mallard wing on a dark red body with ginger legs).

```
 Hook   12. Brown tying silk.
 Body   Dark red wool.
Hackle   Ginger.
 Wing   Bronze mallard.
```

This was the least known and used of the Mallard series. It found favour with some anglers in the Dee valley and was used by some anglers on the river Ceiriog. It has also been used on lakes and reservoirs—though this has not particularly enhanced its reputation.

Aden Ceiliog Hwyaden ar gorff o sidan du main a thraed duon.
(A bronze mallard wing on thin black body with black legs).

>   *Hook 12. Black tying silk.*
>   *Body Black silk.*
> *Hackle Black hen.*
>   *Wing Bronze mallard.*

This is virtually another black fly with a mallard wing. There is no doubt that the popularity of the black body and black hackle was responsible for the creation of this pattern which was invariably used on the point and fished low in the water.

March Brown
(Rhithrogena haarupi)

Hook	*12. Copper coloured silk.*
Tail	*Two strands from partridge tail.*
Rib	*Yellow thick silk.*
Body	*Hare's ear and yellow hair mixed.*
Hackle	*Brown partridge.*
Wing	*Inner quill feather of pheasant wing.*
Location	*Most rivers.*
Time	*Daytime, March & April.*
Conditions	*Normal river flow.*
Method	*Middle fly on three-fly cast, fished downriver.*

The March Brown is one of the most essential flies on the rivers of Wales during the early part of the season. On the rivers Usk and Teifi, the natural March brown hatches in great numbers with the accompaniment of tremendous excitement among the trout. The natural insect has two *satae*, mottled brown wings and a brownish body. The nymphs are to be found in great numbers and, at this stage, are more important food items on Welsh rivers than are either the dun or the spinner stage. In this nymph form the March brown is easily available to trout and wet fly patterns are most effective.

George Scotcher, in his superb little volume, *A Fly Fisher's Legacy*, gives a vivid account of this most important fly for Welsh waters that can hardly be improved on a hundred and seventy years later.

'If, during this season you are early at the river, you must first throw the four-winged brown, then the blue dun, and just before you expect the March brown to come on, throw that, and continue till two o'clock, and then return to the blue dun.

'Natural. In shape like the blue dun, but a larger and bolder fly, and the wings more a-slant. The color of the wings is a blue dune, with a yellow cast in it, and spotted with dark brown; at the root of the larger wings, if you look carefully, you will find two smaller ones. The under part of the body, at the first coming of the fly, is of a redish chocolate, and striped or ribbed with pale yellow; the back is of a deeper chocolate; the six legs are dirty orange-yellow; the two whisks at the tail, of the color of the wings; and its two feelers dark, as well as the head and chest. As the weather gets warmer, the whole fly gets lighter and smaller, till the body at last becomes a light redish buff, ribbed with yellow.

'They seldom appear in any considerable number before the middle of March, and from that till about the middle of April, is their season; after that time they are not so regular in their appearance, and continually lessen in number. They are on strongest in the warm gloomy days, and come in several sudden flights, seldom before eleven, or after two o'clock. If the water is low in their season, the rise of the fish at them is truly astonishing, and is then generally in the heart of the streams; it lasts nearly five or six minutes at a time, and the water appears in such agitation as if two or three persons were continually scattering in handfuls of small gravel. During this rise you can scarcely take any fish, however naturally made may be your fly, but just before the flights come on, and between them, is the principal time; you may sometimes succeed a little during the flight, should the water be in the state of just clearing after a small flood. They are more numerous in rapid rivers than in slower currents. The greatest rise I ever saw at them was on the Usk, near Brecon.

'*Artificial.* The wings may be made from the spotted tail feather of a young partridge, or indeed more satisfactorily from some of the long fibred body feathers, as also the whisks at the tail of the fly; for the body use some of the dark fur which has yellow tips, from off a hare's ear, and tie it on with redish buff silk; if you are inclined to use a hackle for legs, let it be a dun cock's, or a small partridge's feather. As the fly gets lighter alter the body, and use the redish buff fur from a hare's ear, and tie with pale yellow; and let your hackle be a light dun with yellow edges, or a dull ginger one. There is also some part of the woodcock's feathers which match excellently well the wings of this fly, and I have likewise made them well from a speckled hen's feather.'

Edmonds's March Brown

> Hook 12. *Orange silk.*
> Body *Orange silk dubbed with rabbit fur*
> *(from neck) lightly tinged with red.*
> Hackle *Mottled brown feather from snipe's*
> *rump.*

Edmonds's pattern has its followers but, other than on a few tributaries of the Severn and the Wye, it is not so common as the standard March Brown. It is impossible to estimate the value and advantage of the Edmonds's version over other versions before giving it more extensive trials.

D. Evans's Usk March Brown

> Tail *White gallina dyed dark sepia.*
> Body & Hackle *Dubbed black rabbit fur, seal's fur in*
> *black and claret and a little fiery*
> *brown fur.*
> Wing case *Dark turkey feather.*

This very complex pattern is not known to have so much to recommend it when far simpler patterns of the March Brown are used successfully on the river Usk. The angler would be ill advised to go speedily to the trouble of acquiring the pattern suggested here by Mr D. Evans unless he sees some inadequacy in the conventional patterns.

Silver & Gold March Brown—see Sewin flies.
Charlie's March Brown—see Dry flies.

March Brown Quill

Hook *13. Brown silk.*
Body *Peacock quill.*
Hackle *Brown partridge.*
Wing *Hen pheasant wing (optional).*

Location *Most rain-fed rivers, where the natural exists.*
Time *Early season.*
Conditions *Normal & low river flows.*
Method *Wet fly downriver or when river condition is low—then upriver.*

Quill bodies have lost a lot of their appeal for tiers in the last couple of decades. This is probably the result of fly dressers not being prepared to spend as much time and take the same trouble as the fly tyers of old did with their patterns. The March Brown Quill was a fly that served well when the water was clear. It deserves to be better remembered.

The normal season for the March Brown is early Spring and the tendency is for other summer patterns to be more productive thereafter. Yet it is not always advisable to be in too much of a hurry to discard the March Brown as it tends to remain effective long after the natural has disappeared. This is essentially true of the March Brown Quill.

Marlow Buzz
(Phyllopertha Horticola)

Hook *12. Black silk.*
Rib *Flat gold.*
Body *Bronze peacock herl.*
Hackle *Furnace.*

Location *Rivers and lakes of south Wales*
Time *June & July.*
Conditions *Warm weather.*
Method *Wet fly downriver.*

This is a close relation of the Coch-a-bon-ddu; the only difference in the dressing being the ribbing of the body with gold flat tinsel and the use of furnace hackle instead of the coch-a-bon-ddu. It is open to question if the trout are so discerning as to be able to favour one pattern above another. As with the Coch-a-bon-ddu the Marlow Buzz is best fished as a dropper—and, on the highland lakes, it is most productive in late June and July.

George Scotcher makes reference to the 'Marlow Buz' in his article on the 'Fernshaw, Hazle or Button Fly'. This, it seems, must be an early account of the Marlow Buzz as used for dapping.

'*Natural.* They are of the cockchaffer beetle kind, and nearly of the same shape, but rather more round, and a great deal smaller, about the size of half a horse bean. Their outside shell wing cases are of a yellowish red, nearly the color of a cockchaffer's; they have two veined and transparent wings, of a dark smokey color, under the shell cases, which they can extend beyond them; the chest, head, body, and legs are of a varnished substance of a greenish black, and are covered with a kind of short whitish hair or wool, they have two feelers, which are divided at the end into three parts. Their principal season is towards the middle of June, but they may be seen from the end of May, till a fortnight in July, they are frequently found in the mowing grass, and I believe come first out of the earth; they are also seen very abundant on the under-side of young fern, and on the hazle trees. In some seasons they are uncommonly numerous, and fall off in others, wet weather prevents their appearance, and also in some places they are less seen than in others: from nine to about four o'clock is the general time of their appearance.

'*Artificial.* They are made by a red cock's hackle, with a black root, and a black stripe up the stem, commonly called a Marlow

192

buz feather; their bodies are made in a lump, with one black ostrich and two greenish peacock's herls—break the shank of the hook short. This imitation is best taken at their first appearance, for when they come very numerous, the fish are glutted with them, and even refuse the natural.

'They are an excellent bait to dib with.'

The " Carry All " Creel

In this basket the lunch, etc., compartment is above and quite clear of the fish.

The straps are arranged so that the basket may be worn over the shoulder in the ordinary manner, or with strap over both shoulders as a knapsack—a welcome relief when 10 lb. of fish are to be carried any distance.

Made of best brown English wicker.

No. 1.—10 in. × 14 in., for 10 lb. of fish, **32/6**
No. 2.—11 in. × 15 in., for 15 lbs. of fish, **34/6**

Nailer—Dai's

Hook 13. Green silk.
Rib Gold wire.
Body Green silk.
Hackle Blue dun.

Location River Teifi.
Time Early season.
Conditions Windy weather—low water flows.
Method Wet fly downriver.

This is another wet fly from the stable of Dai Lewis, although it must not be regarded as being a favourite of his, neither did it make the top frame very often. It developed a reputation for being a rough-weather fly. In an old tackle box left by one of Dai's contemporaries, the Nailer was found on four of the ready-made casts of three flies—the Nailer in the middle position on three of them. It was clearly one of the early-season flies—and, in those days, fished on a sinking Kingfisher or Corona line. The angler, who kept his tackle box in a position of pride under his huge and very beautiful old Welsh dresser, had, in his day, used those wet-fly casts on a thirteen foot double-handed rod. It is a tragedy that the contents of the valued box were destroyed when a freak flood swamped houses of the area to a height of three feet. Some time later when the box was opened, its contents, alas, were found to have rotted.

Nailer—Usk

Hook *12 & 14. Purple tying silk.*
Tail *Blue dun.*
Rib *Gold wire.*
Body *Five strands of well marked bronze mallard.*
Hackle *Blue dun.*

Location *River Usk.*
Time *Early season.*
Conditions *Normal Spring weather.*
Method *Downriver wet fly.*

Some anglers of late have been using this pattern for lake and reservoir fishing and it is really worthy of a try when the buzzers are hatching in late evening.

The Usk Nailer is a completely different pattern and is used, it seems, on the river Usk when the early olives are about. Dai Gildas Jones of Cwm Tawe is of the opinion that a pattern with a similar dressing to the Usk Nailer was used on the river Tawe in the days of his grandfather. This is a pattern of considerable merit—with grand conquests to its credit on the upper Usk and its tributaries.

It was first devised to fish the river Usk on a three-fly cast. The practice was to cast it downriver and let it swing round with the current. In recent years, more anglers have been fishing this wet fly pattern upriver. The Usk Nailer works well with this approach.

The body of bronze mallard is an attractive colour and is taken for a nymph of some members of the olive family. A darker dun feather works better as the season advances. Some dressers like to show some of the purple silk at the tail-end of the fly.

Oak Fly
(Leptis scolopacea)

Hook   *12 & 13. Orange silk hot orange.*
Body   *Hot orange floss ribbed with grey ostrich*
            herl.
Wings   *Woodcock secondary quill.*
Hackle   *Furnace cock hackle.*

Location   *Rivers of mid Wales.*
Time   *Early season.*
Conditions   *Normal river level.*
Method   *Wet fly, downriver.*

There is some doubt as to whether this fly is really as important as it was formerly generally believed to be. Pryce Tannatt produced an excellent pattern and there is no doubt that the artificial is effective. Another name for the fly is Down-looker, because of the tendency of the natural fly to rest its head downwards.

Scotcher did not tie an artificial but caught the naturals and dapped them.

'*Natural*. About the size of a flesh fly, but not so full in body; the head is like that of a house fly in color, with two long feelers, the chest, back and body where the legs come out of, are of a blueish lead color; the tail part of the body consists of about six rings, the upper back part of it is of an orangy yellow, the belly part rather whiter, it has four or five black spots in rows along its sides, the last two rings of the tail come very taper, and are black all round; it has six legs of a yellow colour, and black marks on them, and two wings of a brownish yellow, veined with black, they lie on the back like those of the large flesh fly, but stand rather more outwards. You will find them principally in May and the beginning of June, and now and then till August, in hot calm days, standing with their heads downwards, generally on the shady side of the trunks of large oak, ash, willow, apple, cherry, and pear trees, in the fields adjoining rivers.

'I use them only in the natural way to dib with.'

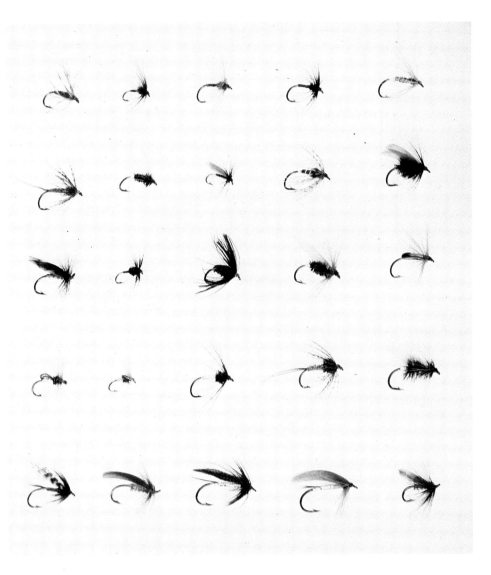

Plate XIII   Trout Wet-flies

Early Brown	Iron Blue Dun	Pheasant Tail	Water Cricket	Smokey Blue
March Brown	Little Chap	Black Midge	Crimson Partridge	Hawthorn Fly
Oak Fly	Black Smut	Tannat's Coch-a-bon-ddu	Coachman	Soldier Beetle
Fire Tail	Tupp's Indis-pensible	Black Spider	August Brown	Cooke's Bogey
Peter Ross	Cinnamon Sedge	Silver Black & Mallard	Green & Gold	Oak Fly

The above fly-patterns, tied by Pryce Tannat, reveal his individual approach even to the most traditional of patterns.

Old Joe

Hook   *13. Black silk.*
Tail   *Three strands of pheasant tail.*
Rib   *Silver wire.*
Body   *Pheasant tail herl.*
Hackle   *Olive.*

Location   *North Wales rivers.*
Time   *Early season.*
Conditions   *Normal river flow.*
Method   *Point fly, fished downriver.*

This was an early-season fly used on the rivers of Mid and North Wales. Many anglers favoured short and dark hackle and some even advocated cock hackle. There is no doubt that it rivalled the better-known Pheasant Tail as a point fly. As Old Joe was used on fast-flowing rivers, there was no great effort made to evaluate what natural fly is represented. But it was at its best when the iron blues were about.

Some of the early dressers of Old Joe insisted that the quality of the body material was important. Cock pheasant tail fibres come in different shades and varying quality. The best shade is that of a deep rich rust with a coppery tinge, and a metalic sheen overall. This then provides the body for the nymph of the dark olive, which many equate with the sepia dun.

Old Joe is used in dry or wet form—depending on the condition of the water. During low river levels the dry fly scores well while the wet fly is far superior in times of high water flows.

Old Warrior

Hook   12. *Black silk.*
Body   *Peacock quill.*
Hackle   *Light blue dun.*

Location   *River Neath.*
Time   *Daytime, mid-day early season.*
Conditions   *Low and mid water.*
Method   *Normal wet fly down or up-river.*
Point fly.

The Old Warrior is a firm favourite with anglers of the Glyn-Neath area and, as with most of the flies devised by Ernest Lewis, they are often as effective on other rivers as they are on the Neath river where they were developed.

Ernest Lewis insisted on acquiring the exact right hackle for all his flies. The Old Warrior, although similar to the normal Blue Upright pattern, differed in that the hackle was of a considerably lighter hue. Ernie bred his own fowls and he cleverly inter-bred the Blue Andalusian with English Game crossed with some Indian Game: thus securing the much-valued blue hackle with reddish tips.

Orl

Hook   12, 14. Red tying silk.
Body   Peacock herl.
Rib   Red tying silk.
Hackle   Blue dun.

Location   River Teifi.
Time   Late season.
Conditions   Normal river flows.
Method   Wet fly, downriver. Middle dropper.

As with the Alder, this pattern came to the Upper Teifi Valley by courtesy of Dan Jones who bought an example in a South Wales tackle shop before the colliers' annual leave. It gained its place on the Teifi, many anglers using it instead of the Alder. It also proved popular on the stillwater lakes of mid Wales which in those days held solid stocks of wild brown trout. The Orl tied on the middle dropper of a three-fly cast was the normal practice.

It is an excellent fly on Talybont reservoir, near Brecon where Dave Cole, an expert fly-dresser from Talybont, who regularly fishes there, recommends the Orl most highly. He stresses that this fly must not be taken as another name for the Alder. Courtney Williams makes this frequent error.

Dave Cole of Orl-fly fame tying-up for Talybont.

Palmer series

Red Palmer

> *Hook*   *10-14. Red tying silk.*
> *Rib*   *Gold wire.*
> *Body*   *Red wool or seal's fur.*
> *Hackle*   *Two red cock hackles tied palmer fashion.*
> *Location*   *All rivers and lakes.*
> *Time*   *Summer.*
> *Conditions*   *Normal.*
> *Method*   *Wet or dry fly.*

The first palmered fly tied in Wales was probably the Drop Fly mentioned by George Scotcher in his little known but wise and charming *The Fly Fisher's Legacy* published in Chepstow around 1820. Scotcher describes how the hackle had to be drawn down with the rib. A century earlier Isaac Walton mentioned Palmers in various colours in *The Compleat Angler*. They were called Palmer after the Crusaders who brought back palms from the Holy Lands. The associated caterpillars were also known as palmers because of their wanderings. In mid Wales the Red Palmer has always been the most popular version of this style of tyings.

Palmered flies are easy to tie but it is advisable to get two hackles of different sizes and to use the smaller to take the hackle down along the body. The shorter fibre, when palmered down along the body, not only makes the fly more pleasing aesthetically but it also facilitates hooking.

Palmered flies are often used as bob flies. The angler casts out some fifteen yards and brings the flies back with the bob fly just skipping the surface of the water. The trout often splash at a palmered fly fished thus: so the angler will find it advantageous to fish the bob fly in the surface layer and, by lifting the rod, pull the bob fly up out of the surface. Frank Owen, a keeper on the Teifi Pools fishery many years ago, used this technique. He would fish with the wind coming over his right shoulder and then move the bob fly skilfully in the surface. His results were almost always creditable, but he tended to favour the herl body for his version of the Red Palmer as opposed to seal's fur.

> *Hook*   *10-14. Red silk.*
> *Rib*   *Gold wire.*
> *Body*   *Peacock herl.*
> *Hackle*   *Two ginger cocks.*

Black Palmer

Hook 10-14. Black silk.
Rib Silver wire.
Body Black wool.
Hackle Two black cocks.

There are numerous lakes in the Harlech area; and on some of these the Black Palmer is used in May and June. It works well especially if the hawthorn is about. The Badger Palmer is a favourite on the small mountain streams in high summer. It is also used increasingly as a sewin fly. Often, on nights when there is a lot of moonlight, a Badger Palmer fished up-river—as one would fish a dry fly—can do quite well.

The custom with dilettante dressers is to add a little tag of other bits and pieces to a pattern in an attempt, no doubt, to improve it. Recently dressed Badger Palmers have sprouted red tags, but this has not especially helped the fly in its role of fishing for sewin at night. Sewin are notorious bottom pinchers, especially so on a moonlit night. Anything that allows them to get a free pinch without touching the hook is a real disadvantage: although it is as often the head of the fly that is the object of their attentions as much as the posterior end.

Badger or Grizzly Palmer

Hook 14 & 16. Black silk.

Rib Silver wire.
Tag Red wool.
Body Black silk.
Hackle Grizzle cocks tied palmer.

The Grizzly Palmer is quite a favourite with anglers in the Corwen area on the river Dee. It is used for fishing the excellent grayling that are there. Mike Green, a dresser of exceptional ability, ties them on sizes 14 & 16 with the short, red tag.

Parry's Black Spider

> Hook 13. Black silk.
> Tag Silver.
> Body Black quill.
> Hackle Starling.
>
> Location Any trout river or lake.
> Time Early season.
> Conditions Normal water level.
> Method Downriver, three-fly cast.

Black flies have always been popular in Wales and Parry's Black Spider is among the best of them. It is always advisable to rib all quill bodies with thin wire as this protects the quill from being damaged by the trout's teeth. The latest device to protect quill bodies is to coat them with a thin layer of Super Glue. This has the effect of binding the whole body into a solid unit and such treated flies have been known to survive the capture of some three dozen trout!

Today, the hackle is generally taken from a black hen—but for anglers who use it in rough water or as a bob fly, then a short cock hackle is to be preferred.

Partridge series
Partridge & Black

      Hook *13 & 14.*
      Body *Black silk.*
   Hackle *Well marked partridge.*

    Location *Rivers of North Wales.*
       Time *All season.*
 Conditions *Normal river flow.*
   Method *Wet fly up or down stream.*

The partridge feather was the most important feather of all for fly dressers in Wales at the turn of the century. In small rivers, the Partridge & Black was a late-season fly used as a dropper. It is now difficult to evaluate the worth of this fly as few anglers are able to comment on it any longer.

This pattern was used to represent the black gnat (*Bibio Johannis*) which suggests an inaccuracy in the dressing somewhere, as the black gnat is not really black: its legs are brownish and the wing-tips rather pale.

Petrisen ar gorff liw gwin.
(Partridge hackle on claret body.) (See February Red on pages 149-50).

Pluen petrisen ar gorff cochddu.
(Partridge hackle on red/black body.)

This fly was reckoned very useful on the lakes of Wales from June onwards. It was dressed very sparsely, which was in keeping with the practice of fishing the pattern towards dusk when it was probably taken as a buzzer. Although the authentic pattern described by the late William Roberts did not include any ribbing, it seems that black cotton was often used to provide a rib to represent the segmented body.

Pluen Petrisen ar gorff llwyd felen.
(A partridge hackle on brownish-yellow body.)

A similar pattern to the better known Partridge & Yellow, except that it is dressed on only half the hook shank—a style similar to that of low-water salmon flies. The colour of the wool body was a fawny yellow. The hackle consisted of a mere two turns, when the fly was held in the sort of runs characteristic of our small, quick-flowing Welsh rivers, the effect was extremely nymph-like—with the body colours visible through this partridge-like lace curtain.

Pluen petrisen ar flewyn glust ysgyfarnog.
(A partridge hackle on a hare's ear body.)

This is another instance of the Partridge family being tied to operate during the stone fly season. It was invariably fished on the first dropper and was, therefore, more often than not, dancing on and in the surface of the running water of the river. In most instances anglers fished wet fly patterns downstream, but sometimes, because of extremely low water conditions, it was necessary to fish it up-river. This pattern did well for the up-river approach.

Pluen petrisen ar gorff lliw rhwd haearn.
(A partridge hackle on a rusty body.)

This rusty-coloured body seems to have been used quite a lot in old Welsh patterns, which suggests that stone flies must formerly have been more plentiful on most Welsh rivers. Many old fly dressers would catch a fly and then make a copy of it on the river bank. They copied the dun stage of the fly and then fished it wet and in a nymph-like manner, which somewhat detracts from the exercise. This pattern remains a great favourite on the Ceiriog and Irfon rivers.

Aden petrisen ar gorff lliw rhwd haearn a thraed cochion.
(A partridge wing on a rusty body with red legs.)

The old Welsh patterns divided themselves into two classes: winged flies and hackle flies. The hackle flies were mainly used for river fishing and the winged flies for lakes. Lake fishing, for obvious reasons, was a highly developed pastime in North Wales and, in some part of the old Merionethshire, we find that winged patterns were, in some instances, fully tied with a tendency towards over-dressing. The old adage that flies, like women, are better under-dressed, was lost on some turn-of-the-century fly dressers, especially when it came to Sedges. The Rusty Partridge was an evening fly, always tied on the bob, which partly explains its rather bulky dressing.

Aden petrisen ar gorff cochddu a thraed du-flaengoch.
(A partridge wing on a black/red body with Coch-a-bon-ddu hackle.)

This pattern was tied very lightly with a thin body and just two turns of hackle. The overall impression suggests a representation of a dark buzzer. The wing is tied short and, when pulled through the water, does look exceedingly like a wing case.

204

Aden betrisen ar gorff blewyn clust sgwarnog a thraed cochion neu lwydion.
(Partridge wing on hare's ear with red or dun legs.)

An old copy of this fly examined, reveals that the dressing was done with yellow silk. This pattern must have been tied as a copy of the lake olive. It would appear that a very much darker version was used during the early part of the season and that it was fished much deeper in the water. It also had a silver wire ribbing and, in some instances, a few extra turns of the wire to form a tag. It was regarded as a point fly and was used mainly in mid summer.

Aden petrisen ar gorff llwyd felyn a thraed llwydion.
(Partridge wing on brownish-yellow body with dun legs.)

This pattern was generally fished in the middle of a three-fly cast and was considered to be best fished just under the surface film. The Welsh words 'Cler Bach' ('small flies') suggest it was used to represent the pupae of the midge. In recent years, work has been done on various creations that seek to represent this pupa stage of the *chronmid*. Could it be that some ancestral Welsh angler stumbled on this solution quite by accident? If so, it would then explain why, in some of the partridge-wing patterns that have come to us, the wings were full—and of normal length—while in others they appeared abnormally short.

Aden petrisen ar gorff lliw gwin a thraed du-flaengoch.
(Partridge wing on claret body with coch-a-bon-ddu legs.)

This was another variant of the midge pupa representation which was very lightly tied. By today, most well known commercial fly dressers have their own patterns for the midge pupa. Those tied some eighty years ago look rather amateurish alongside these modern creations which have been developed primarily on reservoirs and with rainbow trout in mind. Recently Arthur Cove, one of the leading nymph and pupa experts in Britain, maintained that he was reverting to the old spider patterns for representations of the nymphs and pupae he would in future be using. The native brown trout in the highland lakes of Wales have not changed their ideology much, so it is worth giving these old patterns a chance.

Peter Ross

Hook 6, 8 & 10 for sewin, 10, 12 & 14 for trout.
        Black tying silk.
Tail *Golden pheasant tippets.*
Rib *Silver wire.*
Body *Rear half silver, front half red seal's fur.*
Hackle *Black.*
Wing *Teal flank or breast feather.*

Location *All rivers and stillwaters.*
Conditions *All manner of conditions.*
Time *Daytime for sewin in rivers running
        down after spate. All times on
        stillwaters.*
Method *Normal wet fly tactics.*

Mr Peter Ross, a shopkeeper from Killin in Perthshire, is reputed to have said of his newly-created fly that he cared little what the trout took it for as long as they liked it. There existed a school of thought that it was taken by the trout for a shrimp, but others believe that it is a fair representation of a small fish. It certainly is closely connected with the Teal series and differs only slightly from the much older and trusted pattern Teal & Red.

There are certain sewin anglers who have great faith in this pattern. On rivers like the Ystwyth and the Rheidol it will take sewin well when the river is running high during daylight. It also performs well during the hours of darkness and, as is the fashion, it is being dressed in great tandem lengths and on bigger irons.

Some also find that it is a pattern that has never felt a 'touch'.

Many fly dressers have quite a problem with getting the teal wing to sit tidily. Teal feathers are notorious for splaying out on being tied. In recent years the tendency is for wing material to be even more prone to splaying out and refusing to sit in a nice slim manner. All feathers dry out with time and lose the natural oils that keep the feather fibres knitted together. The use of central heating in our homes has increased the speed of this drying-out period. Wildfowl feathers are especially susceptible to this process.

As is the custom with many successful fly patterns, the Peter Ross has been subjected to a host of modifications and variations. Some variations have appeared with orange hackle and orange seal's fur, this being particularly attractive to the angler's eye—and another with gold tinsel instead of silver. It is doubtful if any of the variants are as effective as the original.

206

Pheasant Tail

No. 1 *Hook 12 & 14. Hot orange tying silk.*
    Tail Two or three strands of honey dun
        spade feathers.
    Rib Gold wire.
    Body Two or three strands of rich-coloured
        ruddy fibres from the centre feather of
        a cock pheasant tail.
    Hackle Rusty or sandy dun cock,
        bright and sharp.

No. 2 *Hook 14. Crimson tying silk.*
    Tail Three long herls from saddle hackle.
    Rib Four turns of gold twist.
    Body A very dark herl of cock pheasant tail
        feather.
    Hackle Honey dun.

    Location All rivers and lakes.
    Time Early season.
    Conditions Normal river flows.
    Method Point fly on wet fly cast.

The first pattern was favoured by G. E. M. Skues and possesses the attractive quality of the ruddy herl of cock pheasant tail. The second pattern, tied by Payne Collier, its creator, uses the dark herl from a cock pheasant tail, and this darker version has found more favour with anglers in Wales. On the Teifi and upper Wye, where the pattern is highly regarded, the hackle used is generally of a dark dun, some anglers even favouring black hackle. This pattern is an excellent point fly for the normal three-wet-fly cast fished in the traditional downstream manner early in the season. Many anglers swear that the Pheasant Tail is at its best when the iron blues are about.

Pupil Teacher was a cryptogram for Pheasant Tail in common usage during the thirties and forties, a matter for curiosity now, when we tend to forget that nymph fishing was not considered proper on certain hallowed waters. (See p. 210).

Pluen 'Rhen Law
(The old boy's fly)

Hook 12. Wide gape. Purple silk.
Tail Two strands of horse hair.
Body Reddish purple wool.
Hackle Black.
Wing Hen pheasant tail with a sliver of light
dun on either side.

Location Lakes and, to a lesser extent, rivers.
Time During the day, also late night in June.
Conditions Bright and windy.
Method Point fly on a three-fly cast.

Another local pattern which has travelled well and earned its place on the casts of lake fishers in areas other than its native Ffestiniog, this pattern was sometimes mistakenly called 'Haul a Gwynt' because it was effective when conditions were sunny and windy. As many Ffestiniog anglers were quarrymen in full-time employment from dawn to dusk, it is only natural that Ffestiniog flies earned a reputation for catching well at night.

This fly has enjoyed success as far afield as Lough Conn in Ireland and on some of the remote lochs in northern Scotland. In its stranger environments it has been held effective during the early days of the season. As to the identity of 'yr hen law'—the old hand or old expert—we shall never know. Lost in the mists of Snowdonia.

Poacher

Hook 10, 12 & 14. Brown tying silk.
Tag Red Wool.
Body Rear portion, yellow seal's fur. Front portion, peacock herl.
Hackle Coch-a-bon-ddu hen or cock.

Location Lakes and reservoirs.
Time All season.
Conditions Good wave.
Method On the bob of a normal wet fly cast.

This pattern apparently came from Loch Lomond and was adopted as an alternative to the Coch-a-bon-ddu. In recent years it has proved particularily effective on rainbow trout fisheries. Rainbow trout seem to be attracted to a bob fly and will often follow from afar making big V's in the surface water. To convert that passing interest into firm pulls is quite a problem, and sometimes the Poacher has succeeded in just that function.

Most commercially-produced examples fall short in that they do not carry sufficient hackle on the surface. Bob flies must have lively and bulky enough hackle to appear animated when pulled along the surface. The bob fly is expected to 'kick' as it traverses a pool or a glide. This hop-scotching effect along the top film is meant to give a very life-like impression of an insect trying to fly off.

Pupil Teacher

Hook   12. Black silk.
Rib   Gold wire.
Body   Peacock herl.
Hackle   Blue dun hackle.
Time   Summer.

Location   *Rivers of South Wales.*
Conditions   *Warmish days.*
Method   *Wet fly.*

This fly was a great favourite in South Wales especially on the small rivers which were tributaries of the bigger and often polluted rivers. Dan Jones of Ferndale, Dan the Fisherman, believed that more fish were taken on the 'PT' than on any other fly in the coalmining area of the South.

It was often used on the bob position and it was dressed with cock hackle which greatly helped it to bob on the surface. It was fished on quick flowing rivers and created the necessary disturbance on the surface to attract the trout. While the body is similar to that of the Coch-a-bon-ddu its hackle was rather special.

Dan Jones, insisted that the blue dun hackle had a fair measure of rust on it. He would not take the dun hackle from the cock until it was high summer so that the sun would have added that touch of rust to the hackle.

Dan especially liked this pattern because it could be fished upriver just as effectively as down. It is something of a pity that the Pupil Teacher is no longer so widely used today but its demise is as much to do with the decrease in the practice of fishing the mountain streams as it is with the advent of the more colourful modern flies.

The Sedge Series
Cyfres y Rhwyfwyr

Rhwyfwr Mawr Cochddu (Big Sedge or big boatman)

> *Hook* 8. *Black tying silk.*
> *Body* *Wool from the scrotum of a black ram.*
> *Rib* *Gold thin wire.*
> *Wing* *Brown owl encasing partridge tail.*
> *Hackle* *Brown partridge.*

> *Location* *Lakes in the Blaenau Ffestiniog area.*
> *Time* *Evening and night time.*
> *Conditions* *Warm and dark.*
> *Method* *On the point or bob of a wet-fly cast.*

This was considered to be the most important sedge fly in North Wales. It was dressed bulkily and represented the big mouthful that trout expect in the late evening when the great red sedge is about.

The sedge group of flies is a very large group—representing nearly 200 different species. They are, in the main, nocturnal—with a few of the smaller ones hatching out in the afternoons.

Most of the sedge larvae make cases in which they live and—from school Biology lessons—the caddis larva is to most of us a fairly well-known character. After the larva stage, the insect moves into the pupa stage. This is accomplished after the larva has sealed off the case at both ends. Pupation lasts from a few days to a few weeks according to the species and, when it is ready for transformation into an

adult, it paddles its way up to the surface of the water. The final metamorphosis takes place when the pupa reaches the surface. Many anglers will argue that it is more rewarding to fish the pupa stage of the sedge as it ascends in the water. These men therefore fish with artificials which imitate the insect at this stage of its development (see Longhorns).

This was certainly not the theory held by Welsh anglers fishing the lakes of North Wales in days of yore. They invented patterns that would entice the trout to come up for the big sedges. These patterns in many instances were devised with two pairs of wings as in the sedge fly. The hackle is also put on rather liberally so that the overall effect is of a big bushy insect. The disturbance factor as it skits its progress across the water being an important part of the exercise.

The body material for the Rhwyfwr Mawr Cochddu was from the scrotum of a black ram. As this material is not all that easily available, a mixture of dark brown wool and claret wool is an ideal substitute. This Sedge was used very late at night.

Rhwyfwyr Cochddu Bach
(The small red/black sedge)

> Hook   12. Black tying silk.
> Body   Wool from the scrotum of a black ram.
> Rib   Thin gold wire.
> Wing   Brown owl encasing partridge tail.
> Hackle   Brown partridge.

> Location   Lakes of Blaenau Ffestiniog area.
> Time   Evenings.
> Conditions   Warm and dark.
> Method   On the point or bob of wet-fly cast.

It was an useful ploy by many of the quarrymen of North Wales to use a smaller version of the big Sedge in the early part of the evening. This pattern would be used when the little brown sedge and the little red sedge are in evidence. This pattern has the ability to attract trout that are grubbing amongst the weeds.

Rhwyfwyr Cochddu Aden Telsan

(The red black teal wing sedge)

> *Hook*   *10 & 12. Black tying silk.*
> *Body*   *Wool from scrotum of a black ram.*
> *Rib*   *Thin gold wire.*
> *Hackle*   *Brown partridge.*
> *Wing*   *Teal flank feathers.*

> *Location*   *Lakes of Mid and North Wales.*
> *Time*   *Mid afternoon and early evening.*
> *Conditions*   *Not too windy.*
> *Method*   *As bob fly on two- or three- fly cast.*

This pattern was a late-season performer and fished best in August. The teal wing is of the off-white variety and not the well-marked teal feather which is used for the Teal series. This fly took an impressive basket of fish when fished as a bob fly from a boat on Llysyfran Reservoir.

Rhwyfwyr Clychau Gwyrdd

(The green ringed sedge)

> *Hook*   *10. Green tying silk.*
> *Body*   *Wool from scrotum of a black ram.*
> *Rib*   *Green silk.*
> *Hackle*   *Brown partridge.*
> *Wing*   *Light coloured brown owl.*

> *Location*   *Highland lakes.*
> *Time*   *Summer.*
> *Conditions*   *Evening.*
> *Method*   *Bob fly.*

This is certainly the most cheerful of the sedges. In recent years the brook trout has been introduced into many fisheries in Wales—not always with great success—but this pattern, fished on the bob, has proved effective for taking this new breed of trout. The fly is at its best when brought speedily back along the surface of the water, causing a wake.

Smokey Blue

Hook *13 & 14. Yellow tying silk.*
Body *Mole fur.*
Under *Covert feather from water hen's wing.*

Location *Upper Severn.*
Time *Spring.*
Method *Wet fly downriver, point or bob.*

Pryce Tannatt used this pattern to represent the iron blue dun and the dark olive. The dressing was applied very sparsely with a little mole fur being used and the yellow silk showing through the dressing.

The Smokey Blue is a capital wet fly in the early days of the season. It was often used as a point fly, although some anglers who customarily fish the smaller rivers like it as a bob fly, enabling them to bounce it in the surface film. The hackle was supposed to have a shiny appearance.

The upper Severn holds a good stock of grayling. Smokey Blue is known to have done well with these fish on size 16 hooks.

214

Stone Flies
(Perla maxima)

Hook   *12. Yellow tying silk.*
Body   *Dirty yellow wool.*
Hackle   *Brown partridge.*

Location   *River Ogwen and other North Wales rivers.*
Time   *Late spring.*
Conditions   *Normal river flows.*
Method   *Wet fly downriver.*

There are many rivers in Wales where stone flies represent the most important section of a trout's diet and it is surprising that, on the whole, little attention has been paid to them. On quick-flowing, rain-fed rivers these flies are found in abundance and any angler who does not carry a few artificial representations in his fly box will one day regret it. The most important members of the stone fly order are February red, early brown, large stone fly and the willow fly. Another member is the yellow sally which has fewer adherents piscine or human—from experience.

Stone flies are easy to identify by their hard wings which are somewhat similar to a bee's wings in texture and, when folded, lie close to the body—protruding a little beyond the abdomen. This gives the smaller species, the needle flies, a thin appearance because of the manner in which they are tucked around the body. The wings of the male are stunted and useless as instruments of flight. It is just as well therefore that mating takes place on the ground!

The life history of the stone fly is of interest to anglers in Wales as, it is probably true to say, the nymph stage is of equal importance to the fully mature fly. The egg stage extends from a few days to as much as three months before incubation takes place in the water. The nymphs take some two to three years to mature at this stage, and they have in the past been used in the natural—as opposed to the artificial-form: being known as creepers.

The creepers moult as they grow, moulting about two dozen times. Then, after some three years, they crawl ashore and move quickly among the stones. Some Teifi and upper Severn anglers used to catch these creepers and fish them with light ledgering tackle; and young boys used to earn pocket money catching their creepers for them. When the final moult occurs the ugly creeper gives way to the adult fly. At first the *imago* is very pale but it darkens after a few hours. Adult life is one of inactivity, spent idling among river bank foliage

215

and stones. After fertilisation the female flies over the water and lays her eggs on the surface—sometimes allowing, fatally, the rear of her abdomen to touch the water. The eggs so laid stick to obstacles on the bed of the river. As the stone fly is not one of those flies considered important on the most fashionable dry-fly rivers, the artificial has not been accorded the detailed study that it really deserves. Some anglers are on record as saying that the natural is too difficult to copy, and hence to try to do so is a waste of time. On fast-flowing rivers the artificial does not need to be anywhere near so accurately represented as on more gentle-flowing rivers, so all the angler is really looking for is a match in size and general appearance. A Stone Fly pattern from the river Conway which has been credited to H. C. Holland is a case in point:

> Hook 12. Yellow silk.
> Body Orange seal's fur.

Probably one of the oldest tyings is that given by Alfred Ronalds in his book, *The Fly Fishers' Entomology*, published in 1856.

> Hook 12. Yellow silk.
> Tail Mottled strand of partridge tail.
> Rib Yellow silk.
> Body Rabbit fur or hare's ear mixed with
> yellow.
> Hackle Greenish brown hen.
> Wing Hen pheasant.

On many of the smaller streams of mid Wales, like the Brenig and the upper Aeron, the medium stone fly is an important item in the trout's diet in May and June, it is only half the size of the large stone fly and is of a more brownish colour. Some anglers use the Dogsbody or the Grey Duster to tempt the fish. An old pattern from the box of a once-keen angler known as 'Parry Bach' who had wasted the last years of his life dream-fishing within the confines of an Old People's Home came to light recently. Most of these were beautiful examples of the fly-tyer's art. His fishing had apparently been done on the upper Tawe and upper Usk area. The beautifully-made little brass box, originally designed to hold snuff, was full of examples mostly of the Stone Fly.

Scotcher's Stone Fly

Scotcher in the years leading up to 1819 before he published his classic *The Fly Fisher's Legacy* had developed an original method and technique whereby he varied the intensity of colour as the year progressed.

'*Natural*. From the end of April, till near the middle of July, in rocky and stoney rivers and brooks, you may find under the loose stones near the edge of the water and generally towards the upper part of the stream, first the crab of the stone fly, in shape like an ear-wig, but much larger and of a dark colour nearly inclining to black, with two whisks and two feelers, without wings, and, as I may say, in a kind of case armour. After that towards the middle or end of a warm May, when you perceive their empty cases sticking upon the stones, you will find in the same places, the stone fly, of the same shape, but lighter and larger, being a full inch long, some with four short wings and others with their wings full grown lying flat along the back, one over the other, longer than their bodies, and of a dark dun much vein'd. At their first coming their bodies are nearly black, except under the throat and belly which are of a strong yellow; their six legs are of a dirty yellow. When they are strong on in the middle of June, their wings are lighter, and their bodies of a drab or light stone colour, and light yellow under, and their whisks and legs much lighter.

'*Artificial*. At first I make them of a darker freckled cock's hackle, round the top of the hook, which must be rather large, and the body of black sheep's wool mixed with strong yellow, and ribb'd up with waxed yellow silk. In June I use a lighter hackle, with drab coloured wool and lighter yellow, ribbed with primrose silk.

'If you chuse a winged fly, you will find on the back of a wild mallard, a dark brownish spotted feather, which is very suitable for the wings and whisks; for the legs use a darker dun hackle, and the body of black and yellow wool, ribbed with waxed yellow silk. After that use the lighter part of the feather, or some from a goose's beak feather or dun hen, with a lighter hackle, and drab and pale yellow wool, ribbed with primrose. The time to use them is when the water is rather low, and a heavy wind on, and you perceive them fluttering or paddling along the surface, which is generally early in the morning or towards the evening; throw principally on the ruffled deeps, and particularly on the end of those streams where you know they abound, for though they may be plentifully on the river, they are not found near every stream of the same river. If a heavy flood should happen in their season, or full water continue, they are hardly worth attending to, as it either sweeps them off, or prevents their appearance.

Parry's Stone Fly

> *Hook 12. Yellow silk.*
> *Body Hare's ear.*
> *Hackle A well marked cree and a badger.*
> *(Two turns only).*

By far the most important of the stone flies on rivers Teifi, Severn, Dee and Taf is the February red. In 1856 Alfred Ronalds in his book says:

'This is the earliest fly in North Derbyshire. The tint of the wings is that of a cake of glue held between the eye and the sun. It is best made hackleway with the undercovert feather of a woodcock wing wound upon the above body. In Lancashire it is called Old Joan and the body is made rough with claret coloured wool.'

The pattern used on the river Dee is far less complex and does work well. (See over).

> *Hook 14. Silk crimson.*
> *Body Claret quill.*
> *Hackle A dark rusty dun cock.*

This pattern can be used wet or dry. The dressing of the hackle is confined to two turns only if the fly is to fish below or in the surface.

Another important member of the stone fly family, the early brown, is found in many Welsh rivers. The nymphs live in stony streams, they hatch in early spring, and are of value as a food source to trout when food generally is in short supply. The natural is quite similar to the February red—except that the wings are greyish and there is an absence of the reddish tint in the abdomen.

A pattern suggested by Alan Hudson has proved a success on some North Wales rivers:

218

Dark Stone

Hook 14-16. *Black silk.*
Rib *Silver or gold medium tinsel.*
Body *Hare's ear.*
Hackle *Bad cock front and black cock behind.*

The large stone fly (*Perla carlukiana* & *Perla cephalotes*) is of the greatest interest, since it is very widely distributed in Wales. A pattern mainly used on the Upper Severn, it has, curiously, gained a good reputation on the upper Towy and the Taf.

Hook 12 & 10. *Brown silk.*
Body *Hare's ear ribbed with yellow silk.*
Wing *Woodcock.*
Hackle *A well marked cree with a palmered grizzle.*

This fly is tied rather bulkily—with the wing extending beyond the bend of the hook.

The willow fly is another member of the stone fly family, of which the larger species is commonly to be seen in late summer. It has a long, brownish body of some half an inch and its brownish wings are tucked in—as is characteristic of this family. There are a number of artificials that claim to be effective copies of the natural. Skues gave the dressing for the spent version and, while it has been accepted elsewhere, it has not been widely used in Wales, though Scotcher devised a dressing with hen hackle and purple silk.

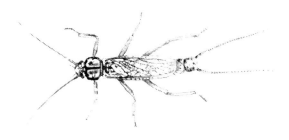

Roger Wooley

Hook 10 & 12. Claret tying silk.
Rib Gold wire.
Body Claret fur.
Hackle Dark green.
Wing Bronze mallard.

Location Ffestiniog area in North Wales.
Time All season.
Conditions All weather.
Method Any position on a wet fly cast.

A very unusual fly with an unusual name for a Welsh fly pattern. Little use was made of dyed hackle in the early part of this century, for trout fly tying, and one wonders whether there may have been some Irish influence in this fly. Salmon flies from Ireland were popular with Welsh anglers at that time, and it is not impossible that this pattern came in with the considerable traffic in flies and feathers that came from Ireland.

Skues's Willow Fly
(Leuctra geniculata)

> Hook 14. *Orange silk.*
> Body *Mole fur.*
> Hackle *Rusty dun cock.*
> Wing *Hen blackbird.*

There is no doubt that this pattern devised by Skues influenced a pattern that was developed in the Tawe valley. Again the pattern came from old Parry's box (see page 212, 218) and it was the same in all its details except that the fur of the water rat had been used on yellow silk.

Scotcher's Willow Fly

> '*Natural*. Like the four winged brown, but much smaller, and the wings slope down more from the back. The wings are of a dark slaty color, and the body of a sooty black, when the flies first come, after that the under part of the tail becomes a little tawny or dirty yellow, and the wings and legs somewhat lighter, then again as the cool weather approaches, they return to their first appearance. They come on tolerably strong in August, and continue so all September, and fall off as October passes. They appear mostly on the water in showery windy weather, but you may see many of them running about on the orl bushes, in the sunny days.
>
> '*Artificial*. They are made by a dark hen's hackle, but not too dark, (as the wings of the fly appear rather light when it is flying,) and dark purple silk, in the showery cool days in August and October, but in the warm days and in September, they are best made by a freckled lighter cock's hackle, with ash colored silk, and a little orangy wool.'

Anglers in North Wales, on the rivers Ogwen and Conway and tributaries of the Dee, discovered the importance of having fly patterns to represent stone flies that apparently hatched in great numbers on those rivers at the turn of century. Most patterns at the time were tied to fish the rough, tumbling sections of those rivers.

Llwyd dywyll ar gorff ysgyfarnog.
(A dark dun hackle on hare's body.)

Aden cyffylog ar lwyd melyn traed llwydion.
(A woodcock wing on a grey/yellow body with dun legs.)

Aden regen yr yd ar gorff llwyd felen a thraed llwydion.
(Corncrake wing on a yellowish/grey body with blue dun legs.)

221

Teal Series

Teal & Black

Hook 8, 10 & 12. Black tying silk.
Tail Golden pheasant tippets.
Rib Silver wire.
Body Black seal's fur.
Hackle Black.
Wing From teal breast or flank.

Location Stillwaters for trout and most rivers for
sewin.
Time All season and at night time in summer
for sewin.
Conditions Normal wet fly river flows.
Method On wet-fly cast fished down river.

Of all the feathers that have been used for a series of flies—such as Partridge, Mallard, Woodcock and Grouse—the Teal is the one that in Wales has the least historical significance. Hearsay has it that Tilsan Werdd (Teal and Green) was used in various parts of North Wales early on in the last century, but it is difficult to understand why the old fly dressers did not make more use of Teal, an excellent winging material, which was presumably so readily available.

It is only to be expected that Teal & Black was to become popular in Wales at some point because of the effectiveness of flies with black bodies. In the early part of this century the Teal & Black in size eight was considered to be the all-important point fly to fish for sewin at night. Its ribbed black body and barred wing make for a very good colour pattern—hence a very attractive fly.

Teal & Green

Hook 8, 10 & 12. Black tying silk.
Tail Golden pheasant tippets.
Rib Silver wire.
Body Green seal's fur.
Hackle Black hen or cock.
Wing Teal flank or breast feather.

The Teal & Green is generally more in use as a lake fly than as a river fly. Dressed on a number twelve hook, it is quite effective as a member of a wet-fly team fished on a slow sinking line on stillwaters. Some anglers like to use it in rough conditions, whilst others feel it is a very good fly to use when the trout are after the minnows. Some ten years ago, an article appeared in one of the angling journals about the great success the writer had experienced with this pattern in fishing for sewin. Almost overnight many fly boxes sprouted a green look, a colour to match those anglers who were proved so gullible! Since then, the Teal & Green has been used modestly for sewin and, as with most ordinary sewin patterns, it has notched up its successes and its failures.

Teal, Blue & Silver

Hook 6, 8, 10 & 12. Tandem and tube style.
Tail Golden pheasant tippets.
Rib Silver wire.
Body Flat wire.
Hackle Bright blue.
Wing Teal breast or flank feathers.

Location All sewin rivers.
Time Day and night time all through the season.
Conditions High and low water conditions provided that the river is fairly clean.
Method Wet fly downriver.

This fly is, without doubt, the fore-runner of all modern sewin flies. Its variants are numerous and collectively take something like fifty per cent of all the sewin taken on a fly in Wales. The standard dressing gives teal feather for the wing but this section has been modified considerably with the increased popularity of hair wings. Hair wings are far more responsive to water currents, and offer vastly more interesting colour ranges than do the more solid fibre wings.

Recent developments with this pattern have seen the growing use of the tandem form with two, or even three, hooks attached to form a lure of some four to six inches long. Just as stillwater flies have given way to bigger lures, so have the standard sewin flies been subjected to change and have become far longer. The practice of adding a wing of two (blue or black) cock hackles tied back-to-back is becoming increasingly frequent. An overlay of peacock herl or peacock's sword feathers is another addition to the basic pattern.

In its tandem form, the Teal, Blue & Silver is designed to be used with a quick-sinking line and to work in the deep section of the pool. Here the big sewin tend to stay, and the deep-sunk Teal, Blue & Silver often tempts them.

In the last two or three years, the Teal, Blue & Silver has surprised quite a number of anglers with its performance on stillwater fisheries. While the pattern was considered to be a definite river pattern, it finds itself being increasingly used on some reservoirs—and anglers using it have taken impressive bags of rainbow trout from places like Clywedog and Elan Valley.

Teal & Red

Hook 8 & 10. Black tying silk.
Tail Golden pheasant tippets.
Rib Silver wire.
Body Red seal's fur.
Hackle Black hen or cock.
Wing **Teal flank or breast feathers.**

Location All sewin rivers.
Time Daytime.
Conditions River running down after flood.
Method Wet fly down river.

This fly could well have been the forerunner of the Peter Ross pattern. It is probably not so extensively used as the other members of the Teal series because of this very similarity to the Peter Ross. Some anglers, though, have a fancy for this pattern and it can do well on the sewin rivers of mid Wales—especially in water which is slightly coloured.

Teal & Mixed

Hook 8 & 10. Black tying silk.
Tail Golden pheasant tippets.
Rib Silver wire.
Body One-third each of yellow, red and blue dubbing of seal's fur.
Hackle Black hen or cock.
Wing Teal flank or breast feathers.

This, the most colourful of the Teal family, is not so widely used as some other members, though it is a fairly useful fly to have in one's box. Not all flies make the 'First Fifteen' but just as a team's strength is dependent on its reserves, an empty creel is often avoided by bringing out an unobtrusive pattern. It is a pattern that has its devotees and, in the days before the Brianne Dam was built on the upper waters of the river Towy, the Teal & Mixed covered considerable mileage there in those beautiful and desolate mountain rapids towards the tail end of the season.

The Teal series also covers flies with body colours of yellow, orange, claret and olive and each and every colour variant has its supporters who are prepared to swear to its virtues. On the other hand, there are some rivers and locations where the Teal series is said to be ineffective: among them, curiously, the middle and lower reaches of the Towy, where sewin are not all that impressed by them.

Teifi Pools Sedge

Hook *10 & 12. Brown silk.*
Body *Orange wool or orange seal's fur.*
Hackle *Dark ginger.*
Wing *Light dun.*

Location *Teifi Pools.*
Time *Late evenings in June.*
Conditions *Warm and calm.*
Method *On bob—worked in and on the surface.*

This pattern was discovered by the late Dr Roderick of Llanelli when, in the fifties, he set about recording the patterns of Welsh flies. Unfortunately, the work was left uncompleted and he has, sadly, not left us any details of the origin of this pattern.

Dr Roderick enjoyed fishing the Teifi Pools especially, and his favourite ploy was to fish the far bank of Llyn Teifi by letting his flies skim along the surface. The wild brown trout responded well to this. It is a pattern worth carrying in the fly box, though Dr Rroderick's faith in it is not always borne out. The secret would seem to lie in the movement of the fly, quickly, on a floating line along the surface when used as a bob fly. It is a fly that works better during the summer months and towards evening after a hot bright day.

The Teifi Pools Sedge has unmistakable resonances of the Grenadier, except that it has the addition of the light dun wing. (See p. 162).

Teify Pools

Nightjar (Troellwr) Series

Troellwr Corff Llygoden Ddŵr
(A Nightjar wing on water rat body)

> Hook *12. Yellow silk.*
> Body *Water rat fur.*
> Hackle *Black hen.*
> Wing *Nightjar.*
>
> Location *Llyn Morynion in North Wales.*
> Time *Early season.*
> Conditions *Cold weather.*
> Method *On point of three-fly cast.*

This pattern, as with indeed most of the Troellwr, Nightjar, series, is not well known outside the Ffestiniog area. The fact that Nightjars are protected and no longer common birds is the reason for this. Most anglers using the pattern today use a grouse, or dark speckled hen, instead of the nightjar feather. This pattern was used in daytime, especially early in the season.

The Alaw reservoir in Anglesey was at one time renowned for its big brown trout. Some anglers even used to come over from Ireland to fish for them. Troellwr flies were the ones that took these trout in the early days of the season. They were also effective on the Brenig reservoir with the native brown trout that are found there. Some flies work better with brown trout than they do with rainbows: this is certainly true of the Troellwr Corff Llygoden Ddŵr.

227

Troellwr Mawr—Dafydd Dafis
(The big Nightjar)

> Hook 10. Claret silk.
> Body Reddish purple seal's fur ribbed with
> golden thread.
> Hackle Black hen.
> Wing Nightjar.

> Location North Wales lakes.
> Time Early season.
> Conditions Wet weather.
> Method Point fly.

This 'wet weather fly' was used extensively in the stony sections of the North Wales lakes where it took fish that were down deep. In the days of silk lines, flies could be worked deep—which paid off in the early season. It is difficult to understand why some flies once gained a reputation for being more effective under certain weather conditions, when modern usage of this fly, for instance, does not confirm its usefulness as a wet-weather fly. It has, however, proved its value on Llwyn-onn reservoir in the Taff Valley in South Wales—amongst the rainbow trout.

North Wales Lake

228

Troellwr Mawr—John Owen 'R Hen Hafod
(The Big Nightjar)

Hook 10. *Red tying silk.*
Body Red seal's fur ribbed with gold wire.
Hackle Dark coch-a-bon-ddu.
Wing Nightjar.

Location Originally on lakes of North Wales.
Time Summer evenings.
Conditions Warm.
Method Wet-fly cast used as point fly.

This pattern was created by John Owen, 'R Hen Hafod, and differs only slightly from the previous one dressed by Dafydd Davies. This is one of those patterns that, like the recipes of the ancient Physicians of Myddfai, were highly confidential family trade secrets. Friendship did not count much when fly patterns were being devised and tested—news of success would often be the cause of animosity. The Troellwr Mawr created by John Owen was held in high esteem and had, no doubt, been in keen competition with the Troellwr Mawr devised by Dafydd Dafis.

229

Snipe Series

Snipe & Purple

> Hook 14. Purple silk.
> Body Purple floss.
> Hackle Snipe hackle.

> Location River Usk.
> Time Spring.
> Conditions Normal river flows.
> Method Wet fly downriver.

The Snipe & Purple pattern is probably better known in other parts of the United Kingdom, but both the Usk Purple and the Macrel Bach are considered better patterns for fast-flowing rivers. The tendency is for the snipe hackle to wrap itself around the purple body, while in the other two patterns the hackle 'kicks' and imbues a little life into the fly. Some anglers of late have been using a well marked cree hackle instead of snipe for the Snipe & Purple.

The snipe hackle is also used with a yellow body thus forming the Snipe & Yellow pattern which does not achieve the same success as the purple version.

Snipe & Yellow

> Hook 14. Yellow tying silk.
> Body Yellow floss.
> Hackle Snipe hackle.

The Snipe & Yellow is taken by the trout for a variety of insects among which are the nymphs of the olive and of the stone flies. It does not work so well in cold water conditions as does the Snipe & Purple. It has the advantage, though, of being a very easily seen fly when the river is slightly coloured.

Dark Blue (Usk)

Hook 12 & 14. Black silk.
Body Mole fur.
Hackle Dark blue hen, nearly black if possible.
Wing Moorhen.

Location River Usk.
Time Early season.
Conditions Normal and above normal river flows.
Method Downriver wet fly.

The Dark Blue in the early days of the season takes trout feeding on
the early and dark olives that hatch in March and April.

The Usk Purple

Hook 12 & 14. Purple silk.
Body Purple floss.
Hackle Dark blue dun.
Wing Snipe wing (blue dun).

This is an old Usk pattern which is deservedly an early season
favourite and is taken for the iron blue nymph. It is quite closely
related to the Snipe & Purple and has the reputation of fishing better
on cold days. The river Usk is difficult to equal, especially on a mild
Spring day; a river which lends itself ideally to wet or dry fly fishing.
The Usk Purple is generally fished in the middle of a three-fly cast.

This pattern is somewhat similar to one in common use in the
Snowdon area of North Wales, known there as 'Macrel Bach' (Small
Mackerel).

Water Cricket
(Velia currens)

Hook 13 & 14. Purple tying silk.
Body Hot orange silk floss ribbed with tying
silk. Three turns of herl from a
peacock's sword feather to represent
thorax.

Hackle Cock starling neck feather.

Pryce Tannatt included this in the personal collection of wet flies which he presented to the Welsh Salmon & Trout Angling Association. He maintained that it took trout on mountain lakes, though his view is not one shared by many anglers!

This dark brown water beetle has two orange stripes on its back and an orange undercarriage. It is to be found in both the winged and the wingless form and is generally found on lakes; although, slow-flowing rivers—like the Teifi in the bogland area of Tregaron—have also been known to produce small colonies of the insect.

Williams's Favourite

Hook 12-14. Black tying silk.
Tail Two or three black whisks.
Rib Silver wire.
Body Black silk body.

Location Rivers of mid Wales.
Time All season.
Conditions Both high and low river levels.
Method Wet fly downriver or dry fly.

One should not here accuse Courtney Williams of paternal favouritism when he praised this pattern—especially as it was created by his father who first tried it out on the Dysynni. Since those days it has travelled far and wide and has travelled well too! Black patterns are pre-eminent in Wales and, of those, this is about the best there is.

It is certainly an all-rounder in that it is effective fished wet or dry, on lake or on river, for brown trout, rainbow trout or sewin. Courtney Williams also praised its ability to take trout in coloured water and was of the interesting opinion that black was probably the best colour from the point of view of visibility in those conditions.

Woodcock series
Woodcock & Yellow

Aden cyffylog ar gorff melyn a thraed cochion.
(Woodcock wing on yellow body with ginger legs.)

> *Hook* 12. *Yellow tying silk.*
> *Body* *Yellow silk.*
> *Hackle* *Ginger.*
> *Wing* *Woodcock.*

> *Location* *Still-waters.*
> *Time* *All season.*
> *Method* *On floating or sinking tip line.*

This is rather an ordinary fly with no great claims made for it. It was commonly used just as the water was changing colour. The yellow body probably made it more visible to the trout. The wing was sometimes tied short—with the yellow body just half-way down the hook.

The woodcock wing was nowhere near as widely used in Wales as was the grouse and the mallard, which is somewhat surprising, as it was easily available.

Aden cyffylog ar gorff lwyd felyn a thraed llwydion tywyll.
(Woodock wing on a fawn yellowish body with dark dun legs.)

> Hook 12. Yellow tying silk.
> Body Yellow silk and fawn wool.
> Hackle Dark dun.
> Wing Woodcock.

This pattern, similar to the above, is a fair representation of the stone fly which is found in abundance on many of the small streams and rivers of North Wales.

Woodcock & Green

> Hook 10 & 12. Green silk.
> Tail Golden pheasant tippets.
> Rib Gold wire.
> Body Green seal's fur.
> Hackle Ginger.
> Wing Woodcock wing.

The Woodcock series is not so widely used in Wales, but there are some anglers who still prefer it to the Mallard or the Teal varieties. Of late, with the sharp increase in the cost of partridge feathers, woodcock feathers have been found useful substitutes.

Woodcock wings are used on yellow bodies, Woodcock & Yellow; red—Woodcock & Red; and with a body of yellow and red which is called Woodcock & Mixed.

Woodcock & Mixed

> Hook 10 & 12. Red tying silk.
> Tail Golden pheasant tippets.
> Rib Gold wire.
> Body Tail half yellow/top half red.
> Hackle Ginger.
> Wing Woodcock.

This pattern is a favourite with anglers on some of the reservoirs in South Wales. It makes for rather a colourful pattern and probably is better equipped to catch the angler—hence its being used more extensively than other members of the series.

York's Special
(Bibio pomonae)

> *Hook* 8, 10 & 12. Black silk.
> *Tag* Red wool.
> *Rib* Gold wire.
> *Body* Black wool.
> *Hackles* Coch-a-bon-ddu or furnace.
>
> *Location* Llyn Trawsfynydd.
> *Time* Mid season onwards.
> *Conditions* All conditions.
> *Method* Fished as bob fly in and on the surface.

This is one of the best bob flies to use on Welsh reservoirs. It first gained its reputation on Llyn Trawsfynydd, primarily among anglers fishing from boats. It is always fished on the bob: the aim is to keep it in the surface or on the surface of the water.

Trawsfynydd anglers use the 'Yorkie', as it is affectionately called, in the bigger sizes. Llyn Trawsfynydd has become principally a rainbow trout fishery and most of the fly patterns exclusively used there are designed to capture these rainbows. Yorkie is equally effective with brown trout.

As a result of National and International competition, anglers from other countries have spread the fame of Yorkie, with the result that it is now used on Scottish and Irish Loughs.

Some anglers have been using a fluorescent wool for the tag which does add an attractive quality to the fly. More and more use is being made of fluorescent material in an effort to make flies more visible under reduced light conditions.

The York's Special fly was first brought into prominence by a man who travelled extensively in North Wales selling fishing tackle. Naturally his name was linked with a number of flies but none has survived in the manner of the above. It is a copy of the heather fly which appears on some stillwaters in late Summer. The red tag is used to suggest the legs of the heather fly which are a vivid red in the upper sections. It is often confused with the hawthorn fly, but the same artificial pattern is used to imitate both the hawthorn and the heather fly.

Emyr Lewis proving the value of York's Special.

Zulu

Hook 12, 10, 8 & 6. Black tying silk.
Tail or Tag Red wool.
Rib Flat silver tinsel.
Body Black seal's fur.
Hackle Two black cock hackles, one palmered
down the body, the second tied as head
hackle.

Location All stillwaters in Wales.
Time All season.
Conditions Big wave for use as bob fly.
Method On the bob of a three- or four-fly cast.

It is very difficult to know where this pattern originated, though not at all hard to guess at how it derived its name. With the love that Welsh anglers have of black fly patterns, it was a natural choice of fly for Welsh waters.

The Zulu is, by now, one of the great standbys for stillwater fishing and invariably it is used on the bob position even in competitive angling. The old anglers who wielded longer rods than are seen today would have the Zulu dribbling along the surface of the water and, fished thus, it had the ability to raise fish from the deep.

The Zulu is also a sewin fly of considerable repute. Here also, it is used as a bob fly on a three-fly cast. Sometimes the wake that it causes as it skims the surface rouses the sewin, and many anglers will claim that, although the fish is often taken on the second fly, it is the bob that has done the work of attracting. Many favour the Blue Zulu when fishing for sewin and there is little difference in the two patterns:

Blue Zulu

Hook 12, 10, 8 & 6. Black tying silk.
Tag Red wool.
Body Black seal's fur ribbed with flat silver
tinsel.
Body Black seal's fur ribbed with flat silver
tinsel.
Hackle Two: one black cock through the body
and one blue at the head.

Gold Zulu

Hook   10 & 12. Black tying silk.
Tag   Red wool.
Rib   Gold tinsel.
Body   Peacock herl.
Hackle   One coch-a-bon-ddu hackle palmered
down the body.

Many use a gold tinsel for the ribbing and call it Gold Zulu which in fact is incorrect as there is another, quite different, pattern correctly known as the Gold Zulu:

Lures

Into a big one in choppy conditions.

Lures took a long time to become adopted in Wales and in some areas they have even yet to earn the respect of local anglers. Lure fishing to some traditional lake anglers of North Wales is closely akin to spinning, and therefore to be regarded with some cynicism, if not contempt.

The story is a different one in South Wales where reservoirs play a more prominent part in the angling scene.

It was only natural that the Black Lure was to become a favourite with Welsh anglers, as they have, throughout the ages, favoured black as a colour for tempting fish. It was discovered, on making a survey, that over eighty per cent of the anglers on one Welsh reservoir on opening day in South Wales were using the Black Lure!

Lures were imported into Wales when reservoir fishing became a popular pastime in the late fifties and early sixties of this century. Like all newcomers they were given, by some, a hostile reception. Some angling bodies even went to the lengths of barring them. Yet they were to prove effective on Welsh reservoirs as they did on the English ones—and with their success came greater usage.

One of the finest of lures, the Sweeny Todd, created by Dick Walker, is nothing but a Jumbo version of a fly tied in Wales over a century ago, known as the Bongoch. The only difference being that Dick Walker's version had a fluorescent spot at the base of the wing. This is not to suggest that Dick Walker copied from the old Welsh pattern, but it does reveal that it is very difficult to invent anything new in the world of fly dressing.

Probably the most popular of all lures to come to Wales in recent years is the Muddler Minnow and today it is to be found on most reservoirs and rivers, fishing for brown and rainbow trout and also for the sewin in our rivers.

Plate XIV   Lures

Ace of Spades	Baby Doll	Pepermint Doll
Black Lure	Worm-fly	Yellow Dog Nobbler
Cenhinen Tony	Jack Frost	Jersey Herd
Appetiser	Gold Muddler	Sweeny Todd

Ace of Spades

Hook Long shank 8 & 10. Black tying silk.
Rib Oval silver wire.
Body Black chenille.
Wing Black hen tied matuka style.
Over wing Bronze mallard.
Hackle Guinea fowl.

Location Welsh reservoirs, Llandegfedd, Brenig, Eglwys Nunydd and Dinas.
Time Early season.
Conditions Cold and rough.
Method Sunk line with lure fishing slow and deep.

The Ace of Spades is one of the most popular early season lures on Welsh reservoirs. In the early days of the season reservoir trout tend to lurk down very low in the water, so the angler has the problem of getting his offerings down to them at the same level. While it is always advisable to vary the speed of retrieve of a lure in the early days, it is generally always best to move the lure slowly.

As the bottom of the reservoir holds the most food during the early months, getting the lure down as low as possible is difficult from a boat. Use a drogue to stop the boat drifting too quickly—and every legitimate method to sink your fly line to the very floor.

Hen hackle tied in over the back—in the Matuka manner—ensures that the hackle does not wrap itself around the hook, as is common with other long-winged patterns.

Baby Doll

Hook 6, 8 & 10 Long shank. White tying silk.
Body White Sirdar wool.
Back White Sirdar wool.

The baby Doll was first used exclusively on reservoirs and was at its best when the fish were feeding on fry. Using a sinking or a floating line, the lure was sometimes left to float or sink, without any retrieve whatsoever, to make it appear like a dead fry.

The former all-white Baby Doll has more recently appeared in guises involving every colour of the rainbow. Probably the most popular of these variations has been the one made with a green fluorescent back, called Peppermint Doll. This variation has been used a lot on the Ynysyfro Reservoir near Newport.

Badger Matuka

Hook 6, 8 or 10 Long shank. Black tying silk.
Rib Silver wire.
Body White chenille.
Thorax Orange wool or chenille.
Wing Two or three pairs of well-marked badger hen hackle.
Hackle Hot orange cock.

Location Reservoir and sewin rivers.
Time Late season on the reservoir and mid summer on the river.
Method On quick sinking line.

The Badger Matuka is a good lure to use in September or October on a reservoir. Generally it is best to fish it from a boat. The technique then is to anchor the boat and to cast the Badger Matuka well out and allow it to sink: then to retrieve it slowly along the bottom of the reservoir. Trout at this time of the year are busy feeding on small fish. These small fish generally congregate in particular locations known to the big predatory trout and, once the angler discovers these, then a big Badger Matuka cast in amongst them will encourage and entice a big trout to strike, out of a sense of rivalry and invaded property.

The Badger Matuka is a good sewin lure to be used on a cold night when the sewin are hugging the river bed. Used on a quick-sinking line, it is often able to move the sewin to take something that is whipped across their field of vision. The Badger Matuka has a good colour pattern which makes it attractive to the sewin. Sometimes, when the sewin have been upriver for some time, it pays to try a smaller version of the lure.

Black Lure

Hook 6, 8 or 10 Long shank. Black tying silk.
Rib Silver tinsel.
Body Black chenille.
Wing Four matching black cock hackle feathers.
Throat hackles Black hackle fibres.

Location Most Welsh reservoirs.
Time Early season and on sewin rivers.
Conditions Cold weather.
Method Generally on a quick sinking line and retrieved either slow or quick.

This is by far the most important lure that is used on Welsh reservoirs in the opening days of the season. It is difficult to imagine what anglers would use if the black lure was for some reason prohibited. On opening day 1983 at Eglwys Nunydd reservoir, Port Talbot, over eighty per cent of the anglers present were using the Black Lure on a quick-sinking line. Over ninety per cent were using black carbon fibre rods and some fifty per cent using black nylon on their shooting heads. A black ceremony, altogether.

Most reservoir fishing in Wales is done from the bank, and use of the Black Lure requires that casting be fairly proficient in order to put the lure some thirty yards out into the water. It must then be allowed time to sink, and only when it has sunk properly should it be brought back: and not too quickly. As the season advances, the speed of retrieve can be increased—and the depth at which it is fished in the water then becomes less critical.

As a sewin lure fished deep and deep into the night towards dawn, the Black Lure has no equal. The same principles apply as for reservoir fishing, except that the later into the night the deeper it should be fished and the larger the size ventured. Chez Wilkes of Newport, a great Towy man for sea trout, used 4" long black lures in this pattern with alternate tying of a silver body with two or three peacock sword feathers tied in. Using a 11½' double-handed rod and a sinking line, Chez would always put back the smaller fish—under two pounds—as his interest lay in the 'big game' sewin which commonly ran above the double-figure barrier in the Towy, in the 1960s and 70s.

Cenhinen Tony

(Tony's leek)

Tail   *Green fluorescent floss.*
Rib   *Gold wire.*
Body   *Green chenille.*
Wing   *White marabou.*
Hackle   *Short orange cock.*
Head   *Deer hair tied muddler fashion.*

Location   *Big reservoirs.*
Time   *Daytime, mid season.*
Conditions   *Big waves fished high in the water.*
Method   *Cast on a long line and fished back quite quickly. Effective on both floating and sinking line.*

When looked at in an upright position this unusual looking lure, devised by Tony Bevan of Llanilar, resembles the Welsh national emblem, the leek: thus the unusual name. Most new reservoir lures, like pop songs, are popular for a fortnight to a month at most and then are forgotten. Cenhinen Tony has done far better than average and, in its fifth season, can claim to be a 'golden-oldie', perhaps. Its real effectiveness is apparent towards the tail end of the season.

As with many other lures, it really moves the fish when it is stripped back very quickly. This is a very tiring form of fishing which many anglers, rightly, do not favour. On its day it can provide excellent sport with rainbow trout, but it is only a technical remove from the monotony of spinning with a fixed spool reel.

Tony Bevan, top-class still water angler whose Cenhinen Tony rides high in the charts, especially late in the season.

244

Fall of the Purthen, nr. Pont Neath Vaughan, Brecknock.

Dog Nobbler—black

Hook 6, 8 & 10 Long shank. Black silk.
Tail Bunch of black marabou.
Body Black chenille.
Head Lead shot or bead fixed with glue.

Location Reservoir
Time Early and late in the season.
Conditions All conditions.
Method Cast well out and retrieve quite quickly.

This was the most popular pattern on big reservoirs in the seasons of 1983 and 1984. Despite being a very new pattern, its fame has spread: and it is used extensively. It is tied in all colours and it is difficult to say which colour is the most effective. Trout seem to vary in their tastes from day to day, so it is advisable for each angler to carry a selection of different colours with him.

As with most lures, the speed of retrieve is important—so the form should be to vary the speed. In high summer when the fish are really difficult, an orange or a yellow Nobbler stripped as fast as the angler possibly can will sometimes get the fish to take. The slow retrieve under such conditions is not productive.

The principle of attaching hackle to the mid and tail section of the fly is certainly not new and the sewin pattern, Night Heron, tied by Lewi Davies of Llandeilo in the forties, used the same technique. Nobblers scored some success with sewin at the end of 1983 season but far more experimentation is required before an exact evaluation can be made. The problem that anglers get with sewin is that they will sometimes just nip the tail of the fly—yet the Dog Nobbler with its long flowing tail has, strangely, not been subject to this aggravating hazard.

Jack Frost

Hook 6, 8 & 10 long shank. Black or white
   tying silk.
Body White Sirdar baby wool covered by
   one-eighth wide strip of polythene.
Tail Crimson wool.
Wing White marabou.
Hackle Long fibres of crimson and white cock
   hackles.

Location Reservoirs of Wales.
Time Early and late season.
Conditions On calm days fished well sunk.
Method Used with quick sinking line in early
   days of the season or on floating line
   in big waves.

The Jack Frost is a first reserve for the Black Lure with many anglers. In the cold days of April when the fish are reluctant to move—even to the Black Lure—the first change is invariably to a white lure. The Jack Frost switch often works. It is a highly visible attractor and, when fished in the deeps in the early days, days of limited light, it does score over the darker coloured lures.

The Jack Frost is fished deep in cold weather but, as the season progresses, it can be fished up nearer the surface. Used from boats on Llandegfedd and on Brenig the Jack Frost, stripped back quickly on a floating line, can take cruising fish. It is also used when the big fish are chasing the fry—when it really *does* do well—on Llandegfedd and Eglwys Newydd.

Jersey Herd

Hook	6, 8 & 10 Long shank. Black tying silk.
Tail and Back	Bronze peacock herl.
Body	Under layer: any coloured floss.
	Over layer: Flat copper gold tinsel.
Hackle	Hot Orange.
Location	Reservoirs.
Time	Early season.
Conditions	All conditions.
Method	Fished slowly on a slow sinking line.

The Jersey Herd is a lure that does not require to be worked quickly through the water for it to take fish. Some lures fish best when they are retrieved slowly, and this one can be fished over the shallows. Some anglers fish the Jersey Herd on a long leader with a floating line—as they would a nymph. This pattern came to the fore when Tom Ivens made his study of reservoir fishing.

There is a tendency for modern fly dressers to use gold tinsel for the body instead of the required copper tinsel. It is important that the original dressing is adhered to, as the copper is vastly superior to the gold body.

Most lures have proved to be quite successful when they have been tied in even smaller sizes or when they have been used after sewin. To date, the Jersey Herd has not proved to be useful for sewin, but it has done quite well in smaller versions with brown trout.

Missionary

Hook *6, 8 & 10 Long shank. Black tying silk.*
Tail *Scarlet dyed hackle.*
Rib *Silver tinsel.*
Body *White chenille.*
Wing *Whole silver mallard breast feather.*
Hackle *Scarlet dyed cock feathers.*

Location *Trawsfynydd, Alaw and Llandegfedd.*
Time *When trout are feeding on fry.*
Conditions *All conditions.*
Method *Worked quickly through the water on sunken line. On a floating line moved jerkily to stimulate injured fry.*

The Missionary, like many other white-bodied lures, imitates the fry on which the larger fish feed—especially towards the end of the season. Most anglers cast it out on a lead-core line which, after being cast, is given enough time fully to sink. As the line sinks, the lure is also pulled under the water. This action is known as the 'drop'. Many trout are taken this way on the drop.

The Missionary is especially suitable for this method of approach in that the whole wing tends to open and slow down the process of the drop. This slow, fluttering action, as the lure sinks, is very attractive to fish.

The Missionary has been used in sewin fishing and here again it is most effective when retrieved along the bottom. Both in stillwaters and in the river it often pays the angler to try and have one continuous pull when retrieving—as opposed to the short, jerking motion achieved with the normal figure-of-eight retrieve.

Muddler Minnow

Hook *6, 8 & 10 long shank; 6, 8 & 10*
      normal shank. Black tying silk.
Tail *Small section of turkey tail.*
Body *Flat gold tinsel.*
Inner wing *Bunch of grey squirrel.*
Outer wing *Two sections of mottled oak turkey wing*
      feather.
Head *Natural deer hair.*

Location *All reservoirs and sewin rivers.*
Time *All through the season.*
Conditions *When water warms up in June and*
      onwards.
Method *Used with all different types of lines and*
      retrieved at different speeds.

This North American salmon and trout lure has, in a very short time, become one of the front-line forces in all arenas of game fishing and has proved to be one of the most versatile of lures. It is a favourite with all boat anglers. It has the distinct advantage of being effective when fished either on the point or on the bob. It produces a very lively effect when used with a sinking line because the deer hair head makes it extremely buoyant: thus it always tends towards an upward movement in the water. When used with a very fast sinking line the Muddler has an advantage in its ability to keep clear of the bottom, thus avoiding snags.

The Muddler Minnow in the beginning was quite a big lure. It is now used in much smaller sizes especially by boat anglers who rarely use it in sizes larger than size eight (normal hook shank).

Sewin anglers have also found the Muddler Minnow to be very useful when used at and just after dusk. Then it is used on a floating or a slow sinking line. The lure should then be kept in the upper layers of the water and fished like a surface lure to resemble a moth or some largish terrestrial, amphibious or aeronautic creature in the throes of a crash-landing trauma.

As with all successful patterns, the Muddler Minnow has many variations, the two most successful being the Black Muddler and the White Muddler.

White Muddler

Hook 6, 8 & 10 Long shank. White tying silk.
Body White flourescent wool.
Wing White marabou.
Head Natural deer hair.

Black Muddler

Hook 6, 8 & 10. Black tying silk.
Body Black floss body.
Wing Black squirrel tail.
Head Natural deer hair.

(See also Allrounder pages 6 & 7).

251

Sweeny Todd

> Hook 6, 8 & 10. Long shank. Black tying silk.
> Body Black floss with a collar of neon magenta
>   fluorescent wool at root of wing.
> Wing Black squirrel.

> Location Reservoirs.
> Time Early and late season.
> Conditions Cold weather.
> Method On quick sinking line stripped quickly.

This is one of the best lures with rainbow trout. It is used in the early days of the season and the spot of magenta wool often triggers off the attack.

It seems that this comparatively modern pattern had a fore-runner at the end of the last century in Wales, known as the Bongoch. This old pattern had a red spot at the base of the wing and many of the quarrymen of Blaenau Ffestiniog were happy to use it in the month of August—especially in a big wind.

The Sweeny Todd can be used in very small sizes on the rivers of Wales in the early days of the season. Many patterns devised for these productive reservoirs in England have not registered the same degree of success when they have been used on Welsh reservoirs. Sweeny Todd has been the exception. Richard Walker, one of the great anglers and angling writers of the last twenty years, claims that the Sweeny Todd is the best pattern recently invented. And he invented it!

Worm-fly

> *Hook* Two size 10 hooks in tandem. Black
> tying silk.
> *Tail* Red wool.
> *Body* Peacock herl ribbed with gold wire.
> *Hackle* Coch-a-bon-ddu.
>
> *Location* Stillwaters.
> *Time* All season.
> *Method* On quick sinking line and worked on the
> floor of the reservoir. On the bob from
> a drifting boat.

Why this lure was called the Worm-fly remains a mystery. Some anglers, not having seen a Worm-fly before, expect something resembling a bunch of worms. It is, in fact, nothing more than two Coch-a-bon-ddu flies tied on in tandem. The answer may lie in the method of fishing it, rather as one would fish a running worm.

It is important to ensure that the trace between the two hooks is one hundred per cent safe. The Worm-fly is a lure which can be fished very slowly. The normal custom is to fish the Worm-fly on the point of a cast used with a sinking line. There are only a few lures that can be fished slowly and yet appear attractive. On the Llysyfran Reservoir in West Wales the Worm-fly does well when fished in this manner.

The Worm-fly can also be used as a bob fly when fished from a boat. The extra hook probably helps with hooking and the extra length of the fly also allows the angler the opportunity of keeping it longer in the surface film. It has also proved successful when stripped quickly on a floating line when fished from a boat.

The Worm-fly has also been used with some success as a sewin fly. In this instance it is used as a normal wet fly and cast downriver and allowed to swing down and across with the current of the water. Here again, the double hook helps with the hooking of sewin which are notorious for their habit of taking short. The Worm-fly has great potential as a sewin fly and, in very small sizes, two size 12 hooks, it is a good daytime fly, fished level with the eyes and mouths of the shoals of newly-arrived 'school' sewin especially.

Whisky Fly

Hook 6, 8 & 10 long shank. Orange tying silk.
Body Flat gold tinsel.
Rib Red floss.
Hackle Hot orange.
Wing Orange bucktail or orange squirrel.

Location Reservoirs such as Trawsfynydd, Brenig, Eglwys Nunydd and Llandegfedd.
Time High summer.
Conditions Warm and still.
Method Stripped quickly in the upper layers of the water.

This pattern was devised by Albert Whillock and it has proved to be very successful for taking rainbows feeding just below the surface. It comes into its own on most Welsh reservoirs by about June when the rainbow trout are fairly active and aggressive; and then a fast—to a very fast—retrieve of the Whisky often seems attractive to them.

The Whisky Fly is sometimes better fished on a slow-sinking line so that it fishes the mid-water levels. It is a fly that does very well in coloured water. On Llyn Brenig it has proved to be a good lure once the water has warmed up. Although it has a good reputation with brown trout, it is with the rainbows that it is most effective in Welsh reservoirs.

Trout
The Dry Fly

There is a notion that dry-fly fishing is a difficult pastime—like playing snooker with the cue behind your back—or driving on ice. It is not. Provided you have reasonable casting competence and a plain man's knowledge of entomology, it is an easy, cooler and more relaxing form, than wet fly. The really difficult forms of fly fishing are the up-stream wet method and night-fishing with a full sunken line. The latter is plain dangerous!

There is, indeed, also even a theory, quoted here from David Jacques, that dry-fly fishing 'was invented by a company of Southern (English) gentlemen to make the capture of trout more difficult in order to display their superiority over less distinguished anglers'. This fails to take into account a rival claim that dry-fly angling was, in fact, developed in Cardiganshire—where the Cardis, a tribe famed for their caution, preferred not to let the fly out of their sight!

The dry-fly method, especially where the flies are of one's own manufacture, is the most pleasureable and satisfying method. It is often the most productive too. It is, however, a method that may have taken longer to come to Wales than elsewhere, though there is every reason to suppose that on the rivers Dee, Wye and Usk the fishing practices generally extant throughout England, were in use from the earliest, and travellers—as well as the landed-gentry classes who had connections in England—were very likely to have brought the dry-fly technique to private waters. The pity is that none of them has left us a clear record of it.

The floating fly is first specifically mentioned by Leonard Mascall who, in 1590, in giving the dressing of a dark fly says 'Thus they are made upon a hooke, lapt about with some corke like each fly afore mentioned'. From that date onwards there are increasingly frequent descriptions of dressings—by Cotton, Barker and George Scotcher—that would undoubtedly float for some time until dried off by false-casting. William Shipley, in his book, *A True Treatise on the Art of Fly Fishing* (1839), advises:-

> 'Let your flies float gently down the water, working them gradually towards you, and making a fresh cast every two or three yards you fish. We distinctly recommend frequent casting. A fish generally takes the fly immediately it has touched the water— provided always it be delicately and lightly flung—and the quick repetition of casting whisks the water out of your flies and line, and consequently keeps them drier and lighter than if they were left to float a longer time in the water'.

A distinction must be made between the 'floating fly' and the dry fly. From reconstruction of early patterns, it is obvious that they were designed to ride on the surface until they became saturated. They were not dry flies. Evidence from printed sources indicates that fly-fishing, until the early decades of the nineteenth century, was practised with a stiff rod—no reel—a horse-hair plaited line, more than the length of the rod, and a knotted gut cast with a single floating fly fast to the leader. This fly was an imitation of the natural hatching on the water, or an actual natural which would be 'dibbed' or dapped.

The method of approach was to stalk your fish carefully and, where possible, cast with the breeze behind you up-stream, retrieving and re-casting frequently. George Agard Hansard in his book *Trout and Salmon Fishing in Wales*, published in London in 1834, advises that 'A stiffer rod is to be preferred, as enabling the angler to throw with more exactness; it is also of great advantage in a strong breeze. It may be observed he who uses a knotted line without a reel (a practice usual in Wales) is more likely to cast his fly with precision, than a man who constantly varies his length'. It can be safely said, though, that in 1834 Hansard was advocating an old-fashioned approach. A 'new' method was in: down-stream wet-fly. Some were also experimenting with up-stream wet-fly: early efforts at nymph fishing —with the aid of reels 'to vary the length'.

Undoubtedly the old and the new would have carried on side-by-side without interruption until the improvements in tackle which came about in the second half of the 19th century made what we now call the classic dry-fly approach possible.

Most angling historians, however, are in accord that it was George Pullman in his book, *Vade Mecum of Fly Fishing for Trout*, in 1851, who has the first description of the classical dry-fly approach. He describes false casting and the fly floating over fish that are on the fin. From then on, dry-fly developed to become an accepted alternative to dibbing the floating fly and to wet-fly and was fully established as the scientific and artistic method of taking trout by the time Halford wrote his final book, *The Dry Fly Man's Handbook* in 1913.

In Wales, the progress of the development of dry-fly fishing is obscure, but thought to be painfully slow. On rivers like the Usk, Dee and the Wye the dry fly did make inroads but, on the quicker flowing rivers of the west and north, the wet fly method was unchallenged. Dry fly design was also generally a problem in the middle of the nineteenth century. Most dry flies were tied on eye-less hooks, despite the fact that eyed-hooks had been introduced around 1845. These dry flies dressed on eyeless hooks, were secured with short, stout gut. On fast running water the gut became worn, in the process of frequent false casting, in drying a fly subjected to considerable wetting when fished in broken water. The redesigned hook with an eye small enough to be used for dry-fly helped enormously in the development of the dry-fly approach to trout fishing in Wales.

Early dry flies designed for fishing the Welsh rivers were bestowed with floatability and visibility as their predominant qualities.

257

Established wet flies like Coch-a-bon-ddu and March Brown were tied with two or three cock hackles and were used as floaters. These early 'dry' flies were expected to sit up well on the water with their hackle and wings giving the right outline. Great care was taken with the body material of these flies: the hackle too, had to be rigid, luminous and bright.

In some instances, dry flies in Wales were dressed with soft hen hackle—as in the Ermine Moth and the Paragon. This should not be seen as a departure from normal practice but rather as a further development in the art of fly dressing. Some local dressers also developed the ploy of dressing the tail of the dry fly around the hook, thus having a tail pointing onto the surface of the water, and achieving greater floatability. Of all the forms of fly dressing, that required for the dry fly is the most demanding.

In the comparatively short time from the publication of *Llawlyfr y Pysgotwr* in 1899, where dry flies do not merit a mention, to the present day, dry-fly fishing has taken its place in Wales and made many important contributions to the art world-wide.

The main lessons to be learned from the great Welsh dresser-innovators, such as Rev Powell and Dai Lewis, are meticulous care in choice of materials and: imagination. There is no doubt that mono-filament nylon, floating plastic lines and fly-floatants have made all the difference in making the dry-fly do its job—namely float —but it still requires an artist-craftsman to make the imitation lively and to present it correctly, sensitively—and cunningly to the trout.

M.M.   L.H.

Alder—Dai's
(Sialis lutaria)

Hook 12. *Black tying silk.*
Body *Peacock herl.*
Hackle *Two black cocks.*
Front hackle *Grouse feather.*

Location *River Teifi.*
Time *Daytime in May and June.*
Conditions *Normal weather and water flows.*
Method *Upriver dry fly.*

The Alder was regarded as an important dry fly for the Summer months on the upper sections of the river Teifi. This insect, with its large black head, dark thorax and heavily-marked brown wings, is easily recognisable and its appearance meant that anglers would immediately fish Dai's Alder in its dry form.

The story of is creation is an interesting one. A collier by the name of Dan Jones, who was known affectionately as 'Dan the Fisherman' in Ferndale where he had made his home after leaving the upper Teifi Valley to look for work, would, as was the custom with most colliers, come back home to the country on his holidays—in Dan's case, for a spot of fishing. Dan used to buy flies at Cardiff and then bring them up-country to experiment with and amaze the locals. On one occasion he brought an Alder fly with him and, immediately Dai Lewis saw it, he set about modifying it.

Dai Lewis had little time for winged flies—and so the wing on the Alder was replaced with a hackle from the grouse body. This hackle was wound in front of the two black hackles. The overall fly was of generous proportions and was an excellent floater. Sometimes Dai would substitute dark ginger hackle for the black one; but this adaptation would often depend on the quality of the hackle available—not so much on the technical requirements of the pattern. The quality of the hackle was of paramount importance to Dai. For the Alder pattern he insisted that the supporting hackle be absolutely perfect.

Dai Lewis, Tregaron, in typical guise,
fishing his beloved Teify.

The Cobbler

Hook *10 & 12. Yellow tying silk.*
Tail *Ginger hackle fibres.*
Body *Dirty yellow wool.*
Rib *Gold wire.*
Hackle *Four ginger cock hackles tied palmer fashion.*

Location *Upper Teifi.*
Conditions *Normal river flow.*
Time *Evening.*
Method *Upriver dry fly.*

The old shoe-shop at Pontrhydfendigaid was an extremely interesting place—a centre for many community activities, not the least of which was preparatory fishing. David Jones, known either as 'Dai Cobbler' or by his nomdeplume 'Glangors', was a man whose approach to fishing was unorthodox but highly effective. He tied his dry flies for one purpose only and that was *visibility*. He maintained that patterns in the upper reaches of rivers were not over-important.

His flies were big by conventional standards and some of his four-hackled flies, tied on number ten hooks, were virtually unsinkable.

David Jones, 'Dai Cobbler' at his work, fly-vice at the ready!

They would hop, skip and jump down the running sections of the river—and it required good eyesight to detect the trout taking them. A light ginger hackle is highly visible, especially in peat-stained water. Dai Cobbler would often tie half-a-dozen flies before he went out, having gone to the bridge just to have a look at the water to ascertain the colour tone of light, sky and waters so that flies were tied to match, later on, after he had closed his shop.

Some anglers, who get to know their patch well, acquire and beget a quiet confidence. They tend to think in terms of 'going out for a few fish'. The flies they use and the methods they employ are products of decades of experience, and to try to copy such masters is folly for the ordinary angler. Dai Cobbler, irrespective of conditions and weather, would use his heavily-hackled dry fly in the quickest of runs and would strike at the slightest suggestion of a disturbance near the fly. The strike was always instantaneous and fairly firm. He did not believe in playing a fish; and as soon as the fish was hooked, it was bounced unceremoniously along the surface until it was on dry land.

The Cobbler's approach to dry fly fishing was an unique one, and certainly worthy of note by anyone who fishes the upper reaches of any of the trout rivers of Wales.

Dan's Supreme

Hook 12. *Yellow tying silk.*
Body *Yellow hind portion. Mole fur front*
        portion.
Hackle *Rusty dun.*

Location *Upper Teifi.*
Time *Daytime in April & May.*
Conditions *Normal river flows.*
Method *Upriver dry fly.*

Dan Jones was one of the many Welsh country men and boys who had to go 'down to South Wales' to find employment in the coal-mines in the twenties. His heart never left the Upper Teifi valley: he was passionately fond of fishing. He devised the 'Supreme' fly as a result of his stock of excellent blue hackle derived from his expertise at the cockfighting pit. The best fighting cocks came from Pembroke-shire where they were known as the Pembrokeshire Blues. In the course of his cockfighting exploits, Dan had been able to collect some very special cock hackles.

Dan's Supreme was his version of the early spring olive for use only in spring. 'Dan the Fisherman' would tend to use this fly in the necks of pools and he required it to bounce along on the surface of the waves and falls. He would also stress that many dry flies tied with inferior hackle would crumble after taking one fish and that it required really good hackle for the fly to retain its form after catching a lot of fish. In evaluating this advantage, it must be remembered that forty years ago, dry fly anglers did not have the floating aids at their disposal that are available today.

Dan's Supreme is a fly that also behaves well on small mountain streams in high summer. Anglers fishing in summer often have to turn to the hills for their comfort when low water conditions leave the main rivers, and even the stillwaters, moribund. Fishing small streams then does offer good sport. Dan's Supreme has the floating qualities and that essential visibility factor which makes it a first choice for fishing these quick-flowing streams where often the fly is tumbling about in, on and under the water. Like Dan's fighting birds the Supreme always comes out on top, ready for more!

Few fly dressers realise that there is as much of an art in producing first quality cock hackles, as there is in producing a top-class fighting cock. Indeed, there is quite a close link between the two! Correctly handled, a cock can produce top class hackle within the space of eighteen months and not, as is generally thought, three years.

Tragedy struck one day. It appears that the one cock which had the most perfect of rusty dun hackles was lost one Sunday morning. The boys were indulging in a little illicit cockfighting when Dan's most favoured cock flew out through a small window that opened from the basement on to the street. Dan galloped out after it only to see 'Dai boots', the local policeman, walking up the street while the missing cock was resolutely walking down to meet him. That was the last Dan heard or saw of the cock. It was said afterwards that the policeman was a great dry-fly angler too!

Dan Jones, 'Dan the fisherman', with one of his supreme champion fighting cocks which provided materials for 'Dan's Supreme'.

Doctor

Hook 14. Black tying silk.
Tag Rabbit flax having been dyed in picric
    acid to make it yellow.
Hackle Two small coch-a-bon-ddu cock hackles.

Location Upper Teifi.
Time Late April & May.
Conditions Normal dry fly.
Method Upriver dry fly.

This is probably one of the best patterns to use on the upper Teifi in the post-grannom period. The trout on the Teifi tend to feed heavily daily during the grannom hatches and become rather difficult to tempt immediately after. Rev Edward Powell on his visits to Tregaron used this pattern to good effect. He was a great angler who devised some superb patterns which, if they have not always proved successful for others, are not themselves necessarily to blame.

In his later years Powell dressed the pattern with a smaller hackle. Another person who tied Doctor flies was Fred Atkins who lived at Lampeter. Rev Edward Powell considered Fred to be one of the finest tyers in Wales. His version of the Doctor was not tied so loosely and bulkily.

It has been suggested that the Doctor is a pattern created to represent one of the many beetles that are found on the rivers in summer. There is no doubt that the Doctor fulfills this role but it is also an all-round pattern that is worth having in one's box to try when the trout are proving difficult to please. It fishes best in the runs leading into the pools and is most effective early in the morning— before the fish have been disturbed and are still at their feeding stations in the shallower runs.

Dogsbody

Hook *12, 14 & 16. Silk: Brown.*
Tail *Three strands of tail of cock pheasant.*
Rib *Oval gold.*
Body *Camel-coloured dog's hair.*
Hackle *Barred Plymouth Rock, with red cock's hackle in front.*

Location *Originally River Usk.*
Time *Early season.*
Conditions *Normal dry-fly weather and water flows.*
Method *Upriver, dry fly.*

The Dogsbody is one of the best dry flies to come from the Usk. It is regarded as a general purpose dry fly with some similarity to the Rough Olive and the hackled Hare's Ear; yet many anglers believe that it is a fair representation of the sand fly. According to the story,

Molly Sweet, of Usk town, demonstrating her tying of the Dogsbody. Note the ancient vice responsible for literally thousands of beautifully-tied specimens annually.

265

the late Harry Powell, fly- and hair-dresser of Usk, was sent, by post, an order from an angler in North Wales, for a dozen flies, the pattern for which was enclosed in the envelope. The body of the pattern proved difficult to match, being of an elusive camel shade. The problem was later solved when a farmer came into Harry's shop for a haircut. At his heels was a dog. The dog's coat was the precise and identical shade that Harry had been hunting! While his assistant went about the business of giving the farmer a haircut, Harry set about collecting the required hair from the dog. The pattern was thus baptised.

Since those days, the fame of the Dogsbody has gone out far and wide, and today it is among the top fifteen dry flies in the British Isles. It becomes most effective after the beginning of May and seems to be a natural follow-on after the grannom period. The river Usk is an ideal trout river. It is of the right size in that the angler can cover every run and pool. It holds good stocks of wild brown trout which, because of the quality of the water, have a sufficient food supply to ensure good growth rates. In such an environment it is not surprising that considerable importance is placed on the fly and its development.

The barber's shop in the town of Usk in Harry Powell's day was an important angling centre which, fortunately, has not disappeared— as many of the old fishing tackle shops have. Molly Sweet followed the tradition set up by Harry Powell and today Jean Williams, taught the art of fly tying by Molly Sweet, ensures that Usk anglers are equipped with the traditional Usk flies, especially the Dogsbody.

Ermine Moth

Hook 12 & 14. Black silk.
Tag Yellowish orange wool.
Rib Thick black cotton.
Body White wool.
Hackle Two grey partridge.

Location River Teifi.
Time Evening.
Conditions Low summer river flow.
Method Normal dry fly method.

This fly was a great favourite with Rev Edward Powell. There is no doubt, however, that the pattern was in existence long before the Rev gentleman developed it. The Vicar was responsible for adding the tag to the original: the tag being short, and divided into two, tended to cause it to curl around the hook as opposed to having it sit on top.

The body is tied full with wool, the black cotton being prominent between the segments of the body. The small grey partridge hackle feathers are found in small numbers on the breast of the bird. To find the right feather, it is advisable to buy a fully feathered (dead) bird from a game dealer. (The partridge will make a nice Sunday dinner after all the valuable feathers have been collected!) Store carefully the small feathers from the mid-back and the mid-chest regions, as they are really valuable and in short supply.

The Ermine Moth is tied with two soft partridge hackles. Some traditionalists among dry-fly anglers did not accept that this fly was a good floater. The tying of the two hackles in the correct manner helps floatability. The two hackles must be tied back to back, thus making the hackle stand upright. The dynamics of the hackle fibres assist buoyancy. Some of the old tyers used to tie in a white cock hackle to support the partridge.

This has developed into an evening pattern, but it should not be neglected during the day. Time was on the Teifi when the signal to put it on was the ten o'clock train which used to run on the track adjoining the river. The visibility of the Ermine Moth during the final thirty minutes was responsible for the downfall of many a bonny trout. Even at the end of June and in early July, little dry-fly fishing proper could be practised after ten-thirty. The form then was to fish the dry fly in the surface film and rely on the pull on the line to register the fish taking. The Ermine Moth fished thus was the pattern that succeeded when all others had failed.

267

Greenwell

Hook   *12 & 14. Yellow tying silk.*
Rib   *Gold wire.*
Body   *Yellow silk waxed (Cobbler's wax).*
Hackle   *Coch-a-bon-ddu cock or Greenwell cock
(Ginger and black).*

Location   *On most fast flowing Welsh rivers.*
Time   *Early and late season.*
Conditions   *Normal river flows.*
Method   *Upriver normal dry fly style.*

On the fast-flowing Welsh rivers little use was made of this winged fly. The dry fly mainly used carried two, three or even four hackles. In short, flies were dressed primarily for floatability and then for visibility. The dry version of the Greenwell, dressed on the upper Teifi by Charles Harries, was dressed on this principle.

Although, in the early part of the season, anglers favoured the darker version of the Greenwell dressed with the coch-a-bon-ddu hackle, as the season progressed, the lighter coloured hackle of the Greenwell (black and ginger) was preferred. Most dry-fly anglers on Welsh rivers and streams would cast the dry fly into the neck of a pool and let it ride the broken water. When olives were in evidence the Greenwell was preferred to other patterns because of its general all-round appeal.

On the rivers of North Wales the term 'corff melyn budr' (a dirty yellow body) was used to describe many of the old traditional patterns, and it shows a relationship to the body of the Greenwell. Most of these dirty yellow bodies tied then were of wool and not of silk as in the original Greenwell pattern.

Grey Duster

Hook *12 & 14. Brown silk.*
Body *Blue rabbit fur.*
Hackle *Well marked badger.*

Location *Originally on rivers of North Wales.*
Time *Day & Evening in Summer.*
Conditions *Low water.*
Method *Upriver dry fly.*

The river Dee in North Wales and its tributaries, the Ceiriog and the Alwen, have been an important nursery school for dry-fly anglers. This has resulted in a number of fly patterns being evolved in those valleys which have proved their value on other fisheries in Wales. Among them is the Grey Duster. It is difficult to say what insect the Grey Duster is intended to represent. It could be an imitation of a member of the *Perlidae* family, like the February red, willow fly, the needle fly or even a moth or a midge-suggesting pattern. Some maintain that it is one of those single-pattern all-rounders that are capable of taking the dry-fly angler right through the season. This rigid approach would seem to dull the fine edge of dry-fly fishing altogether. The one-fly-pattern anger *does* have the advantage that he does not waste time changing flies, and that he has implicit faith in the fly he is using—however wrong-minded.

Grey Duster is a very easy fly to tie, but it is important to have the right colour for the body. Rabbit fur, when on the skin, has three distinct layers of colour. The top layer is brownish with guard fibres; the intermediate layer is fawn and the lower layer is a blue dun colour. This latter is the colour required for the Grey Duster.

The Grey Duster is nowhere as effective a wet fly as it is in its dry form. There are times, however, that it does well when fished semi-dry in the surface film. Maybe then it is taken for a hatching nymph. In recent years the use of the dry fly on stillwaters has increased considerably and the Grey Duster has been known to provide the angler with good sport on those difficult still nights when the surface of the lake loses its ripples and becomes a flat mirror of the sky.

Grizzly Dun

Hook 14. Yellow silk.
Tail Grizzle fibres.
Body Well waxed yellow silk.
Hackle Light grizzle grey badger hackle.

Location Upper Severn.
Time Summer.
Conditions Normal water flow.
Method Upriver dry fly.

This fly gained its reputation on the rivers of mid Wales and the upper reaches of the Wye. It can be fished wet or dry, and does very well when the olives are about. Its advantage is that it is highly visible and, as such, is often put on when the light conditions become difficult.

Visibility on quick-flowing rivers is all-important. Grizzly Dun is also worthy of a try on lakes: it did once score well on Llyn Tarw near Caersws. Llyn Tarw is an unique fishery in that Brook trout breed there naturally and at times they can offer amazing sport.

Imperial

Hook 13 & 14. Purple silk.
Tail Dun fibres.
Rib Gold wire.
Body Heron herl.
Hackle Honey dun.

Location Most rivers with hatches of olives.
Time Early season.
Conditions Normal dry fly water.
Method Dry fly upriver.

The late Oliver Kite, creator of this pattern, was an angler of exceptional ability. He came to fish the upper Teifi in March 1963. Skirting each pool was a crust of ten-week-old ice after that abnormally hard winter and daily, from this harsh environment, Oliver Kite took trout of excellent quality.

The fly that did the trick was his newly-created Imperial—his representation of the early spring olive. Early spring olives hatch every day, even in that sort of weather, and Kite, having studied the natural, produced a first attempt imitation tied with green silk and a light ginger hackle. By the end of the week it had been modified, with the purple silk showing through the heron herl which had been doubled over in order to form a thorax. The hackle was of a dark dun.

The Imperial has, over the years, proved worthy of its name. It has truly reigned supreme over the many other dry flies that purport to represent members of the olive family. The pattern is effective long after the natural insect is gone. Kite advised the use of a rusty dun hackle towards the end of the season.

An important part of the dressing is undoubtedly the doubling of the heron herl in order to make a bulky thorax. This is where so many commercially tied patterns fail. Oliver Kite did not dress his flies very heavily; he only gave four turns of hackle. But Kite liked to fish the Teifi early on. When the trout move out from the pools and into the runs in May the angler fishing for them then is well advised to use quite a few more turns of the hackle.

It is interesting to note that a pattern with an almost identical dressing had earlier been in use in the Tregaron area for quite some time, but as a wet fly. Oliver Kite is quoted as saying that the Imperial could make him a one-fly man. Praise indeed, for 'Kite's Imperial'.

271

Leslie Peters' Special

Hook *12 & 14. Yellow tying silk.*
Whisks *Honey dun.*
Body *Orange and natural wool mixed with tying silk visible through body.*
Hackle *(Tied parachute style) Honey dun.*

Location *River Usk.*
Time *All season.*
Conditions *Normal river flows.*
Method *Upriver dry fly.*

The river Usk is an ideal river for dry-fly fishing. Of pool and riffle nature with ideal glides and runs, it is a river where the dry-fly angler can drop his offering with ease and with reasonable expectation of results.

On Usk glides the parachute fly is ideal—in that it fishes close on the water and has the advantage of no protruding hackle in the surface film. The parachute, although having many advocates in Wales, is certainly confined to particular localities, the Usk being the chief of them.

The parachute style of dressing the hackle of a dry fly is an old style that seems to have lost much favour in the last two decades on most Welsh rivers. A couple of years ago Brian Clark and John Goddard resurrected the principle with their film and book promoting the USD Paraduns. Their novel approach to an old theme had the hackle below the hook, which allowed for very delicate presentation and confronts the trout with a dimpled silhouette. The drawback of this dressing is that, now that the body is below the hackle, it is the reverse of the natural. However, the parachute fly when it, helicopter fashion, lands on the water, can often be taken by trout on hard-fished waters—merely because of its being somewhat unusual.

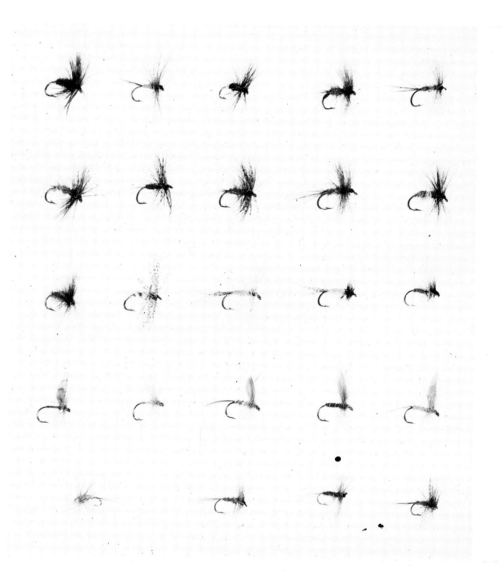

Plate XV   Dry-flies

Dai's Alder	Dan's Supreme	Doctor	Paragon	Dogsbody
Sun Fly	Welsh Partridge	March Brown	Welshman's Button	Caperer
Alder	Ermine Moth	Yellow Badger	Grizzly Dun	Grey Duster
Tannat's Crane Fly	August Dun	Hare's Ear	Dark Olive Dun	Yellow May Dun
Leslie Peters' Parachute	Imperial	Pheasant Tail	Baby Sun Fly	

March Brown

Hook   13. Brown silk.
Tail   Ginger whisks.
Rib   Yellow thread.
Body   Hare's ear.
Hackles   Ginger hackle with two brown partridge
          in front.

Location   River Teifi.
Time   Daytime in early season.
Conditions   Normal river flows.
Method   Dry fly upriver.

Dai Lewis achieved considerable success with his dry fly patterns. This dry March Brown is another superb example. It is dressed rather full with a bulky and a bushy hackle. This pattern is highly visible and a good floater, ideally suited for fishing quick-flowing water in mid summer.

It would be wrong to think of this as just a pattern to use when the March brown is hatching. It must be regarded as a general purpose fly which always offers the trout a good mouthful—thus tempting them to rise to it.

The March brown hatches on rivers like the Usk and the Teifi can extend over quite a long period—thus explaining the durability of this pattern for most of the season. It is conceivable that in late summer the dry March Brown could be taken by the trout for the August dun.

It was customary for Dai Lewis to leave the river Teifi during the months of July and August. He would fish then on the small mountain rivers and Dai's version of the March Brown served him admirably for this purpose.

Paragon

Hook   *12 & 14. Brown silk.*
Tail   *Three or four strands of dark red cock.*
Body   *Rabbit face.*
Hackle   *Two Rhode Island hen, dark chocolate
colour.*

Location   *Upper Teifi Valley.*
Time   *Summer evenings.*
Conditions   *Low water flows.*
Method   *Upriver, dry fly.*

This fly was a great favourite dry fly with anglers on the upper Teifi who went out fishing in the late evening. It was made popular after Vicar Powell advised Courtney Williams about it, who in turn included it in his book, the ever-popular *A Dictionary of Trout Flies.* Its usefulness in the late evening as a sedge decoy earned it is name—which implies perfection.

Many anglers would find a good location, with the river flowing westward, where the very last of the daylight enabled them to see the fly for those all-important last fifteen minutes when flies hatch. Then the fish become active and fishermen often frustrated!

Hen hackles were used—because hen hackle is less shiny and gives a better representation of sedge wings than do the shiny cock hackles.

Dai Lewis, who first tied this fly, although a great believer in having top quality cock hackle for dry-fly patterns, recommended the softer and more hairy hen hackle for his sedge representation: the reason being that he dressed his Sedge flies in order to fish them predominantly in slack water. Let there be no doubt, though, that Dai demanded top quality cock hackles for normal dry-fly fishing in the faster, broken runs.

This method of tying dry flies with soft hen hackles was interesting. The two hackles were placed back-to-back so that the tension of the fibres mobilised against each other. The natural curves of the hackles formed a compact unit, and it was observed that the hen fibres on contact with the surface of the water would bend and thus form a good base for the fly to sit on.

This is a late season Sedge and generally works best after hot summer days in July and August.

Pheasant Tail

Hook 14. Hot orange tying silk.
Tail Two or three strands of honey dun.
Rib Gold wire.
Body Two strands of rich coloured ruddy fibres
from the centre feather of a cock
pheasant tail.
Hackle Rusty dun cock.

Location Usk & Teifi.
Time Evening in Summer.
Conditions Normal water flows.
Method Dry fly upriver.

This is one of the most under-rated flies for use in Wales. In its dry version it probably represents the spinner phase of some of the *ephemera* family. Much has been written about the blue-winged-olive and many have been the debates about the best artificial to tempt the fish when they are feeding on it in the various stages of its development. On the Teifi the Pheasant Tail will outstrip the renowned Orange Quill when the sherry spinners are about.

The Pheasant Tail in its dry form was probably at the height of its fame in the forties. Many dry-fly fishers on the middle reaches of the Teifi would insist on having very dark dun hackle. Often some local fancy can influence the development of a fly. One of the excellent dry-fly anglers of the area, a certain Danny Pryse, would swear by the dark Pheasant Tail—'swear' being the operative word! He would use his dry flies in the necks of the pools and expect his flies to hop-scotch their way over the broken water where the big trout lurked in the warm days of summer.

The Small Harry

Hook 12. Black tying silk.
Tail Red cock fibres.
Body Rabbit face.
Rib Yellow thread.
Hackle Red cock hackle with partridge brown
in front.

Location River Teifi and river Usk.
Time Early season and late.
Conditions Low water.
Method Upriver dry fly approach.

Used as a dry fly version of the March Brown, the Small Harry is dressed rather full with plenty of turns of the red cock. Sometimes two cock hackles were used. The dry-fly version of the March Brown was often used when water flows were low and fishing the wet March Brown proved difficult. This pattern is in contrast to other patterns of Vicar Powell, in that its make-up is extremely simple.

Knee-deep in rununculus the author casts his Sun Fly to the big one in the shadow of the bridge at Pont Llanio.

276

Sun Fly

Hook 10, 12 & 14. Black silk.
Body Rabbit forehead.
Hackle Two coch-a-bon-ddu and a cree.

Location River Teifi.
Time Daytime—mid summer.
Conditions Normal river flows.
Method Dry fly—upriver.

This pattern was tied very full by its creator, the late Dai Lewis of Tregaron. He tied his flies without the aid of a vice, and all his patterns had that 'living' quality which meticulously-tied, clinically-neat flies have not. Body fur, taken from the forehead of a rabbit, gave the fly an overall dark appearance. Cree hackle was used to give the fly a sparkle: this was a ploy often used by Dai on other patterns. Those early Sun Flies were dressed in the days of an abundance of top quality hackle. Floatability was all-important, as little use was then made of floating aids. It is difficult today to appreciate how effective some of these big floating flies were. One of the bigger patterns tied on a number ten hook would be cast into the neck of a broken run and it would come bouncing down like a ping-pong ball with the flow. The dry fly is now earning respect with lake fishers, and it is known that the Sun Fly has been used on stillwater fisheries with considerable success.

It is important that the Sun Fly—which is the creation of Dai Lewis —should not be confused with the Baby Sun Fly which the Rev Edward Powell designed. Mind, there is probably some of Dai in the Baby Sun Fly too!

Baby Sun Fly

Hook 14 & 16. Black silk.
Tail Three strands of coch-a-bon-ddu.
Body Rabbit's face ribbed with tying silk.
Hackle Very small coch-a-bon-ddu cock.

This pattern was tied to represent the black gnat, and an effective pattern it is too. Unlike its bigger brother, it is effective during the early days of the season; and it will be seen to have lost its effectiveness by mid summer. The body of the fly was given the near-black dubbing because of the fur on a rabbit's forehead being black, under the top brownish layer.

Welshman's Button

Hook *12 & 14.*
Body *Five strands of brown turkey tail.*
Centre Ring *Two strands of yellow swan.*
Hackle *Black cock and Red cock.*
Location *Most Welsh river and lakes.*
Time *Evenings in May and June.*
Conditions *Warm and close.*
Method *On the surface.*

The Welshman's Button and the Caperer are often confused by anglers as the same insect. Halford decided to include The Welshman's Button with the Sedges, but in Wales it has always been regarded as a beetle. Lunn's pattern has gained prominence in Wales in recent years, but in the twenties it predecessor was a pattern from the stable of Tom Tom in Mid Wales, who dressed it with brown wool and had two yellow rings of rough cotton in the middle of the body. The hackle of that particular fly was a dark coch-a-bon-ddu, the fly overall was dressed very bushy so that it would float well and be highly visible on the rough waters of the small streams. It was also used as an evening fly on mountain lakes and those reservoirs created by the lead industry. In the later pattern the yellow rings had become far less well-defined and the rear section of the body was all of yellow wool.

In North Wales the Caperer was represented by a small Sedge dressed with a body of cinnamon wool with ginger hackle and mottled hen wing. These Sedges which were known as the Rhwyfawr Series in Welsh varied little in composition and were distinguished by size only, a Small Red Sedge, or a Big Dark Sedge. It was the method of fishing them that classified them as Sedges. Sedge fishing was ideal for the angler who worked all day and could only get out fishing at nightfall. For their river fishing the old anglers would use a hackle version, but would put up a dark brown winged version when fishing stillwaters.

Courtney Williams maintains that the Welshman's Button was a term derived from Welshman's Butty. 'Butty' is an expression used among colliers in the South Wales valleys for a friend. Some claim that the beetle that the Welshman's Button represents, *Sericostoma Personatum*, is not all that common in Wales. A pattern still used on the reservoirs of South Wales is one designed by Eric Taverner:

Hook *12 or 14 Crimson silk.*
Body *Peacock herl (greenish).*

278

Hackle Black cock.
Wing-case Ginger feather from partridge tail.

The Caperer is a very popular fly on some of the North Wales lakes and it is easily recognisable. The body is generally of a cinnamon shade described by the old quarrymen as a 'tobacco' shade: with the thorax like Dark Shagg, the wings mottled and of a yellowish brown colour. Ordinary anglers did not distinguish too carefully between members of the Sedge family and the Caperer. Whether the fly on the water was *Halesus tratiatus* or the *Halesus digitatus* made little odds in the gathering dusk.

Robert Lascelles in his *A Series of Letters on Angling, Shooting & Coursing in three parts*, 1819, says of the Welshman's Button, together with some surprising and illuminating comments on fly-fishing methods a hundred and seventy years ago,

'(It is) called the button fly, or by some the Welshman's button. He is rather a difficult fly to make, from his shape, which is nearly round, and from whence he derives his name. His wings are made from the red feathers of a partridge's tail; his body of peacock's harl, and a black hackle for legs, on a hook (No. 7,) the shank of which should be shortened, to enable you to make a more perfect imitation. He is generally in season from the first to the last week in June; but I have sometimes known him to continue no longer that two days, as the slightest storm of thunder or lightning totally banishes him for the season. This fly, however, to do the most execution, should be used naturally in the following manner:— Your rod must be at least twenty feet long, and of more than common substance; so that if you hook a large fish, which is generally the case, you may throw him out over your head in an instant: your tackle must, of course, be in other respects prop-ortionably strong. During the continuance of these flies, they may be found in great quantities on the willow and hazel bushes: put one, or sometimes a couple on a hook, (No. 7,) in the same manner as I have said of the stone fly, and keeping yourself as much con-cealed as possible behind the bushes, just let out sufficient line to reach the water at the full extent of your rod. A fish will either take your bait the instant he perceives it, or keep following it for some minutes; in which latter case, you must not expect to deceive him, for the weather is, most probably, bright and sultry, and every motion of your rod awakens his suspicions; the best plan will be, to leave him, and try another place; previously, however, throwing in two or three flies, to pave the way for better success. In this manner you may use the cock-chafer and large flesh-fly, which are equally killing, and provokingly tantalizing.'

Welsh Partridge

Hook   12 & 14. Claret silk.
Tail   Two strands from partridge tail.
Body   Claret seal's fur.
Hackle   Claret hackle with three turns of
partridge hackle in front.

Location   Rain-fed rivers.
Time   May & June.
Conditions   Normal dry fly water level.
Method   Dry fly upriver.

Courtney Williams in his *A Dictionary of Trout Flies* claims the Welsh Partridge to be an outstanding dry fly that is capable of taking fish on any river other than the chalk streams. This has proved to be a fair claim for a pattern which is at its best at the latter end of the trout season. It is not known exactly what this fly is supposed to represent, as it is effectively suggestive of a host of different natural flies.

Courtney Williams says that some of his friends found the Welsh Partridge an useful wet fly. It would be a pity if any angler were to judge this fly by just using it as a wet fly as there is no doubt that its primary role is that of a dry fly. One problem anglers encounter using small dry flies is that they are often difficult to see. The Welsh Partridge can be dressed with a grey speckled partridge, a breast feather as opposed to a back one: this makes the fly more visible—especially when the light is poor.

The Welsh Partridge was designed by Courtney Williams's father to fish the rivers of mid Wales, but it is also suited to other parts of the country. It has developed, surprisingly, into a favourite on the Tweed and the Tay in Scotland and also on the Suir in Ireland. Most river flies today are occasionally tried out on stillwaters, but more exacting trials with the Welsh Partridge, on reservoirs particularly, are needed for a full evaluation of its worth.

Whiskers

Hook 10, 12 & 14. Red silk.
Rib Gold wire.
Body Dark red wool or seal's fur.
Hackles Two or three ginger cocks. Hackles tied palmered.

Location Rivers of mid Wales and the Usk.
Time All season.
Conditions Normal river flows.
Method Up river—dry fly.

It is hard to imagine what these balls of fur and feathers are taken for. Some of the bigger patterns resemble nothing other than miniature. feather dusters. Yet they are effective. It was once thought that they worked best at dusk when the moths were about, but they can be equally effective during daytime too, representing, as some believe, the hairy caterpillars, known in Wales as 'Sioni blewog' ('Hairy Johnnies') that get onto the water from time to time.

The only difference between the Whiskers pattern used in North Wales and the one used in the Usk area is that on the Usk it was ribbed with flat gold—and the hackle was stripped on one side. This practice of stripping the fibres from one side of the hackle was common enough in some areas though it might simply have represented the idiocyncrasies of one or two tiers. It takes one productive fly-tier of successful killer flies to set a trend in fly-tying which can exert pervasive influence over the fly-tying style of an area for a long time. This has often happened in Wales, especially in the remote areas where one local expert comes to be regarded as a guru. One such expert was a certain Thomas Thomas who lived and fished the area between Cwmystwyth and Devil's Bridge who supplied flies to many local anglers. A box of his flies, all tied on eyeless hooks, revealed that a lot of his tying was done in the reverse manner: that is, the hackle was at the bend of the hook and the gut came straight down the shank. On stripping one pattern, all the details of tying were found to be identical to the Whiskers pattern. Under the hackle was the knot which ensured that the gut did not pull away. One can see immediately some of the advantages of this practice, though reverse dressing is really a gimmick not to be recommended.

Yellow Badger

Hook 12-14. *Black silk.*
Body *Yellow body.*
Rib *Gold wire.*
Hackle *Well marked badger cock.*

Location *Rain fed rivers of Mid Wales.*
Time *Daytime and dusk.*
Conditions *Low water.*
Method *Upriver, dry fly.*

All small Badger flies are popular with Welsh anglers who like to fish up the smaller rivers during high summer, and the Yellow Badger, on account of its visibility perhaps, is the firm favourite.

This high-visibility property of Badger flies is important and there is, as a result, considerable difference of opinion on the amount of white that should be used in the hackle. Some feel the white should represent about fifty per cent of the hackle, while others just require the tips of the hackle to be white. In recent years the Black Badger has been on the ascendant both on river and lake. Some use it during a buzzer rise and fish it semi-dry in the surface film.

Black Badger

Hook 16 & 18. *Black silk.*
Body *Black silk.*
Hackle *Small badger.*

The success of the Black Badger for buzzer fishing has resulted in the birth of the Red Badger which is used when red buzzers are in evidence.

Red Badger

Hook 16 & 18. *Red silk.*
Body *Red seal's fur.*
Hackle *Small badger.*

Other variations on the Badger hackle include green, olive and peacock herl bodies. The Badger & Silver is an excellent sewin fly (See page 44). Lately, the Badger Quill has found adoption as a dry fly and, such is its promise, that in time this particular variant could develop into becoming more famous than any of the others.

Yellow Sally
(Isoperla grammatica)

Hook 14. Yellow tying silk.
Body Pale yellow wool.
Hackle Yellow cock hackle (dyed).

Location Usk & Teifi.
Time Mid summer.
Conditions Warmish days.
Method Upriver dry fly.

The yellow sally is a member of the stone-fly family and, although quite common and easily recognised by anglers, it is not a favourite with the trout. The small yellow sally *(Choroperta torrentium)* is often found in considerable numbers in the upper reaches of rivers and at times the trout rise to them quite freely. Trout generally take the female just as it is ovipositing or in its spent form.

In the early forties it was not always easy to obtain dyed hackle and some artificial Yellow Sallies of that era are seen to have hackle dyed with a solution prepared from onion skin.

Scotcher, writing in the early decades of the last century, was not all that impressed by the Yellow Sally either:

'*Natural*. In shape like the four winged brown, but much smaller, and has two whisks at the tail, it is all of a lemon yellow, except its black varnished eyes: about the middle of May and beginning of June, is their season, but I have seen them strong on in July; they are seen all day long, and sometimes more numerous towards evening, but they are not a fly of much consequence, that I could ever find.

'*Artificial*. They are generally made with a white hackle, dyed with the inner bark of the barberry tree, and lemon silk for the body, but I have frequently found one of the lighter feathers tipped with yellow from a golden plover's wing, answer full as well.'

Nymphs

The most important item in the trout diet—the subaquatic nymph—has been imitated and fished by Welsh anglers for nearly two centuries. The early Welsh version of the nymph is the old-fashioned spider-style wet fly, a style of dressing that went out with the writings of Skues and Kite but which is now finding favour again with such *eminences grises* among modern-day nymph fishers as Arthur Cove. Fashion in matters piscatorial, as in ladies' hats, tends to travel in circles.

Nymph fishing in Wales originated with the traditional wet fly being cast downstream and worked in a teasing, rhythmic manner back against the river current. The current animated the fly as the hackles responded to the pressure of the water. Some of the more gifted fly dressers ensured that the hackle had the ability to 'kick' out against the water—thus giving the nymph a struggling motion. The hackle would, in some instances, envelope the body—thus giving a very realistic nymph-like shape to the fly. The old Welsh pattern, Petrisen ar gorff lliw rhwd, (Partridge on rust coloured body) was indeed a stone fly nymph.

Not many Welsh anglers of old would have related these old patterns to the nymph stage of the fly. Even today, only a fair percentage of anglers generally, are reasonably well informed about nymph fishing.

A book published in 1660 *Certaine Experiments Concerning Fish and Fruite*, written by John Taverner, explains rather well the role of the nymph in fishing:

'I have seene a young flie swimme in the water too and fro, and in the ende, come up to the upper crusts of the river, and assay to flie up; howbeit, not being perfectly ripe or fledged . . . has twice or thrice fallen downe again into the bottome . . . and on such younge flies before they are able to flie away, do fish feed exceedingly'.

The years that followed did not see a follow-up in the teaching of Taverner and even *The Art of Angling* written in 1780 by Charles Bowker, a book of surprising detail about fly dressing and river craft, makes no mention of nymphs. George Scotcher in his book *A Fly Fisher's Legacy* published in 1819/20 at Chepstow, illustrates a comprehensive selection of flies that were of use to the angler in the South East, but he does not mention nymphs. In 1834 George Agar Hansard went fishing around Wales, killing many a trout but, from his account, none on the nymph. It was therefore left to George Edward Skues in his book *Minor Tactics of the Chalk Stream*, published in 1910, to describe the principles of nymph fishing. He faced considerable opposition in those days as the Chalk Streams were the preserves of the dry-fly purists.

In recent years, a Welshman, the late Major Oliver Kite from Monmouth, did more than most to present the correct image of nymph fishing. His approach was very businesslike, lacking all the frills and trappings of many present-day anglers and celebrated angling writers. He was able to fish the nymph simply: on waters far from the crystalline waters of the chalk downs, a gifted angler with an incredible ability for seeing trout.

Kite explained his approach to nymph fishing in his book *Nymph Fishing in Practice*, 1963, which reveals his considerable knowledge of the natural species and their artificial counterparts. In practice, Oliver Kite had a very easy approach: and this culminated in the ultimate near-absurdity of the 'bare hook' nymph. He visited the river Teifi and the Usk where he would invariably do well with his nymphs. Not many locals followed his teachings on the Teifi; but the river Usk, which also has certain similarities with the chalk streams, provided a better environment for nymph life and for nymph fishing. Leslie Peters, fishing the Usk at Brecon, uses his March Brown Nymph frequently in the early days of the season.

Nymph fishing has become much more popular on stillwaters in Wales. The calm conditions that prevail on lakes and reservoirs have always presented anglers with a problem. The old approach of casting out a three-fly cast, and then retrieving it, was never very entertaining or rewarding under such conditions. Thus nymph fishing, having made a name for itself on reservoirs in England, was tried out. It gained immediate favour on Welsh fisheries. The Buzzer pupa in various shades of black, red, green and yellow was thereafter to be found on many Welsh reservoirs and has happily resulted in a more subtle approach being observed to reservoir angling, which was in severe danger of becoming totally lure-orientated.

The return of the Spider has completed the circle.

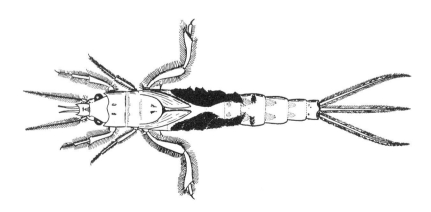

Amber Nymph
(Anthripsodes cinercus)

Hook *10 & 11. Brown tying silk.*
Body *Amber seal's fur tied full for back half of body. Front half, thorax, of brown seal's fur.*
Wing case *Strip of grey feather tied in at tail and finished behind the thorax.*
Legs *A few fibres of pale honey hen hackle, tied under the head.*

Location *Chew Valley Reservoir.*
Time *Mid summer.*
Conditions *Warm evening.*
Method *Used on normal three-fly cast as dropper.*

Dr Bell, a famous fisherman of the Chew Valley Fishery, was responsible for creating this pattern which has subsequently gained much favour on many fisheries in Wales. It bears a close relationship with the Rusty Spider patterns that were used in the Bethesda area at the turn of the century.

On lakes, the Amber Nymph works best from May onwards and is most probably taken for the pupa stage of the brown silverhorns sedge *(Anthripsodes cinereus)*. The brown silverhorns sedge is quite a common sedge with very long antennae which appear as two rather long horns. As the name suggests, the sedge has a brownish body—with wings of brown which have faint black markings. It is doubtful if trout feed much on the adult, but they are often found feeding on the pupa. The pupae have a creamy-brown body with a thorax of brownish orange. The Rusty Spider patterns and the Amber Nymph do well when the brown silverhorns pupa is featuring on the trout's menu.

Sweet's Amber Nymph

> Hook 10 & 12. Brown tying silk.
> Tail Red hen.
> Body Amber floss.
> Rib Gold thread with black thread ribbed alongside.
> Thorax Amber floss.
> Hackle Soft red hen.

This pattern is attributed to Lionel Sweet, an expert caster who, with his wife Molly, ran the famed tackle shop at Usk for many years.

Black Buzzer

> Hook 12. Red tying silk.
> Tail White hackle fibres—tied round the bend of hook.
> Body Black wool.
> Rib Flat lurex.
> Overbody P.V.C.
> Thorax Green peacock herl.
>
> Location Eglwys Nunydd Reservoir.
> Time Evening.
> Conditions Calm.
> Method Slow retrieve on floating line.

In the last two decades many old Welsh Fly patterns have temporarily lost their appeal on Welsh Reservoirs—such as Eglwys Nunydd and Llandegfedd in particular. The influx of angling literature has brought new ideas and modern materials. The Black Buzzer is typical of late twentieth century fly technology, using newly-available materials—in this instance P.V.C. and lurex to create an effect: that of capturing an air bubble—which older practitioners of the fly-tying art had been hard-pressed to achieve with baser materials.

Corixa

Hook 12. White tying silk.
Rib Brown cotton.
Body Cream floss dressed full.
Wing case A strip of dark brown wing fibre tied in
at tail and brought over the back and
tied in at the head.
Legs Cream hen hackle tied in under the
head.

Location Most stillwaters.
Time August & September.
Conditions Fairly shallow water up to three feet
deep.
Method Fished on point and allowed to sink and
then lifted.

The corixa is a common item of food with trout in the late season. They are generally found near weed beds and are fairly active as they move to the surface to get their supply of air. On taking in this fresh supply of oxygen the corixa sinks down with a glistening air sack between its wing and body.

The recognised method of fishing it is to incorporate some lead wire in the dressing, thus ensuring that it sinks quickly. Used on a long leader with a floating line, the angler casts it out near to the weeds and lets it sink. It is then retrieved in short jerks.

There are many dressings which have been used through the years to represent the corixa, but, it must be remembered, that the insect itself varies considerably in the colouring of its back. The abdomen is always off-white in colour. The corixa itself is beetle-shaped with a hard, shiny back and long hind legs. These long legs have been likened to the oars of a boat, hence the origin of the name 'Boatman'.

Tony's Corixa

Hook 12, 14 &' 16. Yellow waxed tying silk.
Body Lime green wool.
Tag Three turns silver thread.
Rib Silver wire.
Back Feathers from magpie tail.
Paddles Large lime green goose biots.
Head Large black varnished eyes.

Location Lishvaen &' Llanishen reservoir.
Conditions Low or high, calm.
Time Evening.
Method On floating line.

Tony Brett and his wife Felicity are a very keen fishing family and more often than not during the season will be found fishing one or other of the Cardiff reservoirs. In recent years the fishing on these two reservoirs has improved immensely due to excellent management by the Welsh Water Authority in the Taff Division.

Tony's Corixa can be fished either low in the water or in the higher levels. It is advisable to add some lead wire to the dressing if it is intended to fish the corixa deep. Tony, being an excellent caster, puts his Corixa well out into the reservoir and then works it back in a series of sink-and-draw movements—which assimilates the natural movement of the corixa.

Tony Brett receives his just-award from Hubert Gwynne, Sec. Welsh Anglers' Council, in the Champion of Champions competition. Felicity Brett looks pleased, she came second!

292

Emyr's Fancy

Hook 12. Black tying silk.
Rib Gold wire.
Body Black seal's fur.
Thorax A mixture of fiery brown, green and
black seal's fur.

Location Llyn Clywedog.
Time Right through the season.
Conditions Calm.
Method On point of thee-nymph cast.

This nymph was developed on the Clywedog fishery and Emyr Lloyd, its creator, a bailiff employed by the Welsh Water Authority, uses it to good effect. During the early days of the season it is fished deep in the water with a little copper wire being added under the dressing to achieve a quick sinking effect. As the water warms up in late spring and summer the nymph is fished closer to the surface. Clywedog is stocked with rainbow as well as with brown trout. In most Welsh fisheries the rainbow does not acquire that silvery sheen which

makes it such a handsome trout: it does do so in Clywedog—and it moves well to nymphs fished near the surface. Brenig reservoir in Clwyd is a fishery of many fish which—unfortunately for the anglers—are very selective in their choice of food. Nevertheless Emyr's Fancy has been the downfall of many.

Emyr Lewis, Llanbrynmair, nymph specialist of Clywedog reservoir.

293

Hare's Ear Nymph

Hook   *10 & 12. Yellow tying silk.*
Rib   *Gold wire.*
Body   *Hare's ear.*
Thorax   *Peacock herl.*

Location   *Rivers where olives hatch and
stillwaters.*
Time   *May & June.*
Conditions   *Low water levels.*
Method   *Upriver.*

The Hare's Ear Nymph has been used for many years on Welsh rivers in its traditional form. The Hare's Ear has always been dressed with a light dun hackle and fished down stream. The new approach is to fish it upriver and let it sink deep to move fish that refuse to respond to downstream fishing.

The great advantage of upriver casting was that it allowed the nymph to sink deep. The shape of the nymph is ideally designed for quick sinking, especially if it has some lead or copper incorporated into the dressing. The thorax of hare's fur gives the body of the nymph its realistic appearance and the peacock herl represents the wing cases.

In fishing stillwaters it is often necessary for the nymph to remain in the upper layer of the water, hence the advisability of having a lightweight pattern with just a turn of hackle at the head instead of the peacock herl.

Ken's Grey Midge

Hook 14-16. Grey tying silk.
Rib Size 14 oval gold wire.
Body Mole fur.
Thorax Mole fur.
Hackle Blue slate hen.
Wing case Pigeon primary feathers.

Location Reservoirs of South East Wales.
Time Evenings from April onwards.
Conditions Warm and calm.
Method On bob of nymph cast.

K en Bowering is one of the most consistent catchers of fish in South Wales. He fishes, in the main, heavily-fished reservoirs, a demanding environment for any fly or nymph pattern. His powers as an International competitive angler are well known, having served in the Welsh team for a number of years and been its captain.

He fishes his Grey Midge on a floating line and thus keeps the nymph in the surface film. The level at which a nymph or fly fishes in the water is critical: a nymph presented an inch or two below the surface can be out of focus for a fish feeding on insects held in the surface. Ken's Grey Midge is presented in the surface film and, by placing it in the bob position, it is held in the right place for surface-cruising fish.

Once the water begins to warm up in late April, the fish in the reservoirs of South Wales move from the deep water and take more interest in insects in the surface and on the surface. Midges are particularly attractive to trout, and this pattern often takes more than its quota on difficult evenings.

Ken Bowring of Cardiff, stillwater specialist and expert trout-catcher and fly-dresser.

295

Oliver Kite in action

March Brown Nymph

(Rhithrogena haarupi)

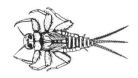

Hook 12. Claret tying silk.
Tail Honey dun whisks.
Rib Gold wire.
Body Claret seal's fur.
Legs Dark honey dun.
Wing case

Location River Usk.
Time Early season.
Conditions Normal river flows.
Method Up-stream in low water.

This is one of the better-known nymphs, common on many rivers in most parts of Wales. The hatches of March brown have, in the early eighties, been extremely encouraging after the poor hatches of the early and mid seventies.

The nymph of the March brown is a stone-clinger and it favours rivers with a stone and gravelly bottom. The nymphs appear in mid April in great numbers and there is little doubt that the trout often take the nymph in preference to the dun: hence the importance of the nymph to the angler. During low flows the up-stream nymph is to be preferred to the down-river-and-across method of fishing where the angler is visible to the fish.

March Brown Nymph

Hook 12. Yellow tying silk.
Tail Two strands of pheasant tail.
Body Orange silk ribbed with gold wire.
Thorax Yellow seal's fur.
Wing case Over seal's fur.
Legs Partridge hackle.

Longhorns
(Anthripsodes cinereus)

> *Hook* 10 & 12. Brown tying silk.
> *Rib* Gold wire over abdomen.
> *Body* Abdomen—Blue, green or amber.
> *Thorax* Chestnut or sepia.
> *Hackle* Brown partridge.
> *Horns* Two pheasant tail fibres tied long.
>
> *Location* Stillwaters.
> *Time* July onwards.
> *Conditions* Calm.
> *Method* Sink and draw on floating line.

Welsh anglers have always looked forward to the sedge fishing time when they would arrive on the river just at nightfall and fish their Sedge patterns on the surface to fairly predictably responsive trout.

In the last decade or so fishing the sedge pupa has become increasingly popular at this time of day with patterns like the Longhorns doing well. The Longhorns fished in the sink-and-draw method on a floating line represents the sedge pupa coming up in the water. The angler can even start fishing in this style well before the sedges start to hatch.

The Longhorns, especially the green version, has done well on Clywedog, Brenig and the Teifi Pools.

Pheasant Tail Nymph

> Hook *10 & 12. Hot orange tying silk.*
> Rib *Gold wire.*
> Tail & Body *Rusty pheasant tail fibres.*
> Thorax *Hare's ear fur.*
>
> Location *River Usk and Teifi and stillwaters.*
> Time *All season.*
> Conditions *All conditions.*
> Method *Upriver on a floating line. On stillwaters*
>   *with floating line with nymph long*
>   *leader.*

Most old Welsh Spider patterns were really nymph represent-ations and it is therefore not surprising that nymph fishing in Wales seemed to take a long time to wake up to it. On the rivers Usk and Teifi, presentation of the Nymph upriver is an ideal formula for success on the cold, early days of the season. The fish are then low in the water and the normal wet fly does not get down to them. Some anglers add a layer of lead under the dressing of the Pheasant Tail in order to help it to sink quickly.

The Pheasant Tail used on stillwaters is generally on a bigger hook and is fished on a long leader with a floating line. The aim of the angler is to get the Nymph down right onto the bed of the reservoir and then work it slowly up and down in the water. The takes by a fish are registered on the floating line. This is, of necessity, a very slow, patient way of fishing and the mistake most anglers make is to tend to move the Nymph too fast.

Shrimp

Shrimp 11. Brown tying silk.
    Body *Underlayer of copper wire. Pale brown wool—tied to form a hump.*
  Hackle *Red cock palmered.*
    Back *Golden pheasant tippet fibres pulled right over body to form a wing case and tied in at head.*

  Location *Teifi, Usk and Severn.*
      Time *Early season.*
Conditions *Cold weather.*
    Method *Downstream on wet fly line.*

This pattern was first created by Eric Horsfall Turner for use on the river Derwent. Eric's creations, because of his association with mid Wales, were soon tried out on the Welsh rivers. The Shrimp pattern found little support when it was fished in the normal wet-fly method. Things improved dramatically, however, when it was fished directly downriver and worked with movement of the rod. Long rods are an asset to this type of fishing. Donald Overfield in his excellent updating of *A Dictionary of Trout Flies* by Courtney Williams, suggests a recent modification of the above pattern is to add slivers of toe-nail parings for the back fibres! Whether the effect of this is visual or olfactory is not made clear, but the new shrimp is said to be more durable and is known as Toe-nail Shrimp.

Grayling

Grayling fishing is not so much practised in Wales as it is in other parts of the United Kingdom—despite the fact that there are a few areas that can offer fishing of very high quality. The development of grayling fishing has been rather spasmodic in Wales, so fly patterns tend to be imported rather than bear the label, 'home made'. Many regular grayling anglers tend to rely on a few standard trout wet-fly patterns with the addition of a red tag.

The quality of the grayling fishing available in Wales has, surprisingly, when everything else is going down-hill, improved considerably in recent years. Some stretches of the river Dee around Corwen now offer grayling of superb quality, with good grayling fishing reported on the Tanat and the Banwy, its tributaries. In mid Wales the Wye and the Severn with their tributaries the Teme, Lugg, Ithon and the Monnow are top-class grayling waters.

The Lugg and the Ithon often fish well when standard trout patterns like the Greenwell's Glory, Pheasant Tail, Iron Blue and the Imperial are used. Some local grayling anglers are quite happy to proceed with the recognised trout patterns in sizes 14 and 16, while on the Dee in North Wales the locals there prefer the fancy patterns, Orange Otter, Red Tag and members of the Witch series.

Many uninitiated anglers who come to grayling fishing from trout believe that the grayling is not quite so well versed in the ways of anglers as is the trout. Let there be no doubt, the grayling is exceedingly perceptive and subjects the fly to far greater scrutiny than does any trout, and is very quick to spit out the unpalatable hook. Flies dressed on very small doubles, sizes 18 and 20 are sometimes required do the trick. The grayling offers the fly dresser the greatest of challenges.

Being past-master at refusing the angler's offering, she will rise consistently and for hours at the natural and completely ignore the artificial copy of it. Suspicion, wariness and distrust have to be overcome if the angler is to succeed against grayling that refuse successively to take the artificial on four or five attempts yet continue to take the naturals all around with rhythmic regularity. Such behaviour tests the mettle of the most able of anglers; and there is, seemingly, nothing that will entice the grayling when in such a mood except the most perfect of flies.

Then there are other times when the grayling will take almost anything that is thrown at them, then the quality and the pattern of the fly seem quite immaterial.

Brookes's Fancy

Hook   *13 & 14. Purple tying silk.*
Body   *Purple floss ribbed with peacock herl.*
Hackle   *White: off-white.*

Location   *Originally Teme, then Severn and Teifi.*
Conditions   *Good river level.*
Time   *Summer and Autumn.*
Method   *Normal wet fly.*

This pattern was originally tied by a well known postman from Ludlow. Brookes, an inventive fly dresser, used it mainly on the river Teme. It was then used on the Severn and earned a considerable reputation there. It has also been used on the few stretches of the river Teifi that hold grayling. As the Teifi is not officially recognised as a grayling river, all fishing closes in early October, hence anglers are at present unable to fish for grayling during the latter months when grayling really come into condition.

The white hackle can often become more effective after the fly has seen some use. Even newly-tied patterns do better if the white hackle used is deprived of that 'whiter than white' appearance.

John Storey

Hook   *14 & 16. Claret tying silk.*
Body   *Peacock herl.*
Hackle   *Medium dark red cock.*
Wing   *Tip of speckled feather from mallard breast.*

Location   *On tributaries of Severn.*
Time   *Autumn.*
Conditions   *Cold sharp mornings.*
Method   *Upriver dry fly.*

Eric Horsfall Turner had a great knowledge of the river Severn in Mid Wales and was responsible for many innovations in the approach to its fishing. He took many fish with his own patented dry flies and with the wet fly fished upriver. He very much liked this John Storey fly pattern from Yorkshire, where he himself spent some years as town clerk of Scarborough. It is claimed that the pattern was devised by a John Storey who was river keeper from the Ryedales Angling Club.

Some of the patterns favoured by Eric Horsfall Turner supported a partridge wing instead of the normal mallard, and a lighter-coloured hackle. This pattern, as indeed with so many other patterns used for grayling fishing in Wales, is also an excellent pattern for trout; the only difference being that they are all used later in the year for grayling.

Dry-fly fishing during the months of November and December under grey dull skies can impose considerable strain on the grayling angler's eyesight. A well-marked wing on a very small pattern is of great help in this respect—and John Storey is one of the most visible of patterns.

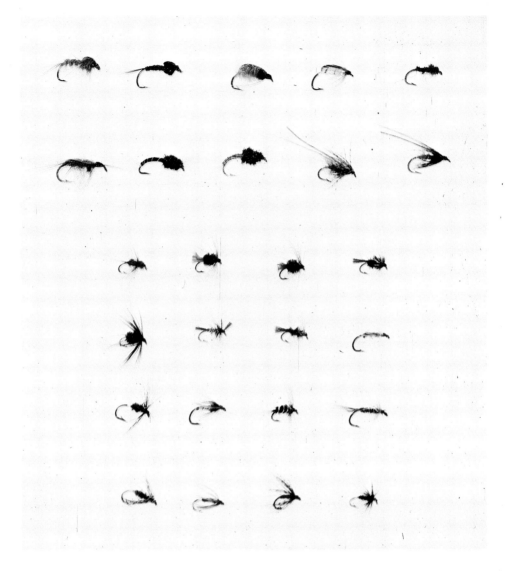

Plate XVI   Nymphs and Grayling Flies

Hare's Ear Nymph	Pheasant Tail Nymph	Amber Nymph	Corixa	Emyr's Fancy
Shrimp	Black Buzzer	Green Buzzer	Green Longhorns	Amber Longhorns
Orange Otter	Red Tag	Crimson Tag	Severn Ke	
Kill Devil Spider	Silver Badger	Rolt's Witch	Brookes's Fancy	
Pluen ddu ar gorff paun	Pluen giach ar gorff lliw rhwd	Pluen goch ceiliog ar gorff paun a weiren aur	Pluen las olau ar gorff plu ffesant	
Pluen petrisen ar gorff lliw llysnafedd yr afon	Pluen giach ar gorff piws	Pluen petrisen ar gorff porffor	Pluen brân ar gorff lliw gwin	

Kill Devil Spider

Hook 14 & 16. Black tying silk.
Body Peacock herl.
Hackle Long black hen.

Location River Dee.
Time Autumn.
Conditions Cold and sharp.
Method Wet fly downriver.

These long hackled flies were first devised by David Foster of Ashbourne. The exceptionally long hackle makes for a very attractive fly when it is worked in a fast-flowing current. The long hackle flows back over the plump peacock herl body and gives a very life-like nymph impression.

As these Kill Devil Spiders are dressed on small hooks, it often becomes a major problem to hook the fast-hitting grayling. Some grayling anglers on the river Dee dress the body to cover only the front portion of the hook—in the low-water salmon fly fashion.

The most popular of the Kill Devil series are of black, brown and blue dun hackle.

Orange Otter

Hook 16, 18. *Orange tying silk.*
Tail *Red cock.*
Body *Pale biscuit colour underpart of an
        otter's throat, soaked in picric acid
        solution and then boiled in the same
        solution for a few minutes—plus equal
        volume of red ink, plus an equal
        amount of water.*
Hackle *Wound around the middle of the hook,
        thus dividing the body in half.*

Location **Border rivers. Teifi at Lampeter till September.**
Time *November after the first frost.*
Conditions *Low water.*
Method *Upriver dry fly.*

This is another fly devised by the late Rev Edward Powell. His patterns are all immensely difficult to tie because of the complex nature of the body material. He found a lot of use for picric acid. His patterns are always worth the trouble, provided one can get them tied with the correct materials.

This pattern, known by its initials O.O., is probably one of the best grayling patterns of all. Anglers have been constantly amazed at its power to get the grayling to come up and strike at it. Its creator was known also to have used it for trout fishing in September.

The grayling is mainly confined to the rivers in Wales that flow eastwards. Most of the short rivers flowing westwards do not have grayling, with the exception of a short area of the river Teifi just below Lampeter. Grayling there average around a pound apiece. For these Teifi grayling the Orange Otter is the top fly and takes these 'game' coarse fish well in the cool September evenings.

Red Tag

Hook *10 & 12. Black silk.*
Tag *Red wool.*
Rib *Gold wire.*
Body *Peacock herl.*
Hackle *Red cock hackle.*

Location *Rivers and lakes.*
Time *High summer. Deep winter.*
Conditions *Normal flows, frost, dull or sunshine.*
Method *Used as the bob fly on a three- or four- wet-fly cast.*

This is a very old fly pattern—going back some hundred and fifty years. It was first used in Wales as a trout fly—with the addition of the red tag to the normal Coch-a-bon-ddu pattern. It has always been a very attractive bob fly and, even when fished on rivers, it has the ability to raise fish that would have ignored other offerings.

It is as a grayling fly that the Red Tag is really outstanding. It is used on the river Dee in the Corwen area and there it takes grayling in either the wet or dry form. When the river is low, and after a November frost, the best fun is had with it in its dry form. Some even use an Orange Tag: a variant seen more frequently on the river Severn.

Grayling fishing is very good on some eastern Welsh rivers. While bait anglers take a lot of grayling, the three-fly cast fished downstream on the Wye and its tributaries provides far better sport.

Severn Ke

Hook 16 & 18. Claret tying silk.
Tail Red fluorescent wool on golden pheasant
      tippets.
Body Peacock herl.
Hackle White cock.

Location Upper Severn.
Time November.
Conditions Cold and sharp.
Method Either upriver as a floater or downriver
        in wet form.

This pattern, used by a few Llanidloes anglers on certain sections of the upper Severn, is an adaptation of the Ke-he fly popular in the Orkneys. The use of the white hackle has been a great advanatage when fishing in late Autumn under poor light conditions. Some keen grayling anglers tie this pattern in two distinct styles. When confronted with swift-flowing water they use much larger versions on hooks 12 and use two hackles. In slack and calm waters they use a very lightly dressed version with only one or two turns of hackle.

Ke-he

Hook 10 & 12. Claret tying silk.
Tail Red tag on golden pheasant tippets.
Body Peacock herl.
Hackle Ginger or brown.

Some anglers use the normal Ke-he pattern for grayling and find it quite an effective fly. So unpredictable are grayling that they will sometimes even take the Black Ke-he in preference to the standard dressing above. The Black Ke-he is identical to the above, except that the hackle is black hen.

Treacle Parkin

Hook *12 & 14. Yellow tying silk.*
Tail *Yellow/Orange wool.*
Body *Peacock herl.*
Hackle *Dark red/brown.*

Location *Monnow and Wye.*
Time *Late Autumn.*
Conditions *Cold and frosty.*
Method *Normal dry fly.*

Grayling anglers disagree about the colour of the tag on this pattern. Some favour the bright yellow above the orange yellow shade. A few even use the rabbit fur dyed in picric acid as recommended by Edward Powell for the tail of the Doctor.

Grayling are not quite as concerned as they imagine with the merits and de-merits of these various shades!

Most serious grayling anglers believe that after the grayling has refused a particular pattern it is advisable to change to something totally different. Treacle Parkin is ideal for this ploy and just as a change of bowler in cricket can drop a wicket, success will often follow similar changes of fly.

The Treakle Parkin originated in Yorkshire where it is a very favoured trout fly. Flies often undergo modification when they travel but, with the exception of the odd grayling angler using coch-a-bonddu hackle instead of the dark red/brown as on the original, Treacle Parkin has remained unaltered.

White Witch

Hook 14 & 16. Black tying silk.
Tail Red wool.
Body Peacock herl.
Hackle White cock tied palmer fashion.

Location Wye and Dee rivers.
Time November.
Conditions Bright and cold.
Method Either wet or dry fly.

This series of Witch patterns can be fished either as wet or dry flies. The White Witch does, however, do far better when fished upriver in its dry state. It is much in use in the Corwen area.

Silver Witch

Hook *14 & 16.*
Tail *Red wool.*
Body *Peacock herl.*
Hackle *Badger cock (palmered).*

This is another use of the Witch series that does better in its dry form. The problem often with these small flies, dressed on number 16 hooks, is in hooking the fish. With the dry fly one has a better chance in that the 'take' is marked.

Rolt's Witch

Hook *14 & 16. Black tying silk.*
Tail *Red wool.*
Body *Peacock herl.*
Hackle *Honey dun.*

This was the original of the Witch series, created by H. A. Rolt whose expertise in grayling fishing is recorded in his book, *Grayling Fishing in South County Streams.* Most of the grayling patterns in the Witch series have followed the principle set by Rolt in this prototype—a small, thick-set body with plenty of red in the dressing.

APPENDIX 1

Patterns from *Llawlyfr y Pysgotwr*, Fisherman's Handbook, by William Roberts first published in Bethesda, 1899.

PARTRIDGE

Petrisen liwgar ar gorff llwyd felyn.
A well marked partridge hackle on a fawn yellow body.

Petrisen liwgar ar gorff o flewyn clust sgwarnog.
A well marked partridge hackle on a hare's ear body.

Petrisen liwgar ar groff o sidan du main.
A well marked partridge on a black silk body.

Petrisen liwgar ar gorff lliw gwin.
A well marked partridge hackle on claret silk.

Petrisen liwgar ar gorff cochddu.
A well marked partridge hackle on black/red body. This black/red body is achieved by either mixing black and (dyed) red wool from the scrotum of a black ram.

Petrisen liwgar ar gorff lliw rhwd haearn.
A well marked partridge hackle on rusty coloured body.

Petrisen liwgar ar gorff melyn.
Partridge hackle on yellow body.

Pluen ddu ar gorff lliw gwin.
Black hackle on claret silk body.

Pluen ddu ar gorff paun.
Black hackle on peacock herl body.

Pluen ddu flaen-goch ar gorff paun.
Furnace hackle on peacock herl body.

Pluen ddu flaen-goch ar gorff clust sgwarnog.
Furnace hackle on a hare's ear body.

Pluen lwyd dywyll ar gorff lliw rhwd haearn.
A dark blue dun hackle on rusty coloured wool body.

311

Pluen lwyd dywyll ar gorff blewyn clust sgarwnog.
A dark dun hackle on hare's ear body.

Pluen lwyd dywyll ar gorff cochddu.
A dark dun hackle on black/red wool body.

Pluen lwyd dywyll ar gorff lliw gwin.
A dark blue dun hackle on claret wool body.

Pluen lwyd dywyll ar gorff du main.
A dark dun hackle on thin black silk body.

Pluen lwyd dywyll ar gorff lliw anisyn.
A dark blue dun hackle on a body of aniseed coloured wool.

Pluen goch ceiliog ar gorff paun.
Ginger hackle on peacock herl body.

Pluen goch ceiliog ar gorff blewyn llwyd clust sgwarnog.
Ginger cock hackle on fawn fur from hare's ear.

Pluen goch ceiliog ar gorff du.
Ginger cock hackle on black wool body.

Pluen lwyd olau ar gorff melyn.
A light blue dun on yellow wool body.

Pluen lwyd olau ar gorff lliw llysnafedd yr afon.
A light blue dun on green wool body (green of the colour of weeds in the river).

Pluen lwyd olau ar gorff sidan du main.
A light blue dun on black silk body.

Pluen lwyd olau ar gorff lliw anisyn.
A light blue dun on body of aniseed coloured wool.

Aden petrisen ar gorff lliw rhwd haearn a thraed cochion.
A partridge tail wing on rusty wool body with ginger hackle.

Aden petrisen ar gorff lliw coch-ddu a thraed du-flaengoch.
A partridge tail wing on black/red body with furnace hackle.

Aden petrisen ar gorff blewyn clust sgwarnog a thraed llwyd neu goch.
A partridge tail wing on hare's ear body with dun or ginger hackle.

Aden petrisen ar gorff llwyd felyn a thraed llwydion.
A partridge tail wing on fawn yellowish body and dun hackle.

Aden petrisen ar gorff lliw gwin a thraed du-flaengoch.
A partridge tail wing on claret body with furnace hackle.

Aden ceiliog hwyaden ar gorff paun a thraed cochion.
Bronze mallard wing on peacock herl body with ginger legs.

Aden ceiliog hwyaden ar gorff lliw coch-ddu a thraed duon.
Bronze mallard wing on black-red wool body with black hackle.

Aden ceiliog hwyaden ar gorff lliw gwin a thraed du-flaengoch.
Bronze mallard wing on claret silk body with furnace hackle.

Aden ceiliog hwyaden ar gorff sidan du main a thraed duon.
Bronze mallard wing on thin black silk body with black hackle.

Aden ceiliog y mynydd ar gorff paun a thraed cochion.
Grouse wing on peacock herl body with ginger hackle.

Aden ceiliog y mynydd ar gorff du a thraed du-flaengoch.
Grouse wing on black silk body with furnace hackle.

Aden iâr ddŵr ar gorff paun a thraed du-flaengoch.
Moorhen's wing on peacock herl body with furnace hackle.

Aden iâr ddŵr ar gorff lliw gwin a thraed cochion.
Moorhen's wing on claret body with ginger hackle.

Aden iâr ddŵr ar gorff coch-ddu a thraed duon.
Moorhen's wing on claret body with ginger hackle.

Aden troellwr ar gorff blewyn clust sgwarnog a thraed cochion.
Nightjar's wing on hare's ear body with ginger hackle.

Aden troellwr ar gorff coch-ddu a thraed du-flaengoch.
Nightjar's wing on black/red body with furnace hackle.

Aden troellwr ar gorff du a thraed duon.
Nightjar's wing on black silk body with black hackle.

Aden pioden ar gorff paun a thraed du-flaengoch.
A magpie's wing on peacock herl body with furnace hackle.

313

Aden pioden ar gorff paun a thraed cochion.
A magpie's wing on peacock herl body with ginger hackle.

Aden cyffylog ar gorff lliw rhwd haearn a thraed cochion.
Woodcock's wing on rusty wool body with ginger hackle.

Aden cyffylog ar gorff llwyd felyn a thraed llwydion.
Woodcock's wing on fawn yellowish body with dun hackle.

Aden cyffylog ar gorff melyn a thraed cochion.
Woodcock's wing on yellow wool body and ginger hackle.

Aden Rhegen yr Ŷd ar gorff paun a thraed cochion.
Corncrake wing on peacock herl body and ginger hackle.

Aden Rhegen yr Ŷd ar gorff melyn a thraed coch.
Corncrake wing on yellow wool body and ginger hackle.

Aden ddu (brân) ar gorff du a thraed duon.
Black crow's wing on black wool body with black hackle.

William Roberts, in addition to giving us an important record of the types of flies used and the local materials used in their manufacture at the turn of the century, also added a number of suggestions that would be of help to anglers. Some of these suggestions are still of use to us today to provide a picture of the methods of fishing extant at the turn of the century. He advises anglers not to use more than three flies on the cast: and to leave at least eighteen inches between the flies. When the water level was low, anglers were advised to work upriver so that they would not be seen by the fish. It would appear that black flies were far more effective towards the tail-end of the season. This advice is repeated many times! The best fishing day even then would seem to have been a damp, wet day. No shortage of those in Bethesda! Winged patterns were considered best for lakes and hackle flies for the rivers.

The interesting feature of these dressings is that they were entirely 'home-made' in that all the materials specified were ready-to-hand in his native Ogwen Valley.

APPENDIX 2

The Welsh Angler's Calendar

In most parts of Wales, Winter lingers until the end of March and even sometimes into early April. Yet many wet fly anglers can do quite well on the odd warm spring day in March. The early spring olives, the stone flies and the March browns are the earliest arrivals and when they appear on the water the trout move to their feeding stations and feed appreciatively.

Later in early April the trout move out from the pools and into the runs from where the angler is able to offer for them with both the wet and the dry fly with much greater chance of success. The iron blue dun is probably the choice item with the hungry trout of early April. Trout tend to feed mainly during the warmer hours of daylight in April with little or no activity before midday, and cease about three in the afternoon.

May is one of the best months for the angler, with most of the water-bred flies and the terrestials appearing on the water. This is the month of the dry fly. Very few Welsh rivers or lakes have the Mayfly but the grannom, stone flies and the alder make up for it. The trout, after the first fortnight in June, tend to become rather difficult—and fly fishing during the day on the rivers becomes very hard. It is more productive for the angler to direct his flies towards the fast-running sections of the river with its well oxygenated water.

Trout in July are generally well-educated in the ways of the angler and are extraordinarily difficult to catch. The nymph fished upriver will often score where the orthodox dry fly has failed. Sedge fishing in the evening is probably the best chance for the angler, especially if the temperatures during the day are high.

August is also a difficult month and the Blue Winged Olive and the Sedges are the best weapons for the angler who would be well advised to fish during the evening. Towards the end of August the trout revert to their spring behaviour and will be feeding quite avidly by the end of the month. It is questionable if anglers should take trout in late September as many trout by then are heavy in spawn.

The yearly pattern for sewin fishing varies from river to river and while rivers like the Towy and the Glaslyn often have a considerable run of sewin in April, this is the exception rather than the rule. Most of the sewin fishing starts in earnest in mid June. Daytime fly fishing for sewin requires an increased water flow with preferably slight colour in it. Fishing at night is for some the most pleasurable method of taking sewin. This requires the water to be clear and at a medium or low height.

315

APPENDIX 3

The list of F. Yates, Neath, 1895

In the early days the fly fishing in various parts of Wales varied quite susbtantially. While in North Wales the lightly dressed style was in vogue in South Wales other than in the Usk area there was a tendency to dress the flies rather heavily. A Mr F. Yates of Neath writing in 1895, produced an impressive list of flies in use in the Neath area which in some cases showed considerable similarity to those used in the West Country.

> 'We do not use a great variety of hackles for trout in South Wales—Blue, honey, copper, brassy, golden-edged dun, grizzle and coch-a-bon-ddu are always in great demand. Materials for bodies are chiefly wools—dirty yellow, olive, buff and brown, various coloured silks; and water rat, mole, and squirrel's fur and peacock herl. Peacock herl is far more difficult to obtain than good hackles.'

It should be noted that the writer was an authority on cock hackles and he bred and sold them for the fly tying trade. Therefore his comments on the availability of hackles and the scarcity of herl should be judged in that light.

Here are some of the patterns recommended:

(1)   *Hook: No. 0 or 1 Kendal. (Larger size for evening)*
        Body: Olive orange or yellow wool or silk.
        Hackle: Silver or honey dun hen.

(2)   *Hook: 1 or 2 Kendal.*
        Tag: One turn silver tinsel.
        Body: Peacock herl.
        Hackle: Sooty blue dun hen.

(3)   *Hook: No. 0 or 2 Kendal.*
        Body: Light olive, primrose or orange silk.
        Hackle: Light dun hen with faint honey tips.

(4)   *Hook: No. 0 or 2 Kendal.*
        Body: Olive yellow, primrose or orange wool or
                hare's ear, mole's fur, or water rat.
        Hackle: Slightly rusty grizzled dun.

316

(5)   Hook: No. 0 to 3 Kendal.
        Body: Silk or wool of yellow, olive primrose or
              orange.
        Hackle: Rusty copper brassy dun hen.

(6)   Hook: No. 0 or 1 Kendal.
        Body: Gut stained bright yellow-gold.
        Hackle: Blue dun.

(7)   Hook: No. 0 or 1 Kendal.
        Body: Hare's ear ribbed with three or four turns of
              gold thread.
        Hackle: Medium brownish blue dun hen.

(8)   Hook: No. 0 or 00.
        Body: Orange or yellow silk.
        Hackle: Cock pheasant neck.

(9)   Hook: No. 0 or 00.
        Body: Orange or yellow silk or mole fur.
        Hackle: Stock Dove.

(10)   Hook: No. 0 or 1.
        Body: Hare's neck dyed yellow ribbed with gold
              thread.
        Hackle: Wren's tail.

(11)   Hook: No. 1 or 2.
        Body: Peacock herl or primrose silk ribbed with herl.
        Hackle: Brassy hen.

(12)   Hook: No. 0 or 1.
        Body: Mole's fur ribbed with yellow silk.
        Hackle: Ring Ousel.

(13)   Hook: No. 2, 3, or 4 Kendal.
        Body: Peacock herl ribbed with gold tinsel.
        Hackle: Pale brassy or honey dun.

(14)   Hook: No. 000 to 3 or 4 long Kendal.
        Body: Hare's ear, mole's fur or quill, with two or
              three turns of peacock herl at the shoulder.
        Hackle: Blue grizzle or rusty dun cock.

317

(15)   Hook: No. 1 Kendal.
          Body: Ruddy brown wool, and five turns of peacock
                 herl.
        Hackle: Blue Coch-a-bon-ddu.

All Mr F. Yates patterns were very simple and no wing was mentioned in any of the patterns. It is very encouraging to realise that the
Neath area in the year 1895 had a good number of fly fishers because
the local rivers at that time must have been polluted by the
industries. Fortunately the rivers of south Wales are improving
annually.

Monthly Fly Emergence Table

	March	April	May	June	July	August	Sept.	Oct.
Alder			x x	x x	x			
Ants					x x	x x		
Beetles				x x	x x	x x		
Blue Winged Olive				x	x x	x x	x x	
Chironomidae (Midges)				x x	x x	x x	x	
Corixa					x x	x x		
Crane Flies					x x	x x	x x	
Grannom		x	x					
Gravel Bed			x x	x				
Hawthorn			x	x				
March Brown	x x	x						
Mayflies			x	x				
Olives (River)	x x	x x	x x	x x	x x	x x	x x	x
Pond Olive				x x	x x	x x		
Sedge-Flies				x	x x	x		
Sepia Dun		x x	x					
Shrimp			x x	x x	x x	x x		
Stoneflies	x x	x x	x x	x x	x x	x x		

*BIBLIOGRAPHY

A Bibliography of Fly-fishing in Wales

Alfieri, Bernard & W. J. M. Menzies. *Where to catch salmon and trout in England, Scotland, Wales, and Ireland.* 1937.

Amateur Angler. See Marston, Edward.

The angler's almanac and pocket-book for 1853: being a hand-book and guide to the principal rivers, lakes, and fisheries in Great Britain, Ireland, and Scotland. By a practical angler. ND[1852].

Angling, and how to obtain it in the Wye and Usk . . . a list of flies and when to use them. ND.

Aquarius. *The battle of the fly laws.* 1875.

Armistead, Joseph J. *An angler's paradise and how to obtain it.* 1895; 1895; 1898.

[Ayrton, William]. *The adventures of a salmon in the river Dee, by a friend of the family. Together with notes for the fly-fisher in North Wales.* [Anonymous]. 1853; ND[1853?].

[—] *A concise practical treatise on artificial fly-fishing for trout. By Grey Drake, an artificial fly-fisher of fifty years' experience.* (1860).

[—] *Mr. Barnacles and his boat.* [Anonymous]. ND[1856].

Bainbridge, George C. *The Fly Fisher's Guide.* 1816.

Barrett, Walter H. *A fisherman's methods & memories.* (1953).

Bashford, Sir Henry H. *Fisherman's progress.* 1946.

Baverstock. Leslie. *Fishing famous rivers. The Wye.* 1961.
                        The Angling Times Book of the Wye. 1984.

B.B. See Watkins-Pitchford, Denys J.

Bickerdyke, John. See Cook, Charles Henry.

Blakey, Robert. *Angling; or, how to angle, and where to go.* 1854; 1865; ND[1871]; ND; ND[1885]; 1898.

Bolam, George. *Wild life in Wales.* 1913.

Bowlker, Charles. *The Art of Angling, and complete Fly-fishing,* 1774.

Bradley, Arthur G. *Clear waters. Trouting days and trouting ways in Wales, the West Country, and the Scottish Borderland.* 1914;

Cadman, Henry. *Harry Druidale, fisherman, from Manxland to England.* 1898.

Canaway, W. H. *A Snowdon stream (the Gwyrfai) and how to fish it.* 1958.

*We are indebted to R. J. W. Coleby for permission to reprint substantially from the 'Wales' section of his comprehensive study, *Regional Angling Literature: a checklist.* (Billinghay—published for the author 1979). This list is supplemented by some Welsh-language titles, referred to in the text, together with a small number of titles of more recent, and some of more obscure, origin.

[Cartwright, W.] *Facts and fancies of salmon fishing. By Clericus.* 1874·

[—] *Rambles and recollections of a fly-fisher . . . With an appendix containing ample instructions to the novice, inclusive of fly-making, and a list of really useful flies. By Clericus.* 1854; 1874.

[Chitty, Edward]. *The fly fisher's text book. By Theophilus South, Gent.* 1841; reissued as:—*The illustrated fly-fisher's text book: a complete guide to the science of fly-fishing for salmon, trout, grayling, &c. . . .*1845.

Clericus. See Cartwright, W.

Cliffe, Charles Frederick. *The book of South Wales.* 1854 and other issues.

Cliffe, John Henry. *Notes and recollections of an angler: rambles among the mountains, valleys, and solitudes of Wales. With sketches of some of the lakes, streams, mountains and scenic attractions in both divisions of the Principality.* 1860; 1870.

Coleby, R. J. W. *Regional Angling Literature: a checklist.*1978.

Connett, Eugene, V., 3rd. Any luck! 1933; 1937; 1937; 1939; 1940.

[Cook, Charles Henry]. *Days of my life on waters fresh and salt, and other papers. By John Bickerdyke.* 1895; 1901.

Cornwallis-West, George F. M. *Edwardians go fishing or many days on many waters.*** 1932; 1933.

Craig, C. W. Thurlow. *Spinner's delight.* 1951; 1954.

Daniel, William Barker. *Rural sports.* 2 vols (1801)-1802; 3 vols (1801)-[1802]; 3 vols 1805; 3 vols 1807; 3 vols 1812. Supplement 1813.

Davies, George Christopher. *Mountain, meadow & mere. A series of outdoor sketches of sport, scenery, adventures, and natural history.* 1873; 1874.

Davies, William. *Llandeilo Vawr and its Neighbourhood, Past & Present.* 1858.

Davies, William E. *Footloose with a fishing rod. Places to fish in Britain and Ireland.* 1853. Subsequently reissued as *Places to fish.*

Deacon, W. F. *The inkeeper's album.* 1883.

Durand, Sir Edward. *Wanderings with a fly-rod.* 1938.

Dutton, T. E. *Salmon and sea trout fishing.* 1972.

Eastwood, Dorothea. *River diary.* 1950.

Edwards, Gareth. *Fishing.* 1984.

Ephemera. See Fitzgibbon, Edward.

Evans, James. *Small-river fly fishing for trout and grayling.* 1972;

Falkus, Hugh. *Sea-Trout Fishing.* 1962; 1977.
                 Salmon Fishing. 1984.

Fielding, J. B. *The salmon question.* ND[1901].

** signifies a chapter or two on Wales.   ND Signifies 'No Date' (of publication).

[Fitzgibbon, Edward]. *The book of the salmon: in two parts. Part I. the theory, principles, and practice of fly-fishing for salmon; with lists of salmon-flies for every good river in the Empire. Part II. The natural history of the salmon, all its known habits described, and the best way of artifically breeding it explained. By Ephemera, assisted by Andrew Young.* ** 1850.

[—] *A handbook of angling: teaching fly-fishing, trolling, bottom-fishing, and salmon-fishing; with the natural history of river fish, and the best modes of catching them. By Ephemera.* 1847; 1848; 1853; 1865.

Francis, Francis. *The angler's register, a list of the come-at-able fisheries in England, Scotland, Ireland and Wales . . .* ** 1858; [1859]; [1860].

—*A book on angling: being a complete treatise on the art of angling in every branch.* ** 1867; 1867; 1872; 1876; 1880; 1885; (1887); 1920; ND[c1930].

Fraser, Sir Hugh. *Amid the high hills.* ** 1923; 1934.

Gallichan, Walter Matthew. *Fishing and shooting on the LMS. England, Wales, Isle of Man, south Scotland and Ireland. A practical guide to sportsmen.* ND[1927].

—*Fishing in mid-Wales. A practical guide.* (1939).

—*Fishing in Wales. A guide to the angler.* 1903; ND[c1905].

—*Fishing waters & quarters in Wales. A practical guide to fishermen with cost of fishing accommodation &c.* ND[1916].

—*The happy fisherman.* 1926.

—*Lake Vyrnwy and around.* 1909.

—*The trout waters of England. A practical guide to the fisherman for sea trout, brown trout and grayling.* ** 1908.

Gammon, Clive, editor. *Angling guide to Wales.* 1974; 1977.

—, editor. *The fisherman's fireside book.* 1961.

—*Hook, line and spinner.* 1959.

—*The Seatrout.* 1974.

Gedney, C. W. *Angling holidays. In pursuit of salmon, trout and pyke.* ** 1896.

Gilbert, H. A. *The tale of a Wye fisherman.* 1929; 1953.

Grey drake. See Ayrton, William.

Grimble, Augustus. *The salmon and sea trout rivers of England and Wales.* 2 vols 1904; 1913.

Gwynn, Stephen Lucius. *River to river. A fisherman's pilgrimage.* ** 1937.

Hancock, C. V. *Rod in hand. An angler's moods & memories.* 1958.

Hansard, George Agar. *Trout and salmon fishing in Wales.* 1834.

Hartman, Robert A. L. *About fishing.* ** 1935; 1938; 1943; 1947.

Haunts and hints for anglers. Fishing resorts along the holiday line. 1914; 2 vols 1925.

Heddon, John S. *Scotcher notes. Bibliographical, biographical and historical notes to George Scotcher's "Fly fisher's legacy . . .", circa 1820; with comments on the fly-dressings.* 1975.

Hicklin, J. *Illustrated hand-book of North Wales; a guide to the tourist, the anti-quarian and the angler.* 1856.

Hill, Laurence C. *The vale of Towy.* 1947.

Hill, Norman E. *A fisherman's notes to his son.* ** ND[1943].

—*A fisherman's recollections.* (1944).

—*A game fisher's days and ways.* 1976.

Hodgson, William Earl. *Salmon fishing.* ** 1906; 1920; 1927.

Hofland, Thomas Christopher. *The British angler's manual, or, the art of angling in England, Scotland, Wales, and Ireland: with some account of the principal rivers, lakes, and trout streams, in the United Kingdom; with instructions in fly-fishing, trolling, and angling at the bottom, and more particularly for the trout.* 1839; 1841; 1848.

Holiday, Frederick William. *Estuary fishing.* ** 1974.

—*Feathering for sea fish.* 1966.

—*Fishing in Wales.* 1964; 1967.

—*River-fishing for sea-trout.* 1960.

Hopkins, F. Powell. *Fishing experiences of half a century. With instructions in the use of the fast reel.* 1893.

Howes, William J., editor. *Fishing waters 1977-1978.* 1977, and earlier editions.

Hughes, Cledwyn. *Poaching down the Dee.* 1960.

Hughes-Parry, J. *Fishing fantasy. A salmon fisherman's note-book.* 1949. Reissued as:—*A salmon fisherman's notebook. A fishing fantasy.* 1955.

Humphrey, William. *The spawning run.* 1970; 1970.

Hunter, William Archibald, editor. *Fisherman's pie. An angling symposium.* 1926; 1929; 1937.

Hutton, James Arthur. *The life-history of the salmon.* 1924; 1925.

—*The life-history of Wye salmon.* 1918; 1918.

—*Mortality among Wye salmon after spawning.* 1922.

—*Our fishing diary, Hampton Bishop, 1908-1933.* 1942; 1948.

—*Rod-fishing for salmon on the Wye with fly, minnow, prawn, etc.* 1920; 1930; ?1976.

—*Rods and nets—catches in the Wye 1906-1925.* 1926.

—*Salmon scale examination and its practical utilty. With notes on the Wye salmon fisheries and the photography of scales.* 1910.

—*Salmon scale examination at Manchester University.* (1911).

—*Salmon scales as indicative of the life history of the fish.* 1909

—*Small spring and summer fish in the Wye.* 1933.

—*Some scales from big salmon.* 1928.

—*The spawning grounds of the Wye.* 1932.

—*Wye parr and smolts. The inverse-ratio theory of river and sea life.* 1937.

—*Wye salmon and other fish.* 1949.

—*Wye salmon; results of scale readings.* 1920 and annually to 1939.

Jardine, Sir William. *On the condition of the salmon fisheries of England and Wales in 1861; with a notice of some of the modes of fishing, especially those practised in the Severn and Wye; and remarks on the natural history of the salmon. From the Edinburgh New Philosophical Journal, New Series for April, 1862.* ND[1862].

Jenkins, J. Geraint. *Nets and coracles.* 1974.

John, D. *Flyfishing on the Usk.* 1968.

Johnson, Arthur Tysilio. *In the land of the beautiful trout.* 1907.

Jones, Griffith Evan. *Confessions of a Welsh salmon poacher.* 1877.

Jones, J. O. Articles in *Y Cymro* on old Welsh fly patterns. 1963-64

Jones, John William. *Fishery research on Llyn Tegid (Lake Bala).* 1960.

—*The salmon.* 1959; 1959; 1961; 1968; 1972.

Kempster, J. W. *Our rivers.* 1948.

[Kent, Charles]. *By Celtic waters. Holiday jaunts with rod, camera & paint brush. By C. K.* 1894.

Kite, Oliver W.A. *A fisherman's diary. Edited by Philip Brown. Nymph Fishing in Practice.* 1963; 1969.

Kneeshaw, W. S. *Sea fishing on the North West coast.* 1918; ?; 1922.

Lascelles, Robert. *Angling, being the first part of a series of familiar letters on sporting.* [1815]; and other issues? Also as part of the next:—

—*A series of letters on angling, shooting, & coursing. In three parts.* 1819. Said to occur also in earlier editions [1815? 1818?] without a collective title.

Lawrie, William Hastie. *English and Welsh trout flies. Essays and analyses.* ** 1967.

Lloyd, J. *The ancient free fishery of the Wye.* 1911.

—*The Severn, Wye, and Usk Districts fishery sketch map.* ND.

Lloyd, John, Jr. *Papers on the river Wye and Lugg.* 1873.

—*The Severn, Wye and Usk Fishery District. Conservation of Wye and Usk, etc.* 1868.

Luard, Geoffrey Dundas. *Fishing. Fact or fantasy?* 1947.

MacArthur, Wilson. *The river Conway.* 1952.

McCaskie, H. B. *The guileless trout.* 1950.

McCraith, Sir Douglas. *By dancing streams.* 1952. (An earlier edition, 1929, without relevant material).

Macdonald, Tom. *Where Silver Salmon Leap.* Gomer 1976.

[McNeillie, John]. *Trout from the hills. The confessions of an addicted fly-fisherman. By Ian Niall.* 1961.

Mansfield, Kenneth F., editor. *The art of angling.* 3 vols. 1957; 1957; 1958; 1962.

Maps. *Map of the trout and salmon waters of England and Wales . . .* 1956 and earlier editions.

—See also Parker, Maude. See Lloyd, J.

Marsh, L. S. *The river Dovey.* 1929.

Marson, Cyril Darby. *Fishing for salmon. Practical modern methods.* 1929.

[Marston, Edward]. *Days in clover. By the Amateur Angler.* 1892.

—*Fishing for pleasure and catching it . . . and two chapters on angling in North Wales by R. B. Marston.* 1906.

[—] *An old man's holidays. By the Amateur Angler.* 1900; 1901.

Medwin, Thomas. *The angler in Wales, or days and nights of sportsmen.* 2 vols 1834.

The Merionethshire angler. ND; 1909.

Mid Wales official holiday guide. ND[1966].

Morgan, Moc. *Fly-Patterns for the Rivers & Lakes of Wales,* 1984.

Yng hysgod Dai. 1956.

Morritt, Henry Edward. *The constant fisherman.* 1957.

Nall, George Herbert. *The sea trout of the Dovey.* 1933.

Nathan, William. *Gone fishing.* 1960.

Niall, Ian. See McNeillie, John.

Norman, John. *101 angling holidays.* 1954.

North Wales—a guide to a holiday region. ND[1966].

Onwhyn, Joseph. *Onwhyn's Welsh tourist, or new guide to North and South Wales and the Wye; describing every object of interest in that most picturesque country, and containing likewise all needful information on the subject of travelling expenses, inns, charges, etc.* 1853 and earlier editions.

Owen, Ieuan D. *Trout fisherman's saga.* 1959.

Palmer, William T. *More odd corners in North Wales.* ND[c1945].

Parker, Maude. *Fisherman's map of salmon catches on the lower Wye.* 1933; ND[1974], the last anonymous. The 1933 edition is usually bound with the following map.

—*Fisherman's map of salmon catches on the upper Wye.* 1933; ND [1974], the last anonymous.

Pearson, Anthony. *Sea fishing. North Wales and Anglesey.* 1968.

Pennell, Harry Cholmondeley (sometimes Cholmondeley-Pennell), editor. *The fisherman's magazine and review.* 2 vols 1864-1865.

Phillips, Ernest. *Trout in lakes and reservoirs. A practical guide to managing, stocking, and fishing.* 1914.

Price, G. V. *The angler's friend. Fishing guide to Merionethshire.* 1939.

Pritchard, W. *The angler's guide to the rivers and lakes of North Wales; with the names of all the fishing stations, arranged in* counties in alphabetical order, together with a list of suitable flies for Welsh rivers and lakes: also a map of North Wales, with the fishing stations marked thereon, etc. (1864); (1865); ND; 1870.

Rees, Alfred W. *Ianto the fisherman and other sketches of country life*. 1904.

Rennie, John. *"I have been fishing."* (1949).

Richards, Coombe. *Tight lines. Fishing anecdotes and incidents*. 1949.

[Roberts, H. W.]. *A guide for anglers to the rivers Clwyd and Elwy, their tributaries and lakes, with full particulars as to licences, &c., how to get to different sections, convenient places to stay at, distances from Rhyl, with maps and illustrations*. (1904).

Roberts, T. R. *The spas of Wales: full information as to facilities for golf, fishing, shooting, &c*. ND.

Roberts, William. *Llawlyfr y Pysgotwr*. 1899.

[Rudd, Donald G. Ferris]. *Game fish records*. By Jock Scott. 1936.

Salter, Robert. *The Modern Angler*. 1802(?); 1811.

Scotcher, George. *The fly fisher's legacy, containing accurate descriptions of all the principal natural flies, that frequent the water, laid down in such familiar manner, that the angler may readily distinguish them; together with the most successful method of imitating them; forming the fisherman's grand desideratum, or, long wished-for instructions: also, an account of sewin, samlet, and salmon pink fishing, and many useful remarks; not selected from books, but deduced from many years real experience and observation. With engravings of the natural flies colored from nature*. ND[c1820]; 1974.

Scott, Jock. See Rudd, Donald G. Ferris.

Senior, William. *Near and far. An angler's sketches of home sport and colonial life*. 1888; 1890.

—*Waterside sketches. A book for wanderers and anglers*. 1875; 1885.

Shaw, Henry. *The fly-fisher's guide, or specimens of artificial flies . . . suitable to the rivers and lakes in England and Wales*. ND [c1850?].

Sheringham, Hugh Tempest. *An open creel*. 1910; 1910.

—*Trout fishing memories and morals*. (1920); (1920).

Silver Doctor. See Smith, Lewis.

[Smith, Lewis]. *Angling from many angles. By "Silver Doctor"*. ND[1950].

—*"Welsh rarebit" by "Silver Doctor". Reprinted from "The Fishing Gazette," November 14th, 1942*. ND[1942].

South & West Wales official holiday guide. ND[1966].

South, Theophilus. See Chitty, Edward.

The state of the rivers Wye and Lugg in Herefordshire, in respect of portation and fishing; concerning which a bill having been passed

by the . . . House of Commons, is now humbly presented to the
. . . Lords . . . ND.
Stewart, Tom. *Fifty popular flies, Volume 2, and how to tie them.*
ND[1964]; 1966; 1970.
—The same, *Volume three.* 1969.
—The same, *Volume four.* 1973.
Taverner, Eric & others. *Salmon fishing.* ** 1931; (1935); (1945);
(1948); (1958); 1972.
—& others. *Trout fishing from all angles. A complete guide to
modern methods.* 1929; (1929); 1933; (1950); (1957); 1969.
Taylor, Samuel. *Angling in all its branches, reduced to a complete
science: being the result of more than forty years real practice and
strict observation throughout the kingdoms of Great Britain and
Ireland* . . . 1800.
The Teify Trout Association. ND[1927]; and other editions.
Threlfall, Richard E. *Lake Vyrnwy Hotel, Montgomeryshire . . .
Notes on trout fishing in Lake Vyrnwy . . . and the upper Vyrnwy
river.* 1947.
Traherne, Michael. See Watkins-Pitchford, Denys J.
Tugwell, George. *On the mountain: being the Welsh experiences of
Abraham Black and Jonas White, Esquires, naturalists, photo-
graphers, fishermen and botanists.* 1862.
Turner, Eric Horsfall. *Angler's cavalcade.* 1966.
Unett, John. *Fishing days.* 1957.
Vahey, John Haslette, editor. *The humane angler. Angling stories
and sketches.* ** ND[1932].
Venables, Bernard. *The angler's companion.* 1958; 1959.
Walker, Charles Frederick, editor. *The complete fly-fisher.* 1963;
1964; 1969; 1972; 1976.
Wallis, H. F., editor. *Stillwater trout fisheries. A guide to reservoirs,
lakes and other still waters in England & Wales.* 1976.
Wallwork, James. *The modern angler; comprising angling in all its
branches: being the result of more than thirty year's practice and
strict observation; together with remarks on the various rivers in
England, Scotland, and Wales . . . with a choice list of the most
killing flies on the various waters of Great Britain and Ireland . . .* **
1847.
Ward, Frank. *The lakes of Wales. A guide for anglers and others. The
fishing, scenery, legends and place names, with some mention of
river fishing.* 1931.
[Watkins-Pitchford, Denys J.] *Be quiet and go a-angling.* [By]
Michael Traherne. 1949.
[—] *The fisherman's bedside book.* Compiled by "B.B" 1945; 1946;
1946; 1950; 1955; 1959.
[—] *Summer road to Wales.* By "B.B." 1964.

327

Wellington, V. Carron. *The adventures of a sporting angler.*** 1952.

Where to fish. Biennially to 1984.

Whittingham, Peter, editor. *Coarse fishing round Britain. 1978 guide to day ticket and free waters.*** 1977.

Wiggin, Maurice, editor. *The angler's bedside book.* 1965.

Williams, Alfred Courtney. *A dictionary of trout flies & of flies for sea-trout and grayling.* 1949; 1950; 1961; 1965; 1968; 1973; 1977.

—*"Fireside fishing." A book of angling yarns.* 1928.

—*Trout flies. A discussion and a dictionary.* 1932.

WNWDA A guide to fresh water fishing in Wales. ND[1977].

Wood, L. G. & J. G. *The Rivers of Wales.* 2 vols 1812.

Wrangles, Alan. *Angling with BP.*** 1965 and later issues.

Yarrell, William. *A history of British fishes.* 2 vols 1836; 2 vols 1841; 2 vols 1859. Supplements 1839 & 1860.

Index

Waters

A WORD ON HOOKS

The selection of a hook for a particular fly is to some extent a matter of personal choice. I can only write from personal experience over many years and I have always found Partridge hooks to be the best for me.

The strength of their hooks and their attention to detail means that the hooks are right if you want to tie good flies.

I have used many different patterns of Partridge hooks over the years but I have listed below the selection of old and new patterns which has now become my shortlist.

ALBERT PARTRIDGE WIDE GAPE DOWN EYE HOOKS (CODE A).
These medium weight, wide gape, slightly offset hooks are ideal for the smaller sewin flies, wide gape trout wet flies, nymphs and tandems.

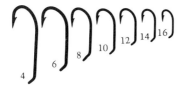

CAPTAIN HAMILTON STANDARD M/W WET FLY HOOKS (CODE L2A).
CAPTAIN HAMILTON STANDARD DRY FLY DOWN EYE HOOKS (CODE L3A).
The medium weight, wide gape, forged bend L2A hooks are perfect for standard wet flies (see also Captain Hamilton International hooks listed below).

For dry flies and buzzers, the fine wire, down eye L3A hooks are my choice.

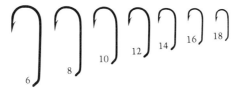

CAPTAIN HAMILTON INTERNATIONAL HOOKS (CODE CS7).
There is an ever increasing interest in competitive fly fishing and to meet this growing demand Partridge recently launched this range of hooks in three wire weights. The size 10 in each wire weight exactly meets the demands for the major competitions which means that the overall length from the outside of the bend to the outside of the eye is not more than ⅝ of an inch. The hooks also have an extra wide gape and are in a black finish.

Those interested in competitive fishing should use these hooks instead of the L2A.

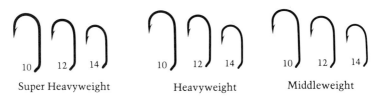

Super Heavyweight   Heavyweight   Middleweight

CAPTAIN HAMILTON STREAMER HOOK (CODE D7A).

For lures and larger sea trout flies, this medium weight, forged bend, wide gape hook is a good choice.

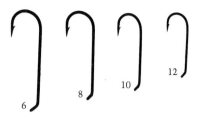

SINGLE WILSON (CODE 01).

These heavyweight, wide gape, loop eye, black hooks are ideal for the larger single hook sewin flies and for salmon flies.

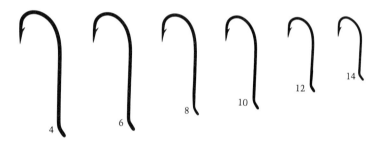

DOUBLE WILSON (CODE 02).

These hooks are the double version of the Single Wilson and are ideal for sewin doubles.

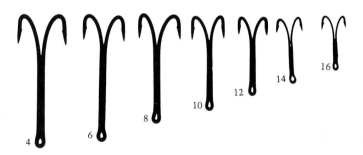

NEEDLE EYE OUTBEND TREBLE (CODE X3).

These trebles are the best choice for flying trebles.

Datblygu'r Canolbarth

Community Projects in Mid Wales

Are you.....

   *buying fishing rights for your local angling club on local
    waters
   *erecting a community television aerial
   *providing equipment for youth organisations
   *floodlighting and improving pitches for rugby and
    football clubs
   *improving community meeting halls
   *organising festivals and drama
   *developing playing fields, swimming pools,sports halls...?

Yes?, then-

Mid Wales Development, who can consider giving financial
support to such projects, would like to hear from you if you have a
scheme of community benefit.

Ladywell House
Newtown
Powys SY16 1JB
Wales, UK
Tel: (0686) 26965
Telex: 35387

Bwrdd Datblygu Cymru Wledig   Development Board for Rural Wales

TACKLE THE TROUT

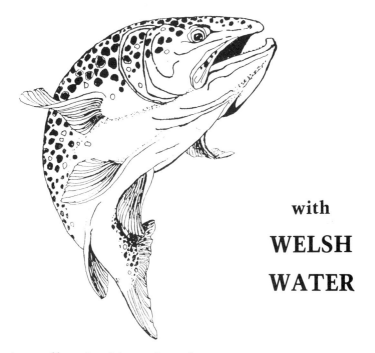

with

WELSH

WATER

As well as looking after the conservation of river fisheries Welsh Water also directly manages the fishing on some of its larger reservoirs.

Some are run as wild brown trout waters and others solely as put-and-take waters.

To find out more about where you can

TACKLE THE TROUT

write or call

Reservoir Fisheries, Welsh Water, Cambrian Way, Brecon, Powys
Tel: 0874 3181

The Fishing Tackle Shop in Pall Mall that offers so much more.

Fishing Tackle, Shooting Accessories and Appropriate clothing.

By Appointment to H.R.H. The Prince of Wales
Suppliers of Fishing Tackle
and Waterproof Clothing.
C. Farlow & Co Ltd London

Farlow's OF PALL MALL

incorporating COGSWELL & HARRISON

5 Pall Mall, London SW1 Tel: 01-839 2423

Now open till 4p.m. on Saturdays and 6p.m. Thursdays.